W9-BGO-803

Passing the ITIL® Intermediate Exams: The Study Guide

Other publications by Van Haren Publishing

Van Haren Publishing (VHP) specializes in titles on Best Practices, methods and standards within four domains:
- IT management
- Architecture (Enterprise and IT)
- Business management and
- Project management

Van Haren Publishing offers a wide collection of whitepapers, templates, free e-books, trainer material etc. in the **VHP Knowledge Base**: www.vanharen.net for more details.

VHP is also publisher on behalf of leading organizations and companies:
ASLBiSL Foundation, CA, Centre Henri Tudor, Gaming Works, Getronics, IACCM, IAOP, IPMA-NL, ITSqc, NAF, Ngi, PMI-NL, PON, Quint, The Open Group, The Sox Institute

Topics are (per domain):

IT (Service) Management / IT Governance	Architecture (Enterprise and IT)	Project/Programme/ Risk Management
ABC of ICT	Archimate®	A4-Projectmanagement
ASL	GEA®	ICB / NCB
BiSL	SOA	MINCE®
CATS	TOGAF®	M_o_R®
CMMI		MSP™
CoBIT	**Business Management**	P3O
ISO 17799	CMMI	*PMBOK® Guide*
ISO 27001	Contract Management	PRINCE2®
ISO 27002	EFQM	
ISO/IEC 20000	eSCM	
ISPL	ISA-95	
IT Service CMM	ISO 9000	
ITIL® V3	ISO 9001:2000	
ITSM	OPBOK	
MOF	Outsourcing	
MSF	SAP	
SABSA	SixSigma	
	SOX	
	SqEME®	

For the latest information on VHP publications, visit our website: www.vanharen.net.

Passing the ITIL®
Intermediate Exams
The Study Guide

Pierre Bernard

Colophon

Title:	Passing the ITIL® Intermediate Exams: The Study Guide
Authors:	Pierre Bernard
Editor:	Jane Chittenden
Publisher:	Van Haren Publishing, Zaltbommel, www.vanharen.net
ISBN:	978 90 8753 0204
Print:	First edition, first impression, May 2011
Design and Layout:	CO2 Premedia bv, Amersfoort - NL
Copyright:	© Van Haren Publishing 2011

For any further enquiries about Van Haren Publishing, please send an e-mail to: info@vanharen.net

Foreword

I was delighted to be asked to present this new title: Passing the ITIL® Intermediate Exams: The Study Guide. Improving the quality of delivering both Public and Private Sector IT services is one of my great passions, but this can only be achieved through one of my other great passions, developing the skills and capabilities of people working in IT service management. This publication can help you with this.

The core ITIL® publications greatly assist by providing a great resource of good practice ideas, but you can't learn how to do service management just by reading. To do this effectively you also need education and training. This should not be approached just by attending the first course that comes along, or by selecting the cheapest. You are making an investment for the future, and like every investment, you should make it wisely. Investment in a correctly structured and professionally delivered education and training program is fundamental to embedding best practices within your organisation, through supporting the on-going development of the skills and capabilities in your service management team.

The ITIL® V3 qualification scheme provides the structure for such an appropriate education and training programme for IT service management. The scheme is professionally delivered worldwide by a range of qualified trainers and training organisations, under the governance of the Accreditor and the Examination Institutes. The different qualifications in the scheme provide students with a balanced progression from understanding the basic concepts at the Foundation Level to applying them at the Intermediate, Expert, and Master Levels.

This publication focuses on the Intermediate Level, which has two streams, the Lifecycle stream and the Capability stream. The ITIL Intermediate qualifications are a natural progression from the Foundation qualification for anyone working in IT service management. Candidates can select courses from either of the Intermediate streams, according to the needs of the individual and the organisation. This provides the flexibility to be able to match the specialist learning requirements of service management professionals to relevant courses.

I have been very fortunate to be involved in the development of the ITIL qualifications as a member of the ITIL V3 Examination Panel since 2007, which is how I first met the author of this publication, Pierre Bernard. Pierre and I share the same passion for improving skills and capability, and have seen the qualifications move from development into widespread worldwide adoption.

I'm sure that at this point in the Foreword you want to know where this publication fits into the ITIL® V3 qualification scheme. The answer is very simple – in this publication Pierre has given insight into the Intermediate Qualifications that can best come from someone who has been actively involved in their development, and who is also very knowledgeable about the subject matter – IT service management.

Through reading this publication and using the sample examination questions you will gain excellent preparation both for your training courses and also for your examinations. You will learn about the syllabus and the types of examination questions, but just as importantly, you will get practical advice on how to approach your learning and how to approach the examinations. I recommend that you use this publication as pre-reading before you attend any ITIL Intermediate course, supplemented by reading complementary publications for the specific courses that you attend.

Note however that there is no 'magic bullet' method to guarantee success in these or in any other qualifications. Only you can guarantee that success, by taking the time and trouble to learn the subject, supported by sample examination questions, and facilitated by this publication and by your trainers. But your education must not stop after the exam – you should continue to develop yourself through application of what you have learned and by exploring other areas of IT service management.

I wish you well in your examinations and your career in IT service management. Both you as a service management professional and your organisation and its customers can reap great benefits from your investment in education and training.
I recommend this title to you.

Kevin Holland
Service Management Consultant Specialist, Department of Health Informatics Directorate (UK)
Chair of UK Government CTO Delivery Group Service Management Domain ITIL V3
Senior Examiner

Acknowledgements

This title was commissioned to serve the needs of many people wishing to use ITIL® training programs to extend their expertise and improve their corporate delivery.

Van Haren Publishing, the Publishers of this title, would like to extend our sincere gratitude to the Author, Pierre Bernard and also to the Reviewers.

Authoring a technical book of this nature and standard demands skill, time and patience and we are extremely fortunate that Pierre Bernard offered to write this work. Pierre's technical professionalism accompanied by an extremely courteous approach means it is a great privilege for us to work with him.

Our reviewers are also extremely professional and kind in reviewing the material we send them. Invariably positive, professional and dedicated, our reviewers put many long hours into finely crafting content and making sure it meets the very highest of standards demanded by the market place. We are extremely fortunate to have had the pleasure of our reviewer's company for many years and owe them a deep debt for the time, professionalism and advice they have given us.

For this title we would like to express our thanks to the following:

Claire Agutter: ITIL Training Zone

Kevin Holland   ITIL V3 Examiner

Mart Rovers: President, InterProm USA

Finally I commend this title to you, if you have any comments please do send them in, we are always delighted to hear from our readers.

Ivo van Haren
CEO, Van Haren Publishing
info@vanharen.net

Preface

The intent of this book is to help people prepare for the ITIL® Intermediate qualification exams. This book contains tips for selecting the appropriate course, preparing for the course, and what to do during the course. Additionally, this book covers tips on reading and understanding the syllabuses, scenarios, supplemental information, the questions and the answers.

About the author of this book:

Pierre Bernard is a Certified Training and Development Professional (CTDP) with the Canadian Society for Training and development (CSTD).

Pierre started his career in IT in 1984. He has been involved with various certifications since 2000 with EXIN, ISEB and LCS before joining APMG in 2007. Pierre was a senior examiner (2007 – 2010) responsible for the creation of the ITIL qualification scheme, and the exam format, and participated in the creation process of many qualifications.

Pierre knows first hand how difficult it is to create exam questions and to make sure that they are understood by others. Being a non-native English speaker, French is his first language; Pierre knows how difficult it is to properly express his thoughts in another language.

Pierre is an ITIL Expert as well as having passed all intermediate qualifications. 'Pierre has taught thousands of people around the world. He knows how stressful examinations can be and hopes this book provides you with insight and tips to help you pass the ITIL qualification exams.

Additionally, Pierre has too much respect for the people who stood up and applied to become examiners to say anything negative about their work. Therefore you will find no negativity about any part of the examination scheme in this book, nor will you find any answers to actual exams.

Pierre makes no promises that you will pass your ITIL Intermediate exam by using this book, nor does he claim that you will fail if you don't.

What you will get is a better understanding of the whole qualification process as well as learning tips on how to properly and adequately prepare for the exams and how to answer the questions during the examination process.

ITIL®[1] Intellectual Property

Throughout this book, every attempt has been made to adhere to the ITIL Intellectual Property (IP) as defined by the owner of ITIL, namely the Office of Government Commerce as well as those defined by the official Accreditor, namely the APM Group Ltd.

Additionally, every attempt has been made to provide the appropriate and accurate references where material is quoted verbatim from another source.

Pierre Bernard
CTDP, ITIL Expert

---

1   'ITIL® is a Registered Trade Mark of the Office of Government Commerce in the United Kingdom and other countries'

Contents

Introduction

The purpose of this book is to assist people to prepare for any of the ITIL Intermediate examinations. The audience includes students, instructors, course designers, and managers.

The book contains information assisting managers and their personnel in selecting the appropriate qualification required for their group and/or their career advancement. The book also contains information on adult learning principles which should provide assistance in understand the format of the scheme as well as the structure of each qualification, the syllabus, the exam papers and the course material developed by the training organizations. Instructors will find information that will help them delivering better exam guidance to the students. Course designers will find information that will help them design course properly aligned to the course syllabus.

The result should be a more enjoyable and practical learning experience for all involved.

Although there are no guarantees, the use of this book should provide the reader with a better understanding of the examination process as well as assisting with the preparation leading up to the examination.

Use of acronyms

Throughout this book, the following acronyms are used

Acronym	Definition
APMG	APM Group Ltd
ATO	Accredited Training Organization
CSI	Continual Service Improvement
EI	Examination Institute
MALC	Managing across the Lifecycle
OGC	Office of Government Commerce
OSA	Operation Support and Analysis
PPO	Planning, Protection and Optimization
RCV	Release, Control and Validation
SD	Service Design

Acronym	Definition
SO	Service Operation
SOA	Service Offerings and Agreements
SS	Service Strategy
ST	Service Transition

Table Introduction.1 List of acronyms used in this book

Referencing the official ITIL books

Due to the dynamic nature of the official ITIL literature and the various available formats, it is not possible to provide precise details such as the page, figure or table number. At the time of publication of this book, the ITIL books are available in three formats: print, electronic, and online subscription. From time to time, an excerpt from a book may be used as an example; however, in case of discrepancy the official book takes precedence and should always be used by the reader. Furthermore, this book is based on the 2007 edition of the ITIL core books although an updated edition was planned for release in the second part of 2011.

Referencing the official syllabuses

Additionally, due to the same dynamic nature of the official syllabuses (syllabi), this book does not contain all syllabuses. From time to time, an excerpt from a syllabus may be used as an example; however, in case of discrepancy the official syllabus takes precedence and should always be used by the reader.

Structure of the book

The book follows a logical progression of topics from understanding the qualification scheme, adult learning principles, and course and examination preparation to understanding and using the various syllabuses, scenarios and question booklets to achieve a thorough exam preparation.

Chapter 1 – The qualification scheme

Chapter 1 introduces the reader to the qualification scheme in simple terms. The chapter provides high level information about each level making up the qualification scheme. Information regarding the relationships between the levels as well as between the intermediate levels provides the reader with a better understanding of what to expect from each level as well as navigating and progressing through the qualification scheme.

Chapter 2 – Selecting the appropriate qualification

Chapter 2 provides the reader with insight about selecting the most appropriate set of qualifications for their personnel or themselves. Additionally, the reader will find relevant information on the following topics

- Clarification regarding various definitions – to clarify misconceptions
- Education and training issues
- Helping an IT professional select the appropriate stream or qualification
- The reasons for a preparatory course before taking an Intermediate level exam
- Competition for your education budget
- The difference between frameworks, methodologies and standards

Chapter 3 – Adult learning principles

Chapter 3 introduces the reader to the principles of adult learning, how adults learn, and how to motivate the adult learner. The chapter provides valuable insight into the Bloom's Taxonomy of Learning. The taxonomy was selected by the senior examiners very early in the creation of the qualification scheme. The Bloom Taxonomy comprises three domains of learning and six levels of learning.

The reader will gain knowledge into understanding teaching and learning and using the taxonomy of educational objectives. The chapter then provides details on each of the domains and levels of learning and their application throughout the qualification scheme.

Chapter 4 – The right qualification for the right people

Chapter 4 provides the reader with information about the five categories of qualifications within the scheme: foundation, complementary, intermediate, capstone and mastery. The reader will gain a deeper appreciation for the four levels: Foundation, Intermediate, Expert and Master. The chapter also provides a high-level description of the complementary set of qualifications that focus on specific topics.

The chapter provides information on the topics covered in each qualification, the learning outcomes to expect from each qualification, and guidance to the reader in mapping the various qualifications to their tasks, roles and responsibilities. Finally the chapter provides valuable information regarding the credit system and the correct meaning of contact hours.

Chapter 5 – Course and examination preparation tips

Chapter 5 starts with providing the reader with a word of caution regarding examinations in general. The chapter provides guidance to the prospective student on what to do prior to attending a course. Using one syllabus as a backdrop, (Operational Support & Analysis) the chapter provides valuable information, insight, and tips on approaching a syllabus.

The reader is encouraged to conduct this exercise on their own for any course syllabus to gain more experience as well as better understanding of that course. The chapter then provides insight on properly understanding the syllabus, what should be done during the course, and tips on properly reading and understanding the material.

Chapter 6 – Understanding the exam paper

Chapter 6 provides the reader with valuable examination information and tips before they start the examination. The chapter covers the characteristics of scenarios, how to properly read and understand a scenario by identifying the relevant information. The reader is then taken through the analysis of two scenarios to reinforce the learning experience.

Chapter 7 – Understanding the question

Chapter 7 provides the reader with invaluable information and tips regarding the proper analysis of a scenario, determining what the question is really asking and what information to look for in the answers in order to better select the 'best' one. The reader is then taken through the analysis of one question from each of the ten qualifications (Question one from Sample paper one) to reinforce the learning experience. The examples cover the four capabilities, the five lifecycle, and the capstone qualifications.

Chapter 8 – Exploring the syllabuses

Chapter 8 first takes the reader on an exploration tour of the structure of the syllabuses for the capabilities stream which covers, the four basic sections: (1) introduction, (2) processes, (3) technology and implementation considerations and (4) challenges, critical success factors and risks. In addition, the chapter provides detailed explanation about each of the four capabilities qualifications.

The reader is then taken on a similar exploration of the structure of the syllabuses for lifecycle stream qualifications which covers eight sections: (1) introduction, (2) principles, (3) processes, (4) activities, (5) organizing, (6) technology considerations, (7) implementation considerations and (8) challenges, critical success factors and risks. Finally the chapter provides detailed explanation about each of the five lifecycle and the capstone qualifications.

Chapter 9 – Using scenarios for practice

Chapter 9 explores how one scenario can be used for all questions within the same sample paper. The reason is quite simple; there are only so many available sample papers (practice exams) available through the examining institutes.

With a little practice and the guidance provided in this chapter, the reader should be able to create multiple additional questions. However, it is not implied here that every scenario will work easily with every question. Nonetheless, this is a good exercise to try.

Chapter 10 – Using exam questions for practice

Chapter 10 uses the same approach as provided in Chapter 9 but from a question perspective. The chapter explores how one question can be used for all scenarios within the same sample paper. Again, as with Chapter 9, the reason is quite simple; there are only so many available sample papers (practice exams) available through the examining institutes.

With a little practice and the guidance provided in this chapter, the reader should be able to create multiple additional questions. However, it is not implied here that every question will work easily with every scenario. Nonetheless, this is a good exercise to try.

Chapter 11 – Using answers & rationales for practice

Chapter 11, although smaller than its two predecessors, provides the reader with a third option to properly prepare for the examination, the answers and rationales.

CHAPTER 1

The qualification scheme

ITIL[2] (The Information Technology Infrastructure Library) advocates that IT services must be aligned to the needs of the business and underpin the core business processes. It provides guidance to organizations on how to use IT as a tool to facilitate business change, transformation and growth.

The ITIL best practices are currently detailed within five core publications which provide a systematic and professional approach to the management of IT services, enabling organizations to deliver appropriate services and continually ensure they are meeting business goals and delivering benefits.

This chapter is not trying to 'sell' you ITIL. This chapter is about helping you make sense of the qualification scheme. It introduces the various groupings making up the qualification scheme. The information in this chapter should help you in the selection process in deciding which ITIL qualification is best suited for you or your personnel.

There are five categories of qualifications within the scheme. There are four levels: the Foundation, the Intermediate, the Expert and the Master. There is also, albeit growing slowly, a complementary set of qualifications centered on specific topics.

The Foundation level
Official name of the certification
•   ITIL V3 Foundation Certificate in IT Service Management

What it is
•   Any foundation level qualification focuses on providing basic and rudimentary knowledge. It is about acquiring a good level of comprehension of the key concepts, structure, and terminology.

What it is not
•   Gaining a detailed understanding of service and / or process adoption and adaptation practices

---

- Gaining a detailed knowledge of how to modify individual and/or organization behavior (culture) when adopting and adapting good practices
- Gaining a detailed knowledge of all the subtleties of the ITIL framework

You should get the point by now...

The ITIL Foundation level qualification

This is an entry level qualification offering candidates a very basic and general awareness of some of the key elements of the Service Lifecycle. The topics covered include high-level linkages (relationships) between the five core lifecycle stages, and between their respective processes. The topics also include the contribution of the five core phases and their processes to the practices involved in Service Management.

A candidate who has completed the education and examination components related to this certification successfully can expect to have gained a general basic knowledge and understanding in the following areas. Please note that the five core books cover more areas and topics not listed here.

- Service Management
- The Service Lifecycle
- Some key principles and models
- Some generic concepts
- Some selected processes
- Some selected roles
- Some selected functions
- Some technology and architectures
- The ITIL qualifications scheme

A candidate's successful completion of the Foundation Level qualification fulfils the pre-requisite entry criteria for the next level of study within the ITIL qualifications scheme, the Intermediate level.

Target group

The ITIL Foundation Certificate in IT Service Management is primarily aimed toward the following:

- Individuals who require a basic understanding of the framework
- Individuals who require an understanding of how the framework can be used to enhance the quality of IT service management within an organization

- IT professionals or any other individual working within an organization that has adopted and adapted the framework
- Those individuals who need to be informed about an ongoing service improvement program
- Those individuals who (may) contribute to an ongoing service improvement program
- Any individuals who may have an interest in the subject

A (strong) word of caution

An individual holding the Foundation level certificate will not be able to apply the Service Management practices without further guidance. The syllabus for this course does not cover all phases, does not cover all processes and certainly does not provide any implementation guidance. The Accredited Training Organizations (ATOs) are free to build their course material to include more than the syllabus requires as well as providing additional guidance. The instructors are certainly free to provide practical examples taken from their experience or that of their colleagues.

Providing information going above and beyond the syllabus might be a great differentiator between ATOs; however, doing so may be detrimental to the success rate of the individual during the exam.

Furthermore, it is not mandatory for an individual to attend a course in order to take the Foundation level qualification exam.

Exam format

The Foundation level exam tests a candidate's ability to demonstrate an understanding of the basic concepts, describe them and demonstrate basic comprehension of the ITIL practices.

In short, the Foundation examination is about 'what is ITIL'. Think of this type of examination as asking you to provide the correct meaning of the road signs in your country.

The Foundation examination consists of the following:
- 40 multiple choice questions
- Only one option can be correct and will be awarded a mark
- No marks are deducted for an incorrect answer
- The duration is 60 minutes
- The pass mark is 65% (26/40)

Another word of caution

The Foundation level exam is not about how candidates currently perform their duties within their organization.

The Foundation level exam is not about how a candidate's organization currently performs practices.

Exam languages

The Foundation level exam has been translated into many languages in order to meet the certification requirements of the global community. See the Accreditor's website Examination Languages area[3] for a full list of languages currently available or undergoing translation. This information or a link to the Accreditor's website should be available on the Examination Institutes' (EIs) and/or ATOs' websites.

The Intermediate level

The Intermediate level makes up the 'core' of the qualifications scheme as it provides in-depth details and focuses on the 'how-to' aspects of the framework.

There are two specific streams at the Intermediate level. There is the Service Lifecycle stream which focuses primarily on the 'management of services and processes' aspect while the Service Capability stream focuses primarily on 'executing the day-to-day process activities related to delivering' aspect. Each stream has its own set of qualifications.

The modular approach of both streams allows you, as a candidate, to select the specific qualification that is of interest to you, based on your own individual educational or career-driven requirements

Depending on your role, whether managerial or not, you can select for yourself or your employees, as few or as many ITIL Intermediate modules as required over time and at the pace desired. This will help you to build a portfolio of certifications tailored to your or your team's requirements.

Each of the Intermediate certifications provides candidates with the knowledge, skills and competencies required to apply or manage the application of specific areas of ITIL best practice, in a Service Management environment.

---

3   http://www.itil-officialsite.com/InternationalActivities/ExaminationLanguages.asp

An additional qualification, 'Managing across the Lifecycle', which is also referred to as the 'capstone' qualification, allows individuals who meet the mandatory requirements to achieve the ITIL Expert qualification.

The Lifecycle stream
This stream consists of five individual qualifications, each based on one of the Service Lifecycle phases – that is, each qualification is based on only one of the five core books. This stream will be of interest to candidates such as (but not limited to) managers, consultants and trainers whose primary focus is on the Lifecycle itself – that is, the Service Lifecycle, the use of processes and the practice elements as well as developing the management capabilities needed to deliver quality Service Management.

The Capability stream
This stream consists of four individual qualifications, each based on a set of clustered process activities, their execution and use throughout specific phases of the Service Lifecycle phases – that is, each qualification is based on two or more of the five core books. This stream will be of interest to people (but not limited to) whose primary focus is on deep level understanding of roles, processes, their implementation and their interactions.

Managing Across the Lifecycle
The ITIL Managing across the Lifecycle qualification completes the Intermediate stream, by focusing on the ancillary knowledge required to implement and manage the necessary skills associated with use of the Lifecycle practices. This particular module is aimed at those candidates interested in achieving ITIL V3 Expert Level, for which this module is a key requirement.

Selecting intermediate modules
Because of the scheme's flexibility candidates can choose modules based entirely on their own individual certification requirements, which can be focused on their current / prospective job roles, or on their own personal educational objectives.

Candidates can take as few, or as many, intermediate qualifications as they require. Each of the Intermediate qualifications is recognized by the industry in their own right, and will be extremely useful to candidates based in, or working towards, a role in IT or Service Management.

Specialization

The modular structure of the Intermediate level allows candidates to select and focus their studies and certifications on specific areas of the Service Lifecycle. An individual can develop a specialty or an organization can develop a center of expertise within a defined area or discipline by selecting various qualifications.

Concentrating on the Lifecycle stream will enable individuals and organizations to focus on the management aspects of Service Management, gaining valuable knowledge and skills to manage, control and coordinate all activities under a specific phase of the Service Lifecycle.

Concentrating on the Capabilities stream will enable individuals and organizations to focus on detailed execution of Service Management, gaining valuable knowledge and skills to plan, design, transition, operate and improve specific aspects of services and processes.

Concentrating entirely on a specific phase of the Service Lifecycle will enable individuals and organizations to gain a holistic perspective of an entire phase from both the high-level management and the detailed execution perspectives. This is achieved by selecting overlapping qualifications from both streams.

The Expert level

The Expert level targets those individuals who are seriously interested in demonstrating a superior level of knowledge in the field of Service Management.

A candidate successful in achieving this qualification benefits at two levels of development, personal and professional. This qualification should aid a candidate's career progression and advancement within the field of Service Management.

Candidates who achieve the Expert level satisfy the pre-requisite entry criteria for the Master Level; which is now the highest level of qualification within the scheme.

Achieving Expert level

As mentioned previously, the qualification scheme is based on a modular approach to certification. Candidates are free to select from a variety of targeted areas of the Service Lifecycle offerings, each focusing one or more major aspects as well as to varying degrees of depth and specialization.

The flexibility offered by the modular approach provides candidates with the freedom to tailor their own individual qualification portfolio to meet their personal and professional needs and requirements.

Although there are many possible module combinations to achieve the Expert level there are four mandatory minimum requirements that all candidates must meet. These are:

1. The candidate must hold the Foundation certificate
   - ITIL V3 Foundation
     – or –
   - Foundation in ITIL Service Management and the V2- V3 Foundation Bridge qualification

2. A minimum total of 22 credits comprised of V3 Intermediate Level qualification and/or earlier qualifications

3. After earning a minimum total of 17 credits, the Managing across the Lifecycle module must be taken and passed

4. It is strongly recommended that the candidate should achieve a balanced knowledge base across the full Service Lifecycle.

These requirements will ensure that all candidates who achieve the Expert Level have successfully completed a series of certifications which span all disciplines consistently.

Applying for the Expert level certificate

Once a candidate has completed all four of the above mandatory requirements successfully, the individual will be eligible to apply for the Expert certificate.

There are several Examination Institutes (EIs). Each EI will have their respective individual processes for application and issuing of the Expert Level certificate. A candidate is free to achieve any of the qualifications through different ATOs as well as through any EI, as not every ATO offers all qualification courses. However, for the sake of simplicity, the EI who administers the highest level of certification (Managing across the Lifecycle or the V3 Managers Bridge) achieved by the candidate will issue the Expert level certificate.

There are no differences between the Expert level certificates issued by any of the EIs as each EI has been official recognized by the official Accreditor. Furthermore, the industry does not make any differentiation between the Expert Level certificates from any of the EIs.

Potential routes to Expert level

As mentioned previously (see mandatory requirement number four above) there are many possible and valid routes available to achieve the Expert level. As time goes by, the qualification scheme evolves. For the latest valid certification combination, please consult the ITIL Credit profiler available on the websites of the Accreditor, the EIs and many ATOs.

A word of caution regarding the Expert level

Not all ITIL experts will be created equal. There are six basic high-level possible paths such as

1. Lifecycle qualifications only
2. Capabilities qualifications only
3. Combination of lifecycle and capabilities qualifications
4. Combination of lifecycle and complementary qualifications
5. Combination of capabilities and complementary qualifications
6. A combination of lifecycle, capabilities and complementary qualifications

Moreover, as there are many qualifications in each stream, the number of accepted combinations is quite large. For a better understanding of the combinations offered, the reader you refer to the credit profiler available on the official ITIL website. See footnote.

The Master level[4]

As IT Service Management grows in maturity, so too do the requirements for developing and recognizing capable individuals in the industry.

The need for increasing levels of IT Service Management (ITSM) knowledge and skills can be seen in the increasing number of jobs that require these skills, the emergence of ITSM academic programs, and formal professional and career frameworks for ITSM practitioners.

The Master qualification meets these growing needs by focusing on the experienced levels of the industry, testing the capabilities of senior IT service managers, executives and practitioners.

---

4   Taken from the official Accreditor's website (http://www.itil-officialsite.com/itilservices/v1/map.asp)

Focus on practice

In an industry that values the ability to work in the real world, advanced qualifications need to test more than application to hypothetical cases.

Candidates for the Master qualification must select one or more real world situations and explain how they were able to apply their knowledge of to implement real solutions. Testing is performed by assessing a written submission describing real-world assignments, augmented by oral examination.

Target group

The Master qualification is aimed at people that are experienced in the industry – typically, but not exclusively, senior practitioners, senior consultants, senior managers or executives, with five or more years' relevant experience. All candidates must hold the Expert qualification.

Curriculum

Since every candidate will have a unique range of experience, principles, methods and techniques that they choose to apply, it is not possible to define a fixed syllabus; instead, the Master qualification allows candidates to determine their own field of study.

A Requirements and Scope document will guide candidates through the process of defining their field of study and which elements they can include.

Achieving the Master qualification

The steps for achieving the qualification are:
- Candidates submit a proposal describing the real life situation they intend to address and the elements they will apply to this situation
- Candidates prepare and submit a Work Package for assessment
- Candidates attend an interview to support the Work Package assessment.

Learning objectives

Although there is no fixed syllabus for this qualification, each candidate is expected to have an in-depth knowledge of the areas of study that they have selected for inclusion in their proposal and Work Package. Candidates are also expected to demonstrate management and planning skills in support of the areas of study that they select.

Why obtain the Master qualification?

- Senior ITSM practitioners and managers are better able to differentiate themselves in an industry that requires ever-increasing demonstration of competence

- Experienced practitioners and managers can identify key areas of study and improvement as they prepare for the qualification
- Organizations will gain value from the benefits achieved during the assignment, and can benefit from the coaching received during preparation of the Work Package
- Organizations that have Masters working for them can claim a level of demonstrable quality, since projects in that organization were independently evaluated
- The Master qualification can be used to differentiate candidates for senior roles

The Complementary level

Managing services involves more than adopting and adapting good practices from only one framework. Additionally, there are instances where an individual or an organization requires a more focused look at a specific component. The qualifications scheme recognizes this fact and this is why it includes supplementary value-adding certifications which link ITIL-base practices to the current certification portfolio. These certifications make up the ITIL Complementary qualifications scheme.

Under this arrangement, any of the officially accredited Examination Institutes may submit a qualification for inclusion. The proposed qualification is then assessed against the following set of criteria:

- It covers one or more topics within the Core and / or Complementary publications
  – or –
- It covers other publicly available Service Management related or relevant publications such as books, standards, papers, etc
- It must not overlap significantly with other ITIL Core qualifications
- It must not simply re-hash topics from a new focus or approach

If the proposed qualification is officially endorsed it will be awarded a credit value, thus recognizing its alignment to the qualification scheme.

Candidates who successfully achieve recognized complementary certifications can use the credits gained (up to a maximum of 6 credits) from complementary certifications towards the ITIL V3 Expert Level of certification.

List of complementary qualifications

The following certifications are endorsed as Complementary and enable a candidate to earn the following number of credits provided they successfully pass the relevant examination.

Qualification	Qualification Overview	Credit Value
ICT Infrastructure Management (ICTIM)	This BCS-ISEB certificate is based on the ITIL best practice guide ICT Infrastructure Management. Successful achievement of the certificate will enable candidates to demonstrate knowledge and application of the processes required to manage an ICT infrastructure, and define the interfaces and dependencies with all other areas involved in the specification, design, development, support, delivery and continuous improvement of ICT services.	3.5 credits
Service Catalogue	This APMG-International certification and associated course is aimed at those with an ITIL Foundation certificate (or above) who have an interest in learning more about how a Service Catalogue could benefit their business, and specifically looks at ways to control demand, publish and track service pricing and cost and automate service request management and fulfillment.	1.5 credits
Foundation Certificate in ITSM according to ISO/IEC20000	The EXIN and TUV-Sued Foundation Certificate in ITSM according to ISO/IEC 20000 demonstrates a student's understanding of the core principles, processes and practices of a quality approach to IT Service Management based on the international standard for IT service provision. The 'IT Service Management according to ISO/IEC 20000' program focuses on the role of people and their activities in achieving quality of IT services and processes.	1.0 credits
Certified Process Design Engineer (CPDE)	This LCS certification will impart, test and validate knowledge on best practices in the assessment, design, implementation, integration and management of IT Service Management processes. The knowledge obtained applies to every Service Management framework, standard and maturity model.	1.5 credits
BCS Specialist Qualifications	The following Specialist Certificates are available: The BCS-ISEB Specialist Qualifications in IT Service Management focus on a single IT Service Management job role and provide detailed knowledge and information on how each particular job role operates within an organization. They embrace a broad range of industry good practice including ITIL, COBIT®, ISO/IEC 20000, SFIA/SFIAplus	1.5 credits
SDI	• Specialist Certificate in Service Desk and Incident Management	
CMS	• Specialist Certificate in Change Management	
SLMS	• Specialist Certificate in Service Level Management	
SBRM	• Specialist Certificate in Business Relationship Management	
SPM	• Specialist Certificate in Problem Management	
SCSM	• Specialist Certificate in Supplier Management	

Qualification	Qualification Overview	Credit Value
Configuration Management Database (CMDB)	This APMG-International certification is aimed at those interested in learning more about how a CMDB could benefit their business, and specifically looks at ways to identify, control report, audit and verify service assets and CIs. It provides a logical model of IT services, linking services to business processes and supporting identification of service improvement opportunities.	1.5 credits
Change Analyst	This APMG-International qualification helps candidates understand the practical implication of change within an IT service environment. Change Analyst gives candidates the knowledge and confidence to assess, authorize and manage changes. They will gain an understanding of how to develop business cases for changes and will have an insight into how to get approval for proposed changes. This is a practical, role based certification for those who already have ITIL Foundation.	1.5 credits

Table 1.1 List of complementary qualifications

CHAPTER 2

Selecting the appropriate qualification

Selecting the appropriate qualification is more complex than one might think. It is important to consider many aspects such as personal interest, and preferences, as well as the needs of the individual, the group, or that of the organization. Additionally the characteristics of the qualification, found in the syllabus, will be determinant factors in the selection process.

In this chapter the reader will find insight about selecting the most appropriate set of qualifications for their personnel or themselves. Additionally, the reader will find relevant information on the following topics

- Clarification regarding various definitions – to clarify misconceptions
- Education and training issues
- Helping an IT professional select the appropriate stream or qualification
- The reasons for a preparatory course before taking an Intermediate level exam
- Competition for your education budget
- The difference between frameworks, methodologies and standards

For many people, the terms certification, designation, diploma and qualification are synonymous. They are not. To ensure proper comprehension about the above terms, here are their respective definitions in alphabetical order. Please note that only the relevant meaning of the definition in the context of the ITIL qualification scheme is provided. All definitions are taken from the Merriam-Webster online dictionary[5].

cer •ti •fi •ca •tion *noun* \ˌsər-tə-fə-ˋkā-shən \
Definition of Certification

The act of certifying: the state of being certified

Figure 2.1 Certification

5 http://www.merriam-webster.com/dictionary/

cer •ti •fy   *noun*   \‚sər-tə-fi\
Definition of Certify

1: to attest authoritatively: as
    a: confirm
    b: to present in formal communication
    c: to attest as being true or as represented or as
       meeting standard

4: to recognize as having met special qualifications such as
    of a governmental agency or professional board within a
    field e.g.: agencies that certify teachers

Synonyms: attest, witness, and vouch

Figure 2.2 Certify

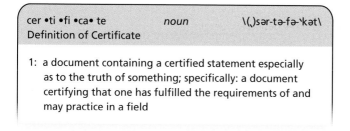

cer •ti •fi •ca• te   *noun*   \(‚)sər-tə-fə-ˈkət\
Definition of Certificate

1: a document containing a certified statement especially
   as to the truth of something; specifically: a document
   certifying that one has fulfilled the requirements of and
   may practice in a field

Figure 2.3 Certificate

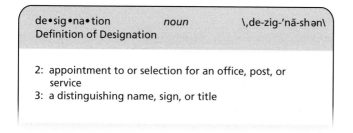

de•sig•na•tion   *noun*   \‚de-zig-ˈnā-shən\
Definition of Designation

2: appointment to or selection for an office, post, or
   service
3: a distinguishing name, sign, or title

Figure 2.4 Designation

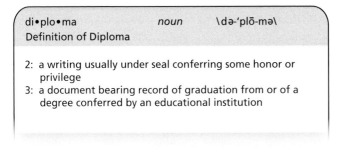

di•plo•ma   *noun*   \də-'plō-mə\
Definition of Diploma

2: a writing usually under seal conferring some honor or
    privilege
3: a document bearing record of graduation from or of a
    degree conferred by an educational institution

Figure 2.5 Diploma

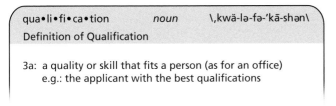

qua•li•fi•ca•tion   *noun*   \,kwä-lə-fə-'kā-shən\
Definition of Qualification

3a: a quality or skill that fits a person (as for an office)
     e.g.: the applicant with the best qualifications

Figure 2.6 Qualification

The ITIL qualification scheme

Using the above definitions, the meaning of the ITIL qualification scheme becomes clearer. Here is how to interpret the meaning.

The ITIL qualification (*a quality or skill that fits a person*) scheme awards certificates which are *documents containing a certified statement especially as to the truth of something; specifically: a document certifying that one has fulfilled the requirements of and may practice in a field to the people.*

The EIs award certificates to individuals who, after attending an accredited course provided by an Accredited Training Provider (ATO), achieve a pass mark (or higher) for an examination based on an established course syllabus. The only exception for the mandatory attendance to an accredited course applies to the Foundation certification.

The EIs award the ITIL Expert certificate to an individual who successfully completes the requirements for this certification[6].

---

6   See the Official ITIL Website for details.

The EIs will award the ITIL Master certificate to an individual who successfully completes the requirements for this certification. Please note this certification is still under development. See the Official ITIL Website[7] for details.

Upon receiving any of the currently available ITIL V3 certificates, individuals do not achieve a designation. They cannot use the course acronym as if it were a designation. The successful candidate can list their achieved certifications in a curriculum vitae (CV) or résumé. It is accepted to add 'ITIL® Expert' on one's email signature or business card or any of the qualification names provided that the '®' (registered trademark) symbol is included after the word 'ITIL'.

The ITIL V2 – V3 bridging certifications and the certification schemes based on the previous versions of ITIL do not provide any designation either.

Please note that the certificates are not diplomas. However, many universities around the world now include ITIL courses as part of their curriculum. So who knows?

Education and training issues
Training organizations, regardless of what topic they cover, seem to face the same issue: too many students come to class unprepared despite the numerous times the training organization instructs them to do so.

The strongly suggested recommendation message about reading the course material before attending the course is reiterated by all three groups involved; the Accreditor, the EIs and the ATOs. This message is actually included in all intermediate level syllabuses.

In the case of ATOs and to comply with accreditation requirements set by their respective EIs, they include this message in numerous locations and documents such as their website, the course description, the confirmation email, the preparation package, the reminder email, or even via a phone call.

Scenario
Imagine for a moment that you are an instructor. If you already are an instructor, you have already lived the following situation.

---

7   http://www.itil-officialsite.com/home/home.asp

- *You welcome the delegates*
- *You discuss the logistics of the course*
- *You facilitate the introduction of each candidate*
- *You start talking about the pre-reading…*

And they all look surprised and tell you they did not know anything about it.

Surprise… Surprise…

One of the biggest issues here is one of culture. Of course, not all cultures are the same and of course, nor is everyone the same. Additionally, the following is not a generalization either but comes from observations from the author.

Fast, fast, fast

It seems we live in a world where everything has to be fast, everything has to be now, and people are working longer hours, and they have more responsibilities than ever. In this world of constant connectivity, social media, and the (very) false perception we can multitask, attending a course undisrupted in nearly impossible because we allow it to be so.

When it comes to continuing education, some believe simply attending a course should entitle them to be awarded a qualification. Additionally it may appear that some people don't want to put in the effort. This is not suggesting that people are lazy; they just don't have the time. People commute long hours stuck in their cars or in public transportation and they work long hours.

However, too often people work on meaningless tasks, so called 'make-work' projects, surf the internet for personal reasons on company time using company equipment, or socialize too much. Lost productivity is everywhere.

Busy, busy, busy

There is also the fact there are too many meetings. The problem with meetings is that there is no action items assigned with a deadline. There is too much talk and too little actual work done. How can one expect people to do any work when they attend meeting after meeting?

Another roadblock is that many people think they have to be connected all the time; they check their cell phones all the time. You speak with someone, his or her phone rings and they answer the phone. This is rude. People do this in meetings, in private conversations and of course in education and training situations.

As instructors, we always hear that people can attend a course but they still have to be available and they have to do their job on top of that. This is non-sense.

Business etiquette is not what it used to be. We fell into the vicious circle of deploying something we know little (or nothing about), overworked staff, too few staff, and the mentality of 'I wanted it yesterday.'

Implementing best practices

Additionally, many organizations still seem to think that implementing any best practice is like installing a video game on a PC from a CD. Common sense tells us this is not the case. Furthermore, the expressions 'implementing ITIL' and 'implementing best practices' are both misleading and incorrect. Here are five simple reasons why.

1. ITIL is a set of books describing services, processes and practices.
2. ITIL is not prescriptive.
3. Organizations are already doing most, if not all, of the activities described in the ITIL core books. The activities may not be executed in a consistent, repeatable and measurable manner across the various functions.
4. There may be a start date when an organization realizes its practices are not as effective and as efficient as they could be but there is no end date when adopting good practices.
5. Adopting good practices (not best) is about accepting to modify our personal and organizational behaviors. Actually, even the expression 'good practice' is misleading. It would be more adequate to utilize '***proven practice***' instead.

Short-term views

Many organizations believe in continuous education for their personnel. They are not afraid to invest time, money and material (books anyone?). They understand that certification is but one step in the grand scheme of things. On the flip side, some organizations refuse to provide education, training, and certification for their personnel.

Pop quiz:

Which is better and more economical?
A. *Educating and training your personnel*
B. *Hiring a consultant to come and do the work, then leave without sharing anything*

Answer 'A'
This answer is better and more economical in the long run as the knowledge will remain within the organization much longer and has a greater probability of being both shared and applied.

To compound the issues, organizations are always looking at ways to cut costs or at least control them. In periods of fiscal restraint, one of the first budget items to be reduced, often drastically, is education and training. It is during difficult times that organizations should focus on education and training so that when recovery is at hand, the personnel are ready for the new challenges.

In tough economic times, slashing the education and training budget is easy and immediately affects the bottom line. This is a huge mistake. Sure, some pundits are going to say this book is obviously biased towards selling education and training. Of course it is. However, it is always a good thing to advocate education and training regardless of the type of industry.

Another narrow view is the belief of some managers and executives that education and training will only serve to make their personnel more marketable to other organizations and encourage people to leave. The view goes something like this.

Narrow-minded manager [1]
'Why should I empty my small budget to educate and train the personnel only to see them leave shortly after? Why would I want to subsidize my competition or any other organization? As soon as my employees get a new certification, they update their résumé (CV) and they leave. I pay and someone else reaps the benefits; no way, not on my watch.'

Narrow-minded manager [2]
'How difficult can this ITIL stuff be? I can only afford so much training. These are intelligent people. They should be able to figure out how to do this when they come back from basic training. Besides, I can only manage to do without them for three days.'

Narrow-minded manager [3]
Speaking to an employee about to leave for a course

'Look, I know this course is important for you and that's it is already paid and that we have already postponed it twice. However, I can ill afford to have you unavailable for the duration of this course. I want you to call in for the meetings you normally attend and to check your email all day.'

Therefore, it is no wonder that people come to class unprepared.

It is like everything in life; without putting in enough effort (what is referred to as sweat equity) there are no results.

Note from the author
The education system is suffering just as well. Kids download essays from the internet, don't study and parents are against homework.

I am a parent and I had to fight many parents who complained that 30 minutes of homework a night stressed out their kids.

How does this reflect on the IT education industry? It is what I call the 'I want you (the instructor) to teach me everything you know about a topic, both theory and practical aspects, in as little time as possible. I want not only to know it but understand it and be able to apply it in my work immediately.'

Now, that is absurdly unrealistic.

So how do we address this? We start at the top. We do a massive communication campaign in as many outlets as possible such as blogs, magazines, conferences, presentations to executives, etc.

Organizations have to invest in developing the knowledge and skill sets of their people. In turn, people must understand the difference between education and training.

Pop quiz:
What is the difference between education and training?

Answer:
- *Education is the acquisition of new knowledge*
- *Training is the practical application of the newly acquired knowledge*
- *Training is the continual practical application of the acquired knowledge*

Example:
Education is the acquisition of knowledge and facts while training is the practical application of that knowledge. Being in the classroom to learn the signs and rules of the road is education. Being in a vehicle under the supervision of an instructor or in a simulator and actually driving/ operating the vehicle is training.

By the way

Have you ever noticed that athletes, performers (actors, singers, or dancers) are always practicing their craft? Why is this not the norm in the business world? We are, after all, performing for our customers and for our organization. What about the old adage that says 'practice makes perfect'? Shouldn't the business world slow down for a second, come up to the surface, breathe a little, look around and actually deliver on it's mantra of 'our people are our greatest assets'.

Well, if people are the greatest assets to an organization, when will the business world actually treat them as something valuable? The easy ways to do this is by educating and training them on a continual basis and allow them to practice their work.

This would result in fewer errors, less faulty products, improved morale, improved productivity and improved profit margin.

This would also result in less stress for employees, fewer sick days, better personnel retention and last but certainly not least, improved work-life balanced.

What a concept!

– Heavy sarcasm from the author

Clear and simple message to every organization

How can someone become an expert in any field just by attending one week-long course? They can't. Give them the resources, money to pay for the course, the books, and the time to prepare and attend the course. By the way, when they attend the course, they are not available.

1. Create and foster a culture based on the acquisition and sharing of knowledge, education and training
2. Provide the means (time, money, and material) to the personnel to achieve <1> above
3. Encourage the dissemination of the knowledge acquired via <1> and <2> above – Knowledge SHARING is power.
4. Enable the employees to acquire the required material such as books, white papers, articles, knowledge bases, etc.

Action items for organizations
- Invest in your people through education and training.
- Stop cutting the education budget, increase it instead.
- Conduct a training needs analysis

- Assess levels of knowledge and skills
- Create an education and training plan
- Execute the education and training plan
- Start again

This will contribute to greater employee retention as well as improving productivity, efficiencies and effectiveness. This should result in a greater job satisfaction level.

This may seem a simplistic view, unrealistic, and out of touch with reality. It is not. If things continue the way they are today, best practice consulting will be around for a long time and companies will pay exorbitant amounts of money and time trying to sort this all out.

Remember the following two old adages

> *'An apple a day, keeps the doctor away'*
> *'A gram of prevention is worth a kilogram of cure'*

Certification for the sake of certification

Don't be seduced by certification for the sake of certification. A wise person should have the knowledge, abilities, attitudes, and aptitudes to take the literature on a specific topic and be able to apply it based on the needs and requirements of the situation.

Organizations should especially be careful about people with too many certifications.

Note from the author

Someone once showed me a 3 inch (about 7.5 cm) binder full of certificates he had achieved in his career. Did this demonstrate that he had the knowledge, the experience, the skills and the aptitudes? In my humble opinion and my dealings with him, it did not. Look, I personally have certificates on technology and software we can probably only find in a box in a basement or in a museum somewhere.

Are these certifications relevant for current needs?

Too many people think holding any foundation level certificate makes them an expert at implementing it. If this was true then someone who took two introductory level accounting courses as electives while attending university should be an accountant. Anyone with a little common sense should agree that two or three measly introduction level courses in accounting do not an accountant make.

Holding any certification means that someone can learn and acquire knowledge. To many, nothing beats experience. Some people are very good at taking and at passing exams. However, can they actually apply the knowledge? On the other side, there are people who do poorly with exams but are very good at what they do.

There are two perspectives to look at here. The first is that people attend certification courses to acquire the knowledge. They will start applying that knowledge once they are back at the office. The second perspective is when very experienced people attend a certification course to 'prove' what they know about something they have already been doing for most of their career. This second reason is often tied to career advancement opportunities.

Pop quiz:
Which of the following is better or best?

1. *Someone learning something, achieving certification then applying it in his or her work*
2. *Someone with a lot of experience achieving a certification on something they already have a lot of experience with*
   a) *1 only*
   b) *2 only*
   c) *Both*
   d) *Neither*
   e) *It depends*
   f) *I don't know*
   g) *Who cares*

The answer is that neither situation is better than the other is and there is no 'best' answer here. Both situations are valid and useful. By the way, answers e), f), and g) should be taken with a grain of salt and actually removed from anyone's vocabulaty.

Which stream or qualification should an IT professional aim for?

First, not everyone in an organization needs to achieve the ITIL Expert level, let alone the ITIL Master. Of course, training and/or consulting organization in the field of Service Management are likely to have many ITIL Experts and eventually ITIL Masters.

Not everyone goes to college or university. For all the people who do go to college or university not everyone registers for and completes the Doctorate (PhD) level. The same logic applies to the ITIL Expert and Master levels.

Although an individual will benefit from achieving a given qualification, the greater benefit is for the organization.

Educating and training a group of people at the same time on a specific topic will help ensure greater consistency and greater understanding of how to apply the material back in the organization.

Sending an employee to a public offering of a qualification will help the individual learn about different perspectives from the other attendees. It could also provide the opportunity to bring back lessons learned about how to apply the material back in the organization.

The following primarily applies to IT personnel who are not ITIL consultants, ITIL trainers or working for an ITSM tool vendor/reseller. There are a few criteria to consider in selecting the right course for you or your personnel.

Criterion No. 1
Look at the primary focus of the job and the primary focus of the selected groups. Is the focus of the personnel in question fixing and supporting something, are they involved with changes, release, and deployment or do they perform analysis and planning (making recommendations)? This will influence which phase of the Service Lifecycle to select.

Criterion No. 2
Are the people at the supervisory/management or are they strictly non-management? This will influence which stream to go for.

Criterion No. 3
Identify the individual primary and secondary learning styles of the people. Are they visual (prefers to read the material), auditory (prefers to listen to a presenter) or tactile (prefers the hands-on approach)? Everyone learns through a combination of these three styles. It is simply a matter of preference. This will influence the type of delivery method for the course.

The current delivery methods for courses include:
- Classroom in a public setting (delegates from different organizations at a public venue)
- Classroom in-house (within your company)
- Computer or web-based – self-paced
- Instructor-led remote – similar to a webcast set-up but with many sessions.

About the IT groups

Although an organization is likely to use other names, there are fundamentally four groups of people within an IT department. It is important for an individual to identify which group they belong to. This, along with their career aspirations, will assist them in determining which certification path to pursue.

The Service Operation book provides an excellent sample of the various groups found in the IT department. First, there are four functions:
- The Service Desk
- Technical Management
- Application Management
- IT Operations

Service Desk

The Service Desk is a function that is crucial to the whole concept of Service Management. It is the Single Point of Contact (SPOC) between the users and customers for the delivery and use of services. The Service Desk is customer-focused and is comprised of people with interpersonal skills, business awareness and a service oriented (value based) perspective.

Technical Management

Technical Management plays an important role in the design, testing, release and improvement of IT services. It provides guidance to IT Operations on how to best accomplish the ongoing operational management of technology and ensures a balance between the skill level, utilization and cost of these resources:

Application Management

Application Management is the function responsible for managing applications throughout their lifecycle and plays a role in all applications, whether purchased or developed in-house. One of the key decisions Application Management personnel contribute to is the decision of whether to buy an application or to build it in-house.

Application Management personnel also play an important role in the design, testing and improvement of applications that form part of IT services. It may be involved in development projects. However, these projects are not usually the same as those involving Applications Development teams.

IT Operations Management
IT Operations Management is the function responsible for executing the activities and performance standards defined during Service Design and tested during Service Transition. In this sense, IT Operations Management's role is primarily to maintain the status quo.

IT Operations Management consists of two roles:
- **IT Operations Control** oversees the day-to-day execution and monitoring of operational activities and events in the IT infrastructure
- **Facilities Management** manages the physical environment of the data center or backup facilities.

The four functions can be summarized in the following diagram. Of course, grouping and names will vary from organization to organization but Figure 2.7 provides a good representation of the primary focus of IT groups.

Why is there a requirement to attend a preparatory course before taking an Intermediate level exam?

The above is a valid question often asked by (prospective) attendees. They are allowed to take the Foundation exam without taking a preparatory course.

However, why would anyone want to 'dumb down' IT's credibility? Just as we are finally turning the corner and becoming more business focused and recognized by the business as an integral part of the organization's success and just as we are getting IT personnel to start thinking in terms of business requirements and business outcomes, this question comes up.

If people are allowed to take an ITIL Intermediate level exam without having to take a preparatory course, the following is likely to happen:

- It would greatly undermine the value of any of qualifications
- It would adversely affect the credibility of anyone who has attended a course

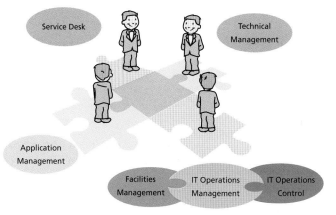

Figure 2.7 Service Operation functions

- ATOs would very likely to go out of business unless they changed their service offerings
- Consulting organizations and consultants would lose credibility
- The Service Management software tool vendors would be able to make all sorts of claims about the compliance or compatibility to the framework
- Book publishers would be unable to recruit reputable authors
- The IT department's credibility would likely to go down the drain

If people are allowed to take an ITIL Intermediate level exam without having to take a preparatory course, it will set the IT industry back about 20 years; right about the time ITIL was launched.

Is there any other businesses group that does not require their members to be properly qualified and/or certified? How can anyone claim to be an expert in any field without…
- Attending the courses?
- Reading the books?
- Passing exams?
- Practicing the knowledge?
- Keeping up-to-date?
- Consulting the literature forming their body of knowledge?

Does a recruiter considers an inexperienced recent graduate of a trade school such as a mechanic, a dental assistant, an electrician, a plumber, a carpenter, etc, to be an expert? These graduates may be very enthusiastic, have the right attitude, possess the right aptitudes for their career of choice and be very good at what they do. However, they lack the so-called 'real-world' experience.

The above does not imply that some people cannot simply read the book, then take the exam and pass it. Many are capable of achieving this. However, allowing people to take the ITIL intermediate exams without attending a course would severely undermine the credibility of the whole qualification scheme.

There are organizations such as the Project Management Institute® (www.pmi.org) and ISACA®, previously known as the Information Systems Audit and Control Association, (www.isaca.org) where people can take exams without taking a course.

However, both these organizations require proof of experience in their domain as well as meeting requirements. It is also strongly suggested that taking a course will greatly increase your chances of passing the exams. Additionally, exam preparation courses are usually mandatory.

In the case of ISACA, the designation is awarded to those individuals with an interest in specific topics who have met and continue to meet the requirements. Please visit their website for exact details on their various certifications and their requirements.

In the case of PMI, individuals have to obtain a credential, prepare for the exam, and maintain their credentials.

Pop quiz
Question: Will you become physically fit if you buy a membership to a gym?
Answer: No

Question: Will you become physically fit if you buy the latest gym-wear fashion clothes and accessories?
Answer: No

Question: Will you become physically fit if you go to the gym?
Answer: No

Question: Why is the answer 'no' for the above questions?
Answer: Because you actually have to use the equipment properly, follow a diverse exercise program and exercise on a regular basis.

Competition for your education budget

There is a myriad of certifications competing for your education, training, and certification budget. A recent search conducted in the fall of 2010 on the internet yielded more than 300 certifications related to IT alone. Here is a list, in alphabetical order, of the most popular categories.

- Architecture (from design to support)
- Assessments
- College and university courses, certificates and degrees
- Consultancy
- Databases
- Executive MBA and management courses
- Frameworks and methodologies
- Governance
- Hardware (from design to support)
- People skills
- Program management
- Programming
- Project management
- Risk management
- Software (from design to support)

    …and many others

To certify or not

Note from the author
Allow me to misquote one of the most well-known lines from William Shakespeare; I am speaking of course of Hamlet, Act 3, Scene 1.

    'To certify or not to certify, that is the question'.

Looking at the spectrum of acceptance of certifications (right hand side) we have organizations who truly believe that educating, training, and certifying their personnel are a worthwhile investment. These organizations usually have formal education and training programs in place. Although they know that some employees may eventually leave, taking their certifications with them, these organizations still promote a nurturing culture that encourages people to acquire and share knowledge.

At the other end of the spectrum (left hand side) are 'paranoid' organizations that refuse spending money or time on education and training. They believe the personnel will leave as soon as they obtain their certification. They do not want any other organizations to be the beneficiary of their education budgets. They prefer to hire people with the appropriate certifications. These organizations also believe that 'on-the-job' training is sufficient. Luckily, there are far more of the former than the latter type of organizations.

Anecdote from the author
A long time ago, I was involved with an organization's Help Desk Manager (this was in the pre-ITIL era) who believed she could simply take someone off the street, put them in front of a phone, give them a procedure manual and 'voila!' a new help desk agent 'auto-magically' appeared.

This did not work very well, as you can imagine. Trust me on that one.

Organizations in general are not necessarily the ones promoting an anti-education culture. Specific individual managers are usually the culprits. These managers, at any level, usually come up with all sorts of reasons against education for their personnel. Some of the reasons are valid such as slow sales, higher costs, unexpected losses, or cash flow issues to name but a few. These managers may simply prefer to hire someone who already has the necessary certifications.

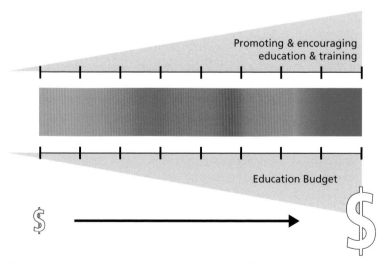

Figure 2.8 Organizational belief in education is proportional to its education budget

Frameworks, methodologies and standards

Before we start looking at ITIL Intermediate qualifications, it is important to differentiate between frameworks and methodologies. Let us start with the following definitions.

Framework[8]

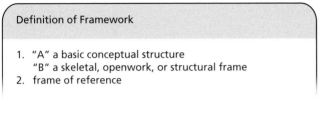

Definition of Framework

1. "A" a basic conceptual structure
   "B" a skeletal, openwork, or structural frame
2. frame of reference

Figure 2.9 Framework

Methodology[9]

Definition of Methodology

1. a body of methods, rules, and postulates employed by a discipline; a particular procedure or set of procedures
2. the analysis of the principles or procedures of inquiry in a particular field

Figure 2.10 Methodology

---

8   Source: www.merriam-webster.com/
9   Source: www.merriam-webster.com/

Method[10]

Definition of Methodology

1. a procedure or process for attaining an object:
    a. (1): a systematic procedure, technique, or mode of inquiry employed by or proper to particular discipline or art
       (2) : a systematic plan followed in presenting material for intruction
    b. (1): a way, technique, or process of or for doing something
       (2) : a body skills or techniques
2. a discipline that deals with the principles and techniques or scientific inquiry

Figure 2.11 Method

ITIL is a framework while PMI or PRINCE2 are methodologies. Two organizations, one large, the other small, and both using the PMI methodology for projects, would end up with very similar supporting documentation regardless of the project type and size. On the other hand, these same two organizations, this time using ITIL, will end up with very different supporting documentation.

A comparative analogy

Process: Two houses are being built side by side. The blueprints, the contractor, the trade people are the same and the materials all come from the same sources. Yet when the two families move in, the houses are different. Their owners have decorated and furnished their home according to their personal taste and available budgets. This is a case of using the same framework (for both houses) yet we have two different results.

Project: A developer has hired an architectural firm and a contracting firm to build an office tower and a housing development. The architect and contractor will use the same project methodology to execute both projects. Of course, the logistics will be different but the project stages will be the same.

---

10   Source: www.merriam-webster.com/

Which framework or methodology should you use?

Some people and organizations still believe they have no need to look at ITIL if they are using PMI and vice versa. This is a narrow view since most methodologies and frameworks are complementary. Other organizations have claimed that they have tried all the frameworks and methodologies to get their IT department 'in order' but things always go back to what they were before.

There are two primary reasons for these failures. One reason is the lack of continuous effort once the 'project' is over; the other reason is failing to embed the changes into the culture of the organization[11]. This means changing the attitudes, behaviors and culture of the organization[12].

There are many methodologies[13] available. Organizations should not simply look at them; they should seriously investigate and consider them. There are many articles, whitepapers, and books on this matter.

A good reference is Frameworks for IT Management[14] available as a book or a pocket guide. This book covers 22 frameworks and methodologies classified into five major categories. They are, in alphabetical order:
• Information Management
• IT Governance
• Project Management
• Quality Improvement
• Quality Management and Business Process Management

See Appendix E for the complete list of frameworks and methodologies.

Evidently, budgets are limited, time is a precious commodity, 'business as usual' is still required, and there are numerous pressures on the organization coming from various internal and external sources. This means that organizations must identify their most pressing needs and address them.

11　For more details on this, please refer to Leading Change and/or The Heart of Change by John P. Kotter
12　The ABC of ICT by Paul Wilkinson, Jan Schilt
13　ITIL V3 Service Design book (OGC, published by TSO)
14　Van Haren Publishing and itSMF International – www.vanharen.net – www.itsmfi.org

Summary: where do you start?

Only you and your organization can answer this question. However, framework and methodology consulting organizations, software tool vendors, and not-for-profit independent and internationally recognized forums and associations will try to influence your decision.

This is normal practice and you will be bombarded with information from every angle. Nevertheless, pay attention to this information. Log on to the websites of these organizations. Compare the information between vendors offering the same framework or methodology. Ask for independent research and journal articles.

Join the recognized independent forums. Most of them have a free membership option providing access to a lot of good information. Attend conferences, if not physically, then webinars are a cheap alternative.

Keep in mind the four Ps of Service Design; People, Process, Products and Partners.

	People skills	Process knowledge	Product knowledge	Partners Relation
Architecture (from design to support)			✓	
Assessments		✓		
College and university courses, certificates and degrees	✓			
Consultancy	✓			✓
Databases			✓	
Executive MBA and management courses	✓			
Frameworks and methodologies	✓	✓		
Governance	✓	✓		✓
Hardware (from design to support)			✓	
People skills (includes negotiation)	✓			✓
Program management	✓			
Programming			✓	
Project management	✓			
Risk management	✓			
Software (from design to support)			✓	

Table 2.1 Mapping 4Ps of Service Design to education

CHAPTER 3

Adult learning principles

Adults as learners

Everyone within an organization, whether managerial or non-managerial, needs to understand how adults learn. The reason is simple; everyone learns in his or her own way. The field of adult learning was pioneered by Malcolm Knowles[15], who identified the following characteristics of adult learners.

Adults are:
- Autonomous and self-directed
- Continuously accumulating a foundation of life experiences and knowledge
- Goal-oriented
- Relevancy-oriented
- Practical

As do all learners, adults need to be shown respect. Instructors must acknowledge the wealth of experiences that adult participants bring to the classroom. These adults should be treated as equals in experience and knowledge and allowed to voice their opinions freely in class. Of course, both instructors and learners must also acknowledge that different cultures in different parts of the world regard and approach education in different ways. Moreover, language plays an important role; it can be a formidable barrier to overcome, especially at exam time.

Motivating the adult learner

Another very important aspect of adult learning is motivation. As a manager, or as an individual, it is important to understand what motivates your personnel or what motivates you. At least six factors serve as sources of motivation for adult learning:

Social relationships	To make new friends, to meet a need for associations and friendships
External expectation	To comply with instructions from someone else; to fulfill the expectations or recommendations of someone with formal authority
Social welfare	To improve ability to serve mankind, prepare for service to the community, and improve ability to participate in community work
Personal advancement	To achieve higher status in a job, secure professional advancement, and stay abreast of competitors
Escape/stimulation	To relieve boredom, provide a break in the routine of home or work, and provide a contrast to other exacting details of life
Cognitive interest	To learn for the sake of learning, seek knowledge for its own sake, and satisfy an inquiring mind

Table 3.1 Sources of motivation for adult learning

The table above is adapted from an article by Stephen Lieb.[16]

Bloom's Taxonomy of Learning

Analysis of use of knowledge

In 1956, Benjamin Bloom[17] headed a group of educational psychologists who developed a taxonomy or classification of levels of intellectual behavior important in learning. (Taxonomy is a classification system.) These levels represented the goals of the educational process. Bloom's work on the taxonomy of learning has been very influential in our understanding of the levels of learning, both in groups and in each individual within a group.

A learning taxonomy is a scale of the degree of difficulty in the learning process. These levels apply to the cognitive, affective and psychomotor domains of learning, but in this section we will deal only with the cognitive sphere.

There is a concept called the Behaviorist perspective which claims that learning occurs when a demonstrated behavior change takes place. This perspective additionally defines three levels, also called domains of learning in which behavioral change occurs.

---

16   http://honolulu.hawaii.edu/intranet/committees/FacDevCom/guidebk/teachtip/adults-2.htm
     Stephen Lieb is Senior Technical Writer and Planner, Arizona Department of Health Services and part-time Instructor, South Mountain Community College – From VISION, Fall 1991

17   http://www.officeport.com/edu/blooms.htm

These three domains of learning are shown in Table 3.2 below.

Cognitive	This refers to mental activities such as thinking and acquisition of knowledge
Psychomotor	This refers to physical activities such as doing or performing a specific activit
Affective	This refers to feelings, emotions and attitudes

Table 3.2 the three domains of learning

Learning often involves a combination and overlap of the three domains. However, acquisition of knowledge and information is often primarily categorized under the Cognitive domain.

Bloom's Taxonomy of Learning is not only very precise but it is easily understood and is therefore one of the most widely used classifications today. According to Bloom's Taxonomy of Learning[18] there are different categories or levels of learning accompanied by behavior descriptions and examples of the activity learned; each step is built on the preceding step.

In other words, the acquisition of knowledge passes through the lowest level of recollection before getting to the highest level of evaluation. The following table illustrates the cognitive domain of Bloom's Taxonomy of Learning.

Note about column 3: Examples of activity to be trained, or demonstration and evidence to be measured

Note about column 4: Key words (verbs describing the activity to be trained or measured at each level)

---

18   Based on the 'Taxonomy Of Educational Objectives: Handbook 1, The Cognitive Domain' (Bloom, Engelhard, First, Hill, Krathwohl) 1956

1. Category or Level	2. Behavior Descriptions	3. Examples of activity...	4. Key words
Knowledge	recall or recognize information	multiple-choice test recount facts or statistics recall a process rules definitions quote law or procedure	arrange define memorize recognize state
Comprehension	understand meaning re-state data in one's own words interpret extrapolate translate	explain or interpret meaning from a given scenario or statement suggest treatment reaction or solution to given problem create examples or metaphors	explain reword / re-write describe classify summarize review report discuss estimate paraphrase
Application	use or apply knowledge put theory into practice use knowledge in response to real circumstances	put a theory into practical effect demonstrate solve a problem manage an activity	use apply relate discover manage solve implement change prepare conduct perform respond
Analysis	interpret elements organizational principles structure construction internal relationships quality reliability of individual components	identify constituent parts and functions of a process or concept or de-construct a methodology or process making qualitative assessment of elements relationships values and effects measure requirements or needs	analyze break down compare quantify measure test examine graph diagram extrapolate value divide
Synthesis (create/ build)	develop new unique structures systems models approaches ideas creative thinking operations	develop plans or procedures design solutions integrate methods resources ideas parts create teams or new approaches write protocols or contingencies	develop plan build design organize revise formulate propose establish integrate modify

1. Category or Level	2. Behavior Descriptions	3. Examples of activity...	4. Key words
Evaluation	assess effectiveness of whole concepts in relation to values outputs efficacy viability critical thinking strategic comparison and review judgment relating to external criteria	review strategic options or plans in terms of efficacy return on investment or cost-effectiveness practicability assess sustainability perform a SWOT analysis in relation to alternatives produce a financial justification for a proposition or venture calculate the effects of a plan or strategy perform a detailed risk analysis with recommendations and justifications	review justify assess critique present a case for defend report on investigate direct appraise argue project-manage

Table 3.3 Cognitive domains of Bloom's Taxonomy of Learning

Bloom created this taxonomy for categorizing levels of abstraction of questions that commonly occur in educational settings. In addition to the cognitive domain he, and others, developed the classification for the affective domain. The classification of the psychomotor domain was designed at a later time by others.

More on the categories or domains of learning

The **cognitive domain** of learning involves intellectual or 'head' learning. This involves the acquisition of information, concepts, data or theory. The learning is essentially abstract in nature.

The **affective domain** involves learning values, attitudes, feelings, appreciations and emotions. This may be intentional or unintentional teaching on the part of the instructor. Instructors may transmit to their students a love of learning, enthusiasm, eagerness in questioning and zest for life as well as a love of their discipline or they may convey to them bored or negative attitudes to all these things. Instructors are a 'significant other' in the lives of their students. A good instructor must try to remain aware of their own attitudes, values and levels of enthusiasm and present them to their students as such rather than as 'definitive aspects' which students must accept and value if they are to succeed. This domain of learning encompasses the instinctive (or 'gut') feelings which so affect every day living and behavior.

The third domain of learning is the **psychomotor**. This area involves the acquisition of physical skills or 'hand' learning. Examples of this type of learning are: typing, cartooning, heavy equipment operation, graphic design and craft work, automobile repair, etc.

The three domains of learning are not always separate entities but may well occur within any one of many courses offered to adults. The affective domain is the one most likely to be both in cognitive and psychomotor spheres and the one which instructors must bear in mind as one which goes on concurrently with any other activity.

The levels of learning in Bloom's taxonomy

The Bloom's taxonomy defines six levels of learning in the cognitive domain which are both sequential and cumulative. They move from the simple to the complex. This implies that in order to achieve the sixth level of learning, for example, the instructor must ensure that the previous five levels have been mastered.

1. The **knowing** level. Here the student is able to bring to mind or remember the appropriate material. The behavioral tasks associated with this level tax the student's memory and include such tasks as defining, recalling, listing, recognizing, describing and naming.

2. The **comprehending** level. Here the student is able to understand or grasp the meaning of what is being communicated and make use of the idea without relating it to other ideas or materials and without seeing the fullest possible meaning or translation of the idea. Behavioral tasks at this level would include stating in the student's own words, giving examples of, illustrating, inferring, summarizing and interpreting. These actions involve the knowing that has taken place at the first level.

3. The **applying** level. Here the student should be able to use ideas, principles and theories in new, particular and concrete situations. Behavioral tasks at this level involve both knowing and comprehension and might include choosing appropriate procedures, applying principles, using an approach or identifying the selection of options.

4. **Analyzing** is the fourth level of learning described by Bloom. At this level the student is able to break down a communication (rendered in any form) into constituent parts

in order to make the organization and significance of the whole clear. Breaking down, discriminating, diagramming, detecting, differentiating and illustrating are important behavioral tasks at this level and can be seen to include the previous levels of knowing, comprehending and applying. Here the significance of the constituent parts of an entity are examined in order to understand the whole more fully.

5. The **synthesis** level. At this level the student is able to re-assemble the various parts or elements of a concept into a unified organization or whole. This putting together again and making sense of small parts is a crucial factor in intelligence and learning. Behavioral tasks at this level would include creating, writing, designing, combining, composing, organizing, revising and planning. In order for this level of learning to occur, it must include the first four levels – knowing, comprehending, analyzing and applying. This level of learning is probably the most intense and exciting for student and teacher alike.

6. The **evaluating** level. In this phase the student is able to arrive at an overview and to judge the value and relative merit of ideas or procedures by using appropriate criteria. At this level of learning the student will be able to compare, judge, appraise, justify, criticize and contrast theories, procedures, methods and concepts. This level involves mastery of the five previous levels of knowing, comprehending, applying analyzing and synthesizing.

Remember that the levels are sequential and cumulative.

Bloom and the ITIL V3 qualification scheme

The qualification scheme uses Bloom's taxonomy as part of the construct of all syllabuses and exams. Since the qualification scheme is about acquiring knowledge and learning how to apply it, examiners, training organizations, instructors and those responsible for the procurement of education services need to understand how people learn. This becomes extremely useful when selecting the delivery method for the selected qualifications.

Every level of the ITIL V3 qualification scheme focuses primarily on two levels of the Bloom's taxonomy.
- The Foundation level qualification uses Bloom's levels 1 and 2
- The Intermediate level qualification use Bloom's levels 3 and 4
- The Master level uses Bloom's levels 5 and 6
- The complementary qualifications are the exception as they may cover Bloom's level 1, 2 and 3.

The following table, about the three domains of learning, provides a good view of what a person does at each level based on their predominant domain. Remember that everyone uses all three domains in various learning situations.

THREE DOMAINS OF LEARNING A tool for classification of learning To assist in the writing of learning outcomes and critical performances		
Cognitive domain knowledge, facts, information, ideas, concepts, principles, theories, systems of knowledge, procedures, processes, products	**Psychomotor domain** skills, hands-on, practice, application; basic operations, complex operations, integrated operations	**Affective domain** feelings, emotions, values, beliefs
Knowledge remembers previously learned material		
Comprehension grasp the information, and possibly create it in a different form	*Recognize requirements to perform an action* a beginner – different internal feelings	*Receive information* listen to different ideas that create a response of positive/negative feelings
Application use the information in some manner	*Explain the required performance* interim beginner	*Respond/accept/reject* react to and accept/reject ideas
Analysis break down an item into manageable parts	*Perform a single action independently* moving toward competence	*Recognize value or worth* beginning to identify personal and societal values
Synthesis put something together, create something new	*Combine several operations independently* competent; moving toward mastery	*Organize* conceptualize the value and resolve conflict between it and other values
Evaluation make sound reasoned judgments	*Perform the skill automatically* mastery of the skill	*Internalize* beliefs become part of who you are

Table 3.4 Cognitive domains mapped to the levels of learning

Understanding teaching and learning

Bloom, and others after him, found that most people retain the following.

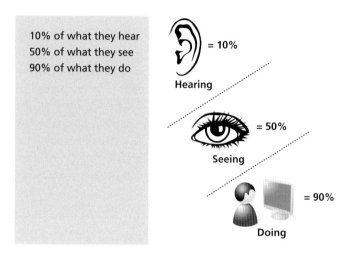

Figure 3.1 Understanding teaching and learning

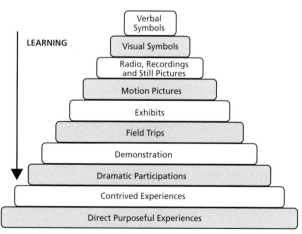

The greatest amount of learning usually takes place at the wide end of the cone.

Figure 3.2 Dale's Cone of Experience

Look carefully at the following diagram and observe the activities at the base for students.

Using the taxonomy of educational objectives

Once we understand the levels of learning, we can begin to use this information to write learning objectives, which ensure that participants gain the level of learning they need in order to meet the goals of the course.

One of the most helpful guides in identifying and defining learning objectives is the Taxonomy of Educational Objectives (Bloom, 1956; Krathwohl, 1964). This provides a classification of educational objectives that organizes the learning objectives into levels of comprehension and skill. It consists of a set of general and specific categories that encompass all possible learning outcomes that might be expected from instruction. The classification system was developed by psychologists, teachers, and test experts for use in curriculum development, teaching and testing. Because the system is based on the assumption that learning outcomes can be best described in terms of changes in student behavior, it is especially useful to trainers who are attempting to state their instructional objectives in behavioral terms.

The taxonomy is divided into three parts:
• The cognitive domain
• The affective domain
• The psychomotor domain

As outlined earlier, the cognitive domain includes those objectives that emphasize intellectual outcomes, such as knowledge, understanding and thinking skills. The affective domain includes those objectives that emphasize feeling and emotion, such as interest, attitudes, appreciation and methods of adjustment. The psychomotor domain includes those objectives that emphasize motor skills, such as handwriting, typing, swimming and operating machinery. Bloom developed a classification only for the cognitive and affective domains. Since then, there have been several authors of classifications of the psychomotor domain.

Learning objectives for the cognitive and affective domains

On the following pages are brief descriptions of each of the major categories in the cognitive and affective domains. The accompanying tables also present examples of objectives and illustrative behavioral terms (for stating the specific learning outcomes) for each of the categories. These examples should help clarify the meaning of each category and suggest types of learning outcomes to consider when identifying and defining instructional objectives.

It should be noted that the categories for classifying objectives in each domain of the taxonomy are arranged in hierarchical order, from the simplest behavioral outcomes to the most complex. For example, the cognitive domain starts with simple knowledge outcomes and then proceeds through the increasingly complex levels of comprehension, application, analysis, synthesis and evaluation. Each category is assumed to include the behavior at the previous levels. For example, a learning objective written for the application level assumes that the participant has already mastered both the knowledge and comprehension levels, and so on. The affective domain follows a similar hierarchical pattern.

The illustrative general instructional objectives (see Tables 3.7 and 3.9) are, of course, not exhaustive and are meant to serve as guides only. They should aid in further clarifying the taxonomy categories and should stimulate you to think of a broader range of objectives for your particular area of instruction.

The illustrative behavioral terms for stating specific learning outcomes also help clarify the taxonomy categories. It should be noted, however, that only a sample of the more relevant terms has been included in each category. It must also be kept in mind that the same behavioral term may be appropriately used at several different levels. The term identified, for example, is appropriate in each of the following cases:
- Knowledge: Identifies the correct definition of the term.
- Understanding: Identifies examples of the principle.
- Application: Identifies proper grammar usage.
- Analysis: Identifies the parts of a sentence.

Despite this considerable overlap in the use of behavioral terms, there are some terms that are more directly relevant to one taxonomy category than to another. Those listed in Tables 3.7 and 3.9 are merely suggestions, but they can assist in selecting the behavioral terms that most clearly convey the instructional intent of a given objective.

Learning objectives for the psychomotor domain

The psychomotor domain is concerned with motor skills. Bloom's team did not develop levels for this category; they felt they did not have the experience necessary to describe the levels. Dave (1970), Harrow and Simpson (1972) each developed taxonomies.

Although this domain (see Table 3.10) includes some learning outcomes that are common to most subjects (writing, speaking, laboratory skills), it receives major emphasis in courses such as home economics, trades education, physical education, art and music. Performance skills play a prominent role in the instructional objectives in these areas.

Learning objectives tables

The five tables which follow are designed to assist instructional designers in writing learning objectives.

Table No.	Table Name	Description
Table 3.6	Cognitive domain – major categories	Describes the six levels or categories of the Cognitive Domain and summarizes the learning content that is associated with each level.
Table 3.7	Cognitive domain – general instructional objectives	Describes the Cognitive Domain and provides examples of learning objectives of this domain. Each row represents a level of the domain, i.e. row 1 refers to the first level, Knowledge, and so on. The left column gives general information on the learning objective for that level. The right column provides specific wording that can be used for objectives at that level.
Table 3.8	Affective domain – major categories	Describes the five levels of the Affective Domain and summarizes the learning content that is associated with each level of that domain.
Table 3.9	Affective domain – general instructional objectives	Describes the Affective Domain and provides examples of learning objectives of this domain. Each row represents a level of the domain, i.e. row 1 refers to the first level, receiving, and so on. The left column gives general information on the learning objective for that level. The right column provides specific wording that can be used for objectives at that level.
Table 3.10	Psychomotor domain – general instructional objectives	Describes the Psychomotor Domain and provides examples of general and specific wording that can be used to write learning objectives at each level.

Table 3.5 List of tables for learning objectives

Cognitive Domain – major categories

Major categories of educational objectives in the COGNITIVE DOMAIN[19] are shown in Table 3.6 below.

1. Knowledge	Knowledge is defined as the remembering of previously learned material. This may involve the recall of a wide range of material, from specific facts to complete theories, but all that is required is the bringing to mind of the appropriate information. Knowledge represents the lowest level of learning outcomes in the cognitive domain.
2. Comprehension	Comprehension is defined as the ability to grasp the meaning of material. This may be shown by translating material from one form to another (words to numbers), by interpreting material (explaining or summarizing), and by estimating future trends (predicting consequences or effects). These learning outcomes go one step beyond the simple remembering of material and represent the lowest level of understanding.
3. Application	Application refers to the ability to use learned material in new and concrete situations. This may include the application of such things as rules, methods, concepts, principles, laws, and theories. Learning outcomes in this area require a higher level of understanding than those under comprehension.
4. Analysis	Analysis refers to the ability to break down material into its component parts so that its organizational structure may be understood. This may include the identification of the parts, analysis of the relationships between parts and recognition of the organizational principles involved. Learning outcomes here represent a higher intellectual level than comprehension and application because they require an understanding of both the content and the structural form of the material.
5. Synthesis	Synthesis refers to the ability to put parts together to form a new whole. This may involve the production of a unique communication (theme or speech), a plan of operations (research proposal), or a set of abstract relations (scheme for classifying information). Learning outcomes in this area stress creative behaviors, with major emphasis on the formulation of new patterns or structures.
6. Evaluation	Evaluation is concerned with the ability to judge the value of material (statement, novel, poem, research report) for a given purpose. The judgments are to be based on definite criteria. These may be internal criteria (organization) or external criteria (relevance to the purpose) and the student may determine the criteria or be given them. Learning outcomes in this area are highest in the cognitive hierarchy because they contain elements of all of the other categories, plus conscious value judgments based on clearly defined criteria.

Table 3.6 Cognitive domain – major categories

---

19   Bloom, 1956

Cognitive Domain – general instructional objectives

Examples of General Instructional Objectives and behavioral terms for the COGNITIVE DOMAIN of the taxonomy are shown in Table 3.7 below.

Illustrative General Instructional Objectives	Illustrative behavioral terms for stating specific learning outcomes
Knows common terms Knows specific facts Knows methods and procedures Knows basic concepts	Defines, describes, identifies, labels, lists, matches, names, outlines, produces, selects, states
Understands facts and principles Interprets verbal material Interprets charts and graphs Translates verbal material to mathematical formulas Estimates future consequences implied in data Justifies methods and procedures	Converts, defends, distinguishes, intimates, explains, extends, generalizes, gives examples, infers, paraphrases, predicts, rewrites, summarizes
Applies concepts and principles to new situations Applies laws and theories to practical situations Solves mathematical problems Constructs charts and graphs Demonstrates correct usage of a method or procedure	Changes, computes, demonstrates, discovers, manipulates, modifies, predicts, prepares, relates, shows, solves, uses
Recognizes unstated assumptions Recognizes logical fallacies in reasoning Distinguishes between facts and inferences Evaluates the relevancy of data Analyzes the organizational structure of a work	Breaks down, diagrams, differentiates, discriminates, distinguishes, identifies, illustrates, infers, lines, points out, relates, separates, subdivides
Writes a well organized theme or speech Writes a creative short story (or poem or music) Proposes a plan for an experiment Integrates learning from different areas into a plan for solving a problem Formulates a new scheme for classifying objects (or events, or ideas)	Categorizes, combines, computes, composes, creates, devises, designs, explains, generates, modifies, organizes, plans, rearranges, reconstructs, relates, reorganizes, revises, rewrites, summarizes, tells, writes
Judges the logical consistency of written material Judges the adequacy with which conclusions are supported by data Judges the value of a work by use of internal criteria Judges the value of a work by use of external standards of excellence	Appraises, compares, concludes, contrasts, criticizes, describes, discriminates, explains, justifies, interprets, relates, summarizes, supports

Table 3.7 Cognitive domain – general instructional objectives

Affective Domain – major categories

Major categories in the AFFECTIVE DOMAIN of the Taxonomy of Educational Objectives[20] are shown in Table 3.8 below.

Receiving	This refers to the student's willingness to attend to particular phenomena or stimuli (classroom activities, textbook, music, etc.). From a teaching standpoint, it is concerned with getting, holding and directing the student's attention. Learning outcomes in this area range from the simple awareness that a thing exists to selective attention on the part of the learner. Receiving represents the lowest level of learning outcomes in the affective domain.
Responding	This refers to active participation on the part of the student. At this level they not only attend to a particular phenomenon but also react to it in some way. Learning outcomes in this area may emphasize acquiescence in responding (reads assigned material), willingness to respond (voluntarily read beyond assignment) or satisfaction in responding (reads for pleasure or enjoyment). The higher levels of this category include those instruction objectives that are commonly classified under 'interests'; that is, those that stress the seeking out and enjoyment of particular activities.
Valuing	This is concerned with the worth or value a student attaches to a particular object, phenomenon, or behavior. This ranges in degree from the more simple acceptance of a value (desires to improve group skills) to the more complex level of commitment (assumes responsibility for the effective functioning of the group). Valuing is based on the internalization of a set of specified values, but clues to these values are expressed in the student's overt behavior. Learning outcomes in this area are concerned with behavior that is consistent and stable enough to make the value clearly identifiable. Instructional objectives that are commonly classified under 'attitudes' and 'appreciation' would fall into this category.
Organization	This is concerned with bringing together different values, resolving conflicts between them and beginning the building of an internally consistent value system. Thus the emphasis is on comparing, relating and synthesizing values. Learning outcomes may be concerned with the conceptualization of a value (recognizes the responsibility of each individual for improving human relations) or with the organization of a value system (develops a vocational plan that satisfies his/her need for both economic security and social service). Instruction objectives relating to the development of a philosophy of life would fall into this category.
Characterization by a Value or Value Complex	At this level of the affective domain, the individual has a value system that has controlled his/her behavior for a sufficiently long time for him/her to have developed a characteristic 'life style'. Thus, the behavior is pervasive, consistent, and predictable. Learning outcomes at this level cover a broad range of activities, but the major emphasis is on the fact that the behavior is typical or characteristic of the student. Instructional objectives that are concerned with the student's general patterns of adjustment (personal, social, emotional) would be appropriate here.

Table 3.8 Affective domain – major categories

---

20   Krathwohl, 1964

Affective Domain – general instructional objectives

Examples of General Instructional Objectives and behavioral terms for the AFFECTIVE DOMAIN of the taxonomy are shown in Table 3.9 below.

Illustrative General Instructional Objectives	Illustrative behavioral terms for stating specific learning outcomes
Listens attentively Shows awareness of the importance of learning Shows sensitivity to human needs and social problems Accepts differences of race and culture Attends closely to the classroom activities	Asks, chooses, describes, follows, gives, holds, identifies, locates, names, points to, selects, sits erect, replies, uses
Completes assigned homework Obeys school rules Participates in class discussion Completes laboratory work Volunteers for special tasks Shows interest in subject Enjoys helping others	Answers, assists, compiles, conforms, discusses, greets, helps, labels, performs, practices, presents, reads, recites, reports, selects, tells, writes
Demonstrates belief in the democratic process Appreciates good literature (art or music) Appreciates the role of science (or other subjects) in everyday life Shows concern for the welfare of others Demonstrates problem-solving attitude Demonstrates commitment to social improvement	Completes, describes, differentiates, explains, follows, forms, initiates, invites, joins, justifies, proposes, reads, reports, selects, shares, studies, works
Recognizes the need for balance between freedom and responsibility in a democracy Recognizes the role of systematic planning in solving problems Accepts responsibility for his/her own behavior Understands and accepts his/her own strengths and limitations Formulates a life plan in harmony with his/her abilities, interests and beliefs	Adheres, alters, arranges, combines, compares, completes, defends, explains, generalizes, identifies, integrates, modifies, orders, organizes, prepares, relates, synthesizes
Displays safety consciousness Demonstrates self-reliance in working independently Practices cooperation in group activities Uses objective approach in group activities Demonstrates industry, punctuality and self-discipline Maintains good health habits	Acts, discriminates, displays, influences, listens, modifies, performs, practices, proposes, qualifies, questions, revises, serves, solves, uses

Table 3.9 the affective domain – general instructional objectives

Psychomotor Domain – general instructional objectives

Examples of General Instructional Objectives and behavioral terms for the PSYCHO-MOTOR DOMAIN of the taxonomy are shown in Table 3.10 below.

Taxonomy Categories	Illustrative General Instructional Objectives	Illustrative behavioral terms for stating specific learning outcomes
Receive	The learner notices the activity.	Detect, recognize, relate, respond, react
Observe	The learner observes a more experienced person in his/her performance of the skill. Asked to observe sequences and relationships and to pay particular attention to the finished product.	Identifies, describes, explains,
Imitate	The learner begins to acquire the rudiments of the skill. The learner follows directions and sequences under close supervision. The learner is conscious of deliberate effort to imitate the model.	Assembles, builds, calibrates, changes, cleans, composes, connects, constructs, mends, mixes, nails, paints, sands, weighs, wraps, saws, sharpens
Practice	The entire sequence is performed repeatedly. All aspects of the act are performed in sequence. Conscious effort fades as the performance becomes more or less habitual. Timing and coordination are emphasized. Here, the person has acquired the skill but is not an expert.	Practices, matches, repeats, operates, monitors, sets up
Adapt	Perfection of the skill. Creates new patterns to perfect the skill or develop new method.	Adapts, alters, rearranges, organizes, revises, manipulates, corrects

Table 3.10 Psychomotor domain – general instructional objectives

Summary

In summary, the Taxonomy of Educational Objectives provides a three-domain scheme (cognitive, affective and psychomotor) for classifying all possible instructional objectives. Each domain is subdivided into a series of categories that are arranged in hierarchical order – from simple to complex. A review of these categories and the illustrative objectives and behavioral terms accompanying those (Tables 3.6 to 3.10) should aid in:

- Identifying objectives for a particular instruction unit
- Stating objectives at the proper level of generality
- Defining objectives in the most relevant behavioral terms

- Checking on the comprehensiveness of a list of objectives
- Communicating with others concerning the nature and level of learning objectives

As useful as the taxonomy may be, don't become a slave to the system classification. Some objectives will include elements of all three taxonomy domains. Such objectives should not be discarded simply because they are difficult to classify. If revision will increase their usefulness, as well as identification with one of the domains, then revision may be the way. But if revision of the objectives distorts rather than clarifies their instructor intent, the original statements should be retained. In short, the taxonomy should serve as a guide – not as a master.

CHAPTER 4

The right qualification for the right people

This chapter is not trying to 'sell' you ITIL. It is about helping you make sense of the qualification scheme. The chapter focuses on the considerations about which ITIL V3 track/stream or qualification to select for you or your IT personnel. This information should help you decide which ITIL qualification to select if you decide to follow that route.

ITIL V3 qualifications highlights

There are five categories of qualifications within the scheme. There are four levels: Foundation, Intermediate, Expert and Master. There is also a growing, albeit slowly, complementary set of qualifications centered on specific topics.

There are two streams or groupings of qualifications within the qualification scheme. They are the Service Lifecycle, which has a management focus, and the Service Capabilities stream which focuses more on the practitioner aspects.

Qualifications with a management focus (Lifecycle stream)	Qualifications with a practitioner focus (Capabilities stream)
Service Strategy Service Design Service Transition Service Operation Continual Service Improvement	Service Offerings and Agreements Planning, Protection and Optimization Release, Control and validation Operational support and analysis

Table 4.1 Primary focus of the intermediate qualification streams

Management focus (Service Lifecycle)

In the management stream, the qualifications focus on topics that include planning, designing, building, deploying, and improving both services and processes as part of each lifecycle phase. Each of the management qualification covers a particular phase of the Service Lifecycle. The management qualifications only cover the material found in the core book relevant to that phase. No other books are referenced in any of the management stream syllabuses.

This series will be of interest to candidates wishing to obtain knowledge of ITIL V3 practices within the Service Lifecycle context. The primary focus is the Service Lifecycle itself, the use of process and practice elements used within it and the management capabilities needed to deliver quality Service Management practices in an organization.

The Service Lifecycle series is focused on each stage of the Service Lifecycle and syllabuses are matched to each of the five core practice areas. Each module of the Service Lifecycle series covers an introduction to the Service Lifecycle, the principles, processes, functions and activities within that stage of the ITIL Service Management Lifecycle, and the technology and implementation considerations.

Other than the individual's job title, which usually includes words such as director, managers, and supervisor, it is proposed that individuals whose job function currently includes or will soon include the following elements should pursue the Service Lifecycle qualifications.

Service/process
- Service/process documentation and awareness
- Defining service/process metrics
- Reviewing service/process metrics and taking action
- Service/process design
- Improving service/process effectiveness and efficiency
- Reviewing proposed enhancements
- Providing input to the Service Improvement Plan
- Addressing issues with the service/process
- Identifying staff training needs and role awareness
- Ensure service/process reviews and audits take place
- Interfaces with line management
- Ensuring staffing resources are adequate

Service/process policy
If an individual is responsible for defining, documenting and enforcing policies around services and processes, this individual should pursue the Service Lifecycle qualifications. A policy is a formally documented set of management expectations and intentions about a service or process. Policies are used to direct decisions and to ensure consistent and appropriate development and implementation of:

- Service/process
- Standards, either internal or external
- Roles of the people involved with the service or the process
- Activities of the process

Process objectives

If an individual is responsible for defining, documenting and enforcing process objectives in support of services, this individual should pursue the Service Lifecycle qualifications. It is the defined purpose or aim of a process that governs the process activities. The objectives are also sometimes referred to as the process goals. The objective of a process is realized to the degree that the Critical Success Factors for that process are achieved.

Service/process documentation

Some individuals are responsible for a service or process that is properly documented in order to achieve a service or process that:
- Is consistent across the organization
- Is provided and conducted with integrity
- Utilizes a common language understood across the organization
- Performs knowledge transfer in a consistent and repeatable manner
- Has people complying to the appropriate policies
- Has verifiable and measurable activities

These individuals should pursue the Service Lifecycle qualifications. These individuals do not have to create or maintain the documents but are responsible for the appropriate personnel to do so. The documents include policies, flows, procedures, and work instructions, templates for records, reports and models for escalation, prioritization and assessment.

Process feedback

If an individual is responsible for providing consolidated feedback (reporting) about a service or process from an internal or external perspective (in-sourced or outsourced) or from a quality, performance, value or compliance perspective, then this individual should pursue the Service Lifecycle qualifications.

Service/process resources and capabilities

All services and processes require resources in order to function. The resources fall into the following categories: financial capital, infrastructure, applications, information and people.

All services and processes develop capabilities that are achieved over time and are demonstrated in their respective ability to support the management team, the organization, the processes themselves, the organizational and individual knowledge and the people.

If an individual is responsible for providing resources or developing the capabilities then this individual should pursue the Service Lifecycle qualifications.

Practitioner focus (Service Capabilities)

The practitioner stream qualifications are focused on the management and execution of the day-to-day activities required to provide services. Each practitioner qualification covers a particular cluster of processes. Each cluster focuses on one of four practical application of the framework.

The four areas are:
- Business relationships
- Designing services, processes and architectures
- Building, testing, deploying service solutions
- Operational support of the services

By their very nature, the four areas above cover material found in the other ITIL core books.

The series is focused on role-based clusters in a modular set. Each cluster contains groupings of processes and roles from within Service Management, intended to offer candidates a balanced knowledge of ITIL practices that have direct interaction and dependencies in their daily use.

The series will be of interest to candidates who wish to become qualified at a deeper level of understanding of processes and roles. Attention to the Service Lifecycle is illustrated as part of the curriculum; however, the primary focus is the process activities, execution, and use throughout the Service Lifecycle.

If an individual is not considered to be in a managerial or supervisor role and if this individual's primary focus is to execute the activities and work instructions of processes, gather, process, and analyze data, or perform the various techniques described is the core books, then this individual should pursue the Service Capabilities qualifications.

ITIL V3 qualifications acronyms

MANAGEMENT (Lifecycle)		PRACTITIONERS (Capabilities)	
SS	Service Strategy	SOA	Service Offerings and Agreements
SD	Service Design	PPO	Plan, Protect and Optimize
ST	Service Transition	RCV	Release, Control and Validation
SO	Service Operation	OSA	Operational Support & Analysis
CSI	Continual Service Operation		
CAPSTONE			
MALC	Managing across the Lifecycle		

Table 4.2 ITIL V3 qualification acronyms

Syllabus coverage for Practitioner qualifications

For people interested in the Practitioner qualifications, the following table provides a list of the chapters from each core book referenced in the syllabus for that Practitioner.

Practitioner	Service Strategy	Service Design	Service Transition	Service Operation	Continual Service Improvement
OSA	2, 3	7, 9	2, 9	2, 4, 6, 7, 8, 9	3, 4, 7, 9
RCV	2, 3	7	2, 4, 6, 7, 9	2, 4, 6, 7, 8	3, 5
PPO	2, 5, 9	2, 3, 4, 6, 7, 8, 9	2, 9	2, 7, 9	
SOA	2, 3, 4, 5	2, 3, 4, 6, 7, 8, 9,	2, 9	8, 9	3

Table 4.3 Core book chapter for each Capability/Practitioner qualification

As one can see, the OSA qualification primarily focuses on the Service Operation and Continual Service Improvement books while the RCV qualification focuses on the Service Transition and Service Operation books. This makes a lot of sense since the 'operational' activities center around support and handling changes.

The PPO and SOA qualifications primarily focus on the Service Strategy and Service Design books. This also makes perfect sense since designing services and managing agreements are usually executed by more senior staff and management.

Processes covered

The following table provides the list of the processes covered in each of the five ITIL core books. The Management-focused qualifications will cover the processes identified in each of the five phases in addition to other relevant management concepts for each phase.

Note: A course acronym beside a book title indicates that only certain sections from this book are used. They usually exclude the sections on the processes.

	Management (Lifecycle)	Practitioner (Capabilities)
SERVICE STRATEGY		
Other sections of this book are also used as part of the OSA, RCV & PPO practitioners		
Service Strategy	SS	n/a
Financial Management	SS	SOA
Service Portfolio Management	SS	SOA
Demand Management	SS	PPO, SOA
SERVICE DESIGN		
Other sections of this book are also used as part of the OSA, RCV & SOA practitioners		
Service Catalogue Management	SD	SOA
Service Level Management	SD	SOA
Capacity Management	SD	PPO
Availability Management	SD	PPO
IT Service Continuity Management	SD	PPO
Information Security Management	SD	PPO
Supplier Management	SD	SOA
SERVICE TRANSITION		
Other sections of this book are also used as part of the OSA, PPO & SOA practitioners		
Transition Planning and Support	ST	n/a
Change Management	ST	RCV
Service Asset and Configuration Management	ST	RCV
Release & Deployment Management	ST	RCV
Service Validation and Testing	ST	RCV
Evaluation	ST	RCV
Knowledge Management	ST	RCV
SERVICE OPERATION		
Other sections of this book are also used as part of the OSA, RCV & PPO practitioners		
Event Management	SO	OSA
Incident Management	SO	OSA
Request Fulfillment	SO	OSA, RCV
Problem Management	SO	OSA

	Management (Lifecycle)	Practitioner (Capabilities)
Access Management	SO	OSA
Functions		
Service Desk	SO	OSA
Technical Management	SO	OSA
IT Operations Management	SO	OSA
Application Management	SO	OSA
CONTINUAL SERVICE IMPROVEMENT		
Other sections of this book are also used as part of the RCV, PPO & SOA practitioners		
Seven Step Improvement	CSI	

Table 4.4 Processes covered for Intermediate qualification

Learning outcomes

The learning outcomes for all five Management and all four Practitioners qualifications are basically the same. The wording may vary slightly from syllabus to syllabus but the intent is the same. The common learning outcomes are:

- Understanding of the importance of Service Management as a practice concept and <qualification name> principles, purpose and objective
- How ITIL <qualification name> interacts with other Service Lifecycle processes
- The activities, methods and functions used in each of the ITIL <qualification name> processes
- The roles and responsibilities within ITIL <qualification name> and the activities and functions to achieve operational excellence
- Explain how to measure ITIL <qualification name>
- Understanding of technology and implementation considerations surrounding ITIL <qualification name>
- Challenges, critical success factors and risks associated with ITIL <qualification name>

The four Practitioner qualifications also contain the following two additional learning outcomes:

- The importance of ITIL <qualification name> while providing service
- The importance of IT Security and its contributions to ITIL <qualification name>

Mapping qualifications to job focus

The following section primarily applies to IT personnel who are not ITIL consultants, ITIL trainers or working for an ITSM tool vendor/reseller. The reason is that ITIL education, training, and certification is usually either mandatory or part of the job for these individuals.

The following is a mapping of the qualifications to a person's primary role or focus. In larger organizations, people tend to focus on one area only. Some people may of course focus on more than one area. In small to medium-sized organizations, people may be focusing on many areas.

There is no perfect matching method. We recommend considering your current primary business needs in order to determine which qualification to attend yourself or which qualification to procure for your staff.

Before looking at the specific audience, it must be understood that each qualification is also aimed at people looking to achieve the ITIL Expert and/or the ITIL Master qualifications. To avoid repetition, the following provides the three general target audiences for each of the Management and Practitioner qualifications. The only differences are the Service Phase in the first bullet for the Management qualification and the Practitioner name in the second bullet for the Practitioner qualifications.

For all Management qualifications (Service Lifecycle)
- IT professionals working within or about to enter a <Service phase> environment and requiring a detailed understanding of the processes, functions and activities involved
- Individuals seeking the ITIL Expert in IT Service Management for which this qualification is one of the prerequisite modules
- Individuals seeking progress towards the ITIL Master in IT Service Management for which the ITIL Expert is a prerequisite

For all Practitioner qualifications (Service Capabilities)
- Individuals who have attained the ITIL V3 Foundation certificate in Service Management, or the ITIL V2 Foundation plus the V3 Foundation Bridge certificate and who wish to advance to higher level ITIL certifications
- IT professionals that are working within an organization that has adopted and adapted ITIL who need to be informed about and thereafter contribute to an ongoing service improvement program

Of course, most IT organizations will be looking to increase the knowledge and understanding of their personnel in some specific area first. The following table provides the most appropriate target audience for IT managers and/or their IT personnel.

Qualification	Primary target audience
Service Strategy	Individuals who require a deeper understanding of the ITIL Service Strategy stage of the Service Lifecycle and how activities in it may be implemented to enhance the quality of IT service management within an organization
Service Design	Individuals who require a detailed understanding of the ITIL Service Design phase of the Service Lifecycle and how it may be implemented to enhance the quality of IT service provision within an organization.
Service Transition	Individuals who require a detailed understanding of the ITIL Service Transition phase of the Service Lifecycle and how it may be implemented to enhance the quality of IT service provision within an organization
Service Operation	Individuals who require a detailed understanding of the ITIL Service Operation phase of the Service Lifecycle and how it may be implemented to enhance the quality of IT service provision within an organization
Continual Service Improvement	Individuals who require a detailed understanding of the ITIL Continual Service Improvement phase of the Service Lifecycle and how it may be implemented to enhance the quality of IT service provision within an organization
Service Offerings and Agreements	Operational personnel involved in Service Portfolio Management; Service Catalogue Management; Service Level Management; Demand Management; Supplier Management; Financial Management and Business Relationship Management who wish to enhance their role-based capabilities.
Planning, Protection and Optimization	Operational personnel involved in Capacity Management, Availability Management, IT Service Continuity Management, Information Security Management, Demand Management and Risk Management, who wish to enhance their role-based capabilities.
Release, Control and Validation	Operational personnel involved in Change Management, Release and Deployment Management, Service Validation and Testing, Service Asset and Configuration Management, Request Fulfillment, Service Evaluation and Knowledge Management, who wish to enhance their role based capabilities.
Operational Support and Analysis	Operational personnel involved in Event Management Process, Incident Management Process, Request Fulfillment Process, Problem Management Process, Access Management Process, Service Desk, Technical Management, IT Operations Management and Application Management

Table 4.5 Primary target audiences for Intermediate qualifications

Managing across the lifecycle (MALC)
This qualification is aimed at individuals who require a business and management level understanding of the ITIL V3 Lifecycle and how it may be implemented to enhance the quality of IT service provision within an organization.

Different job focus means different courses

First, for everyone on the team it is mandatory to start with the ITIL V3 Foundation qualification. 'Everyone' includes all of IT personnel, supervisory roles, middle management, senior management and even the CIO. Yes, the CIO. It is fully understandable that many people will claim lack of time or lack of applicability to their roles. This is utter nonsense. In order to properly adopt and adapt good practices everyone must understand the basics. This certification is a requirement for all intermediate ITIL V3 certifications. It is usually offered over a three-day period and is often brought in-house to reduce costs; it is also readily available in computer-based or web-based format.

For non-management personnel	Management personnel such as team leads, supervisors and managers
ITIL V3 Foundation	ITIL V3 Foundation Continual Service Improvement is recommended for team leads, supervisors and managers to assist them in identifying and prioritizing improvement opportunities, as well as service measurement and reporting
If the focus of this person or group	**If the focus or this person (or persons) is managing**
is technical or application support (fixing things); go for *Operational Support and Analysis*	a support group or groups (fixing things), go for *Service Operation*
centers around changes, releases and deployment; go for *Release, Control and Validation*	personnel involved in handling changes, releases and deployment; go for *Service Transition*
is about ensuring the correct levels of availability, capacity, service continuity and security *Planning, Protection and Optimization* *Continual Service Improvement* These qualifications are usually more useful for more senior analysts-type personnel	people involved in translating business requirements into IT requirements, propose significant changes and improvements; go for *Service Design*
	agreements, with the business or with other internal parties, or about contracts with external organizations; go for *Service Offerings and Agreement*

Table 4.6 Different qualification for different job focus

Credit value and system

Each ITIL qualification is worth a certain number of credits. These credits can be accumulated toward the ITIL Expert qualification. The calculation is simple.

Foundation	2 credits
Intermediate	Accumulate 15 or more credits
Capstone (MALC)	5 credits
Expert (minimum credit requirement)	22 credits

Table 4.7 Credit system

With the ITIL Expert qualification, there are additional rules such as a balanced mix of topics. Individuals should only attempt to acquire credits from non-overlapping qualifications. For example, you could go for the OSA qualification but should avoid the Service Operation qualification as they both cover primarily on a common set of topics: the Service Operation book.

Clarification:

Individuals can take and achieve overlapping qualifications. There is nothing against this. If a candidate needs both the Management and the Practitioner courses for a particular topic, then they should go for it.

	Management	Practitioners
Number of credits	3	4

Table 4.8 Credit by stream

Contact hours

The Management and the Practitioner streams have different requirements for contact hours.

Contact hours are those spent:
A. In a classroom with an instructor
B. In an instructor-led online (virtual) classroom
   'a' and 'b' can be in a public setting or an onsite setting (brought inside the organization)
C. A self paced computer-based (CBT) or web-based (WBT) designed course

The following are <u>excluded</u> from the official contact hours:
- Syllabus recommended self study time
- Reading assignments or assignments before the course
- Homework between sessions
- Breaks and lunch periods
- Exam period

	Management	Practitioner
Contact hours	21	30
Recommended hours of self study	21	12

Table 4.9 Contact hours by stream

Focus of the qualifications

To help you to select the qualification to pursue, it is recommended that you compare the target audience and the topics covered by the Management and the Practitioner qualifications for the phase of the lifecycle of interest.

Note: all times are in hours and minutes format (HH:MM)

Focus on Service Operation

SERVICE OPERATION SO (Management)		OPERATIONAL SUPPORT & ANALYSIS OSA (Practitioner)	
Introduction	0:45	Introduction	1:30
Principles	1:00	Event Management	2:30
Processes	6:00	Incident Management	5:00
Common activities	3:30	Request Fulfillment	4:00
Organizing	4:00	Problem Management	5:00
Technology	1:00	Access Management	2:30
Implementation	2:00	Service Desk	3:30
Challenges, etc	0:15	Functions	4:00
Summary, Exam Preparation and Directed Studies	2:00	Technology and Implementation considerations	2:00
		Summary, Exam Preparation and Directed Studies	2:00
TOTAL	20:30	TOTAL	32:00

Table 4.10 Service Operation focus

Focus on Service Transition

SERVICE TRANSITION ST (Management)		RELEASE, CONTROL & VALIDATION RCV (Practitioner)	
Introduction to Service Transition	2:30	Introduction	1:30
Service Transition Principles	2:00	Change Management	4:00
Service Transition Processes	7:00	Service Asset and Configuration Management	3:30
Service Transition related activities	3:00	Service Validation and Testing	4:00
Organizing for Service Transition	1:30	Release and Deployment Management	4:00
Consideration of Technology	1:00	Request Fulfillment	2:00
Implementation and improvement of Service Transition	2:00	Service Evaluation	2:00
Summary, Exam Preparation and Directed Studies	2:00	Knowledge Management	3:30
		Service Release, Control and Validation Roles and Responsibilities	2:00
		Technology and Implementation Considerations	3:30
		Summary, Exam Preparation and Directed Studies	2:00
TOTAL	21:00	TOTAL	32:00

Table 4.11 Service Transition focus

Focus on Service Design

SERVICE DESIGN SD (Management)		PLANNING, PROTECTION, & OPTIMIZATION PPO (Practitioner)	
Introduction to Service Design	2:00	Introduction	1:30
Service Design Principles	4:00	Capacity Management	4:00
Service Design Processes	7:00	Availability Management	5:00
Service Design technology related activities	2:00	IT Service Continuity Management	5:00
Organizing for Service Design	1:30	Information Security Management	4:00
Consideration of Technology	0:30	Demand Management	2:00
Implementation and improvement of Service Design	2:00	Challenges, Critical Success Factors, and Risks	2:00

SERVICE DESIGN SD (Management)		PLANNING, PROTECTION, & OPTIMIZATION PPO (Practitioner)	
Summary, Exam Preparation and Directed Studies	2:00	Planning, Protection and Optimization Roles and Responsibilities	2:00
		Technology and Implementation Considerations	3:00
		Summary, Exam Preparation and Directed Studies	2:00
TOTAL	**21:00**	**TOTAL**	**30:30**

Table 4.12 Service Design focus

Focus on Service Strategy

SERVICE STRATEGY SS (Management)		SERVICE OFFERINGS & AGREEMENTS SOA (Practitioner)	
Service Strategy Principles	2:30	Introduction	1:30
Defining Services and Market Spaces	3:00	Service Portfolio Management	2:30
Conducting Strategic Assessments	3:30	Service Catalogue Management	3:00
Financial Management	2:00	Service Level Management	8:00
Service Portfolio Management	1:00	Demand Management	2:30
Managing Demand	3:30	Supplier Management	3:00
Driving Strategy Through The Service Lifecycle	2:00	Financial Management	5:30
Critical Success Factors and Risks	2:00	Business Relationship Manager	1:00
Summary, Exam Preparation and Directed Studies	1:30	Service Offerings and Agreement Roles and Responsibilities	1:00
		Technology and Implementation Considerations	2:00
		Summary, Exam Preparation and Directed Studies	2:00
TOTAL	**21:00**	**TOTAL**	**32:00**

Table 4.13 Service Strategy focus

Focus on Continual Service Improvement – CSI

Continual Service Improvement CSI (Management)	
Introduction to Continual Service Improvement	2:00
Continual Service Improvement Principles	2:00
Continual Service Improvement Process	5:30
Continual Service Improvement Methods and Techniques	4:30
Organization for Continual Service Improvement	1:30
Technology for Continual Service Improvement	1:30
Implementing Continual Service Improvement	2:00
Critical success factors and risks	2:00
Summary, Exam Preparation and Directed Studies	2:00
TOTAL	**23:00**

Table 4.14 Continual Service Improvement focus

Focus on Managing Across the Lifecycle – MALC

Managing across the lifecycle MAL (Capstone)	
Introduction to IT Service Management Business and Managerial Issues	2:00
Management of Strategic Change	2:00
Risk management	5:30
Managing the Planning and Implementation of IT Service Management	4:30
Understanding Organizational Challenges	1:30
Service assessment	1:30
Understanding Complementary Industry Guidance and Tool Strategies	2:00
Summary, Exam Preparation and Directed Studies	2:00
TOTAL	**30:00**

Table 4.15 Managing across the Lifecycle focus

Summary

When looking at your education budget, try not to allocate it into only one category of certification. Of course, you know what your requirements are. Nonetheless, it is important to keep in mind the five aspects of service design and the four Ps of process design. Both complement each other and actually overlap each other.

Select a training organization that uses adult learning best practices as well as Bloom's taxonomy in all their delivery methods. Make sure the organization has a solid reputation and make sure the instructors are truly qualified.

Select the method of delivery carefully. First, a computer or web-based approach is cheaper than an instructor led one. However, a computer or web-based course does not offer the opportunity for interaction with other attendees. This is a major benefit of an instructor-led course.

Second, an instructor-led online course does offer interaction but it is not the same as being physically in the same room as everyone else. Thirdly, a public course offers the opportunity for learning about the experiences of other organizations while an in-house course provides the opportunity for focusing the discussions on your organization's situation if so desired.

Finally, make sure to identify the primary focus of an individual candidate and their personnel interest before sending them to a certification course.

CHAPTER 5

Course and examination preparation tips

A note about examinations
Note from the author

As the author of this book and as a former Senior Examiner for the ITIL V3 qualification scheme I cannot, in good conscience, claim the following advice will ensure that you will pass the exam. I was involved and instrumental in the development of the exam format and I was also involved in the various development stages of some exam papers.

Furthermore, I have no more access to the pool of scenarios and questions. This right belongs to the Accreditor and to the EIs. Moreover, I did sign a non-disclosure agreement with the Accreditor.

However, what I can do is to show you how to break down scenarios into relevant pieces of information that will be useful in helping you select the best answer to the question at hand.

Although it would be nice to provide absolutes, reality tells us otherwise. Nothing in life is certain, everything is fluid. The qualification scheme is indeed dynamic and undergoes regular reviews. The chief examiner and the team leads for each qualification review the syllabus, the live papers and the sample papers regularly to ensure they are free from grammatical and syntax errors. They also review the results of papers over time, looking at items such as the individual success rate of a particular question. They use statistics as well as feedback from the EIs and the ATOs.

There are always at least two live papers for each qualification. The results are analyzed for statistical anomalies. Let us assume that a particular question is answered correctly 100% of the time all the time. Is this good or bad? Before this can be answered, further analysis is required.

- How long has the question been in circulation?
- What is the size of the sample?
- What is the exam language?
- What is the geographical dispersion of the question?
- Is only one EI involved?
- Is only one ATO involved?

- Is only one instructor involved?
- Is only one customer organization involved?

These questions and others need to be explored and answered before it can be said that the perfect success rate of a question is valid or not.

The same logic applies to a question with an abysmal success rate.

If required, errors are corrected as appropriate. The EIs will receive an update about modifications to live papers. The ATOs only receive information about updates to sample papers. If deemed necessary, a question may be retired and replaced with another one.

It is important to mention the above to dispel the false rumors that nothing is being done to correct errors or that papers are deliberately engineered to fail people. This is absolutely not true.

An exam paper is not designed to be so easy that anyone will be successful. Neither is an exam paper designed to fail everyone. To optimize credibility, the expectations from the Qualification Board, the EIs and the examiners (the people who create the exam questions) are that a certain number of people will, for various reasons, fail the examination. Another expectation is that not everyone should pass on the first attempt either. There needs to be a high enough level of difficulty.

Before you attend the course

The candidate's manager has approved the course and signed off the related expenses. The three most popular delivery methods are:
- Onsite brought into the organization
- Public conference venue, often in a hotel conference room
- Online, whether instructor-led, self-paced or blended approach

Each of the above three delivery methods brings its own set of benefits and challenges.

Benefits

Onsite
- Group and team dynamics
- Candidates know each other
- Same message heard at the same time

- Can be used as part of practical adoption and adaptation of good practices
- Many people, cost effective

Public
- Different view points by candidates from other organizations
- Networking opportunities
- Learn from other's experiences, challenges and successes

Online
- An organization using this method should achieve the same benefits as the onsite delivery method. Candidates from various offices/regions can attend training at same time
- Using the instructor-led or blended methods for a public delivery will save on travel costs for all
- The self-paced method allows a candidate to learn at their own pace and is very cost effective

Challenges

Onsite
- Can lead to group frictions
- Distractions caused by the proximity of work environment
- Lack of other view points
- Too much or too little emphasis on either examination or practical aspects

Public
- Distractions caused by perceived need to remain in contact with work environment
- Discussions being monopolized by a few individuals
- Too much or too little emphasis on either examination or practical aspects
- Various degrees of knowledge and experience regarding good practices may isolate those individuals newer to the topic
- Travel requirements, especially on last day

Online
- In a group setting, are people really participating or are they working instead
- Handling questions and answers
- Technology issues may arise
- Scheduling issues when individuals are in various time zones
- Need to schedule more frequent breaks and course may be delivered on more days

- Self-paced can become boring, leading to skipping sections
- Distractions from work environment may be frequent

Arguably, there are more potential benefits and certainly more challenges may arise. It is up to management to determine which approach is best suited for their organization and for their personnel. Demonstrated management commitment to education and training is invaluable in proactively addressing the challenges.

Note from the author
With onsite delivery, it is important that management must be present at the beginning of every session to communicate why the instructor is there and why the individuals are there; what are the benefits to the individuals and what are the benefits for the organization. Additionally, management must show up at various intervals to inquire how the learning is progressing. It does not have to be the same manager, although continuity is more desirable.

I have too often seen candidate arriving to class having no clue why they are there. Either there was no communication as to the reasons and goals of the course or they were told just a few minutes before the start of the class to replace someone at the last minute in order to keep costs down. This is what I call the 'there's-an-empty-seat-let's-fill-it-up' mentality. That's not very conducive to proper learning. The organization suffers in many ways. The person identified as requiring the qualification will not receive it. The replacement person may have had important deliverables to complete at that time.

Sure, it saves money. Sure, it is possible the missing candidate may be ill. However, this contingency needs to be planned ahead of time. If there is an available seat, make sure that the replacement is identified ahead of time and the information communicated in order to get them prepared.

Other than for the self-paced online method, I have seen too many situations where people still had to attend meetings and having to complete their daily work at night instead of being in class and preparing for the next day.

I don't know if things are going to change but management needs to understand that learning is part of someone's job. When they are attending a course, let them attend the course undisturbed.

To the individual candidates, unless you are self-employed, here is a newsflash; no one is that 'indispensable'. The organization existed before you joined it and will exist after you are gone.

Let's not forget that a good instructor can play a large part in addressing many of the challenges if they are properly introduced by management as well as being respected by the candidates. It goes without saying that the instructor must respect the organization and the individuals.

Let's be honest here. Individuals will get ill and thus miss part of or even the whole course. Individuals will need to attend meetings physically or via conference calls. Individuals will have to work in the evening for various reasons. It does not matter whether it is part of the organization's culture or the individual's decision.

Logistics

There are many logistical aspects to consider such as venue, catering, scheduling, travel, work, security, access, delays, technology failures, etc. It is not within the scope of this book to cover these but they are worth mentioning.

Books

Understandably, purchasing the five core books in any of the presently available formats (hardcopy, electronic and online subscription) is, relatively speaking, a major expense for anyone and for most organizations. Purchasing many sets of books for one organization and distributing them to those who need it is one thing. Ensuring they remain available is another.

Attending a course and having to carry one book is simple enough, but carrying all five books is another – especially if the candidate is traveling. Carrying the books in electronic format is much easier but many people are still uncomfortable reading online instead of having a book in their hands.

Moreover, physical space in a classroom setting is always at a premium. Books, course binders (workbooks) provided by the training organization, paper notepad, computer, mobile phone, and beverages add up to a significant footprint. Depending on the type of table used, the room setup and size, the number of participants, and the often uncomfortable chairs contribute to a difficult learning environment.

It is up to the *organization* to provide the best learning atmosphere, conditions and environment as possible. It is up to the *individual* to make the most of what is being provided.

Understanding the syllabus

The candidate has received the green light to attend a course. The logistics are in place and the course schedule is confirmed.

So what is a candidate to do? Of course they should not wait. The next step is to get the syllabus. This is usually available through the training organizations or the examination institutes.

Now that the candidate has the syllabus, how do they use it?

It would be nice to analyze every syllabus. However, it is not the intent of this book to do so. There are many ways to look at a syllabus and there are ten syllabuses. The following section analyses the Operational Support and Analysis syllabus. There is no real need to conduct this analysis for every syllabus; a candidate should be able to repeat the analysis for the qualification being pursued.

Moreover, it is in the best interest of the candidate to conduct the analysis on their own. Simply looking at someone else's analysis of a particular syllabus is likely to provide the candidate with a false sense of security. There are – and there should be – no shortcuts when it comes to pursuing a qualification. The heavy lifting must be done by the individual pursuing the qualification.

Lastly, as was previously mentioned in this book, the syllabuses are dynamic and do change overtime. There is no logic to include them all in this book when they are subject to change. Of course the changes are not always significant but can be important enough to alter the analysis if it is provided in a book.

What is important is learning how to properly approach, analyze and use a syllabus at exam time.

The following syllabus is from the fall of 2010. Some information has been stripped away as it does not come into play during the analysis or at exam time.

Foundation certificate

Attending a foundation class whether in the classroom, online instructor-led or self-paced computer training is not mandatory to sit the exam. However, it is strongly recommended to attend a class.

If a candidate decides to attend a preparatory course before sitting the exam, it is possible to select any training organization, accredited or not. A candidate must be mindful of a few things if they decide to use the services of a non-accredited training organization. It is not implied here that non-accredited training organizations do a poor job or are very bad or are deceitful. From the perspective of the Official Accreditor and that of the Examination Institutes, a candidate has basically no recourse if they have a complaint about the quality of the course delivery or of the exam results. If a candidate or an organization decides to hire a non-accredited organization for the delivery of a foundation-level course, it is their decision and they will have to live with it.

On the other hand, using the service of an Accredited Training Organization (ATO) provides some warranties for the candidate. Some of those warranties include:
- The EI is in good standing with the Official Accreditor
- The ATO has fulfilled all of the EI's business requirements
- The ATO is in good standings with the EI
- The instructor meets all of the requirements
- The course material meets all of the requirements, which includes:
  - Correct description of concepts
  - Correct definitions
  - Proper explanations and examples
  - Proper coverage of the latest version of the syllabus
  - Latest versions of the sample papers

Of course, not all ATOs are the same. While some are large corporations, others may be a single individual. While the course material of any ATO meets the syllabus coverage requirements, the content requirements and the Intellectual Property Rights (IPR) as set by the Official Accreditor, there are many aspects to consider. Among these are:
- The overall quality of the course material
- The presentation material
- The order in which the material is presented
- The presentation skills of the instructor
- The personality of the instructor
- The experience of the instructor
- The examples provided by the instructor

Additionally, the following aspects also need to be taken into consideration:
- The primary learning style of the candidate
- The organization's belief in education and training
- The candidate's workload at the time of the course
- The physical location of the course whether public or onsite
- For online learning, is the candidate isolated from co-workers to be able to concentrate on the course?

So why take a course and how do you prepare for the exam?
Let's find out.

The Foundation exam

The examination format is simple.
- There are forty (40) questions
- All questions are multiple-choice
- There is only one (1) correct answer for each question
- No marks are deducted for an incorrect answer
- The pass score is set at 65% or 26 out of 40 (26/40)

Additionally, the number of questions for each topic is based on the suggested duration of each section as a proportion of the overall time.

Before you attend the course

Question: Is there any pre-reading to do before attending a foundation course?
Answer: No

Question: Is there a need to read all the core books cover to cover during the course?
Answer: No

Question: Do the pocket guides contain enough information?
Answer: Not enough, but they are a good study aid

Question: Can a candidate use the Introduction[21] book to prepare for the exam?
Answer: It can be used however, the book is not a summary of the five core books and its content may not cover some of the elements from the syllabus.

---

21 The Introduction to the ITIL Service Lifecycle book (OGC/TSO)

Question: Can a candidate use the Foundation exam book[22] book to prepare for the exam?

Answer: Of course, however, make sure to use the appropriate edition based on the most current syllabus

Question: Is the workbook provided by the ATO sufficient to prepare for the examination?

Answer: It should be sufficient or it would not be accredited by an EI in the first place

Question: Are any other books that can be used to prepare for the exam?

Answer: Yes. They include[23]
- ITIL® V3 – A Pocket Guide
- Foundations of ITIL® V3
- ITIL® V3 Foundation Exam: The Study Guide

As you can see, there are many publications that can be used to prepare for the Foundation level exam.

However, how do you know what to study? The answer is to turn to the syllabus.

The Foundation level exam

As already mentioned, the syllabuses change frequently so it is with some reservation that some of the content is presented here. However, the syllabus is unlikely to change drastically so the material that follows should be useful for a long time.

Each section in the syllabus contains a suggested duration. The number of questions is apportioned based on the suggested duration. Table 5.1 shows a breakdown of the duration of each section.

Section	Duration (HH:MM)	Percentage of total time	Number of questions
1	00:45	5%	2
2	01:00	6%	3
3	01:00	6%	3
4	01:50	9%	4
5	10:00	63%	25
6	01:00	6%	3

---

22 'Passing your ITIL® Foundation Exam (OGC/TSO)
23 All three books from Van Haren Publishing

Section	Duration (HH:MM)	Percentage of total time	Number of questions
7	00:50	3%	1
8	00:25	2%	1
Totals	16:00	100%	40

Table 5.1 Foundation syllabus analysis

The total course duration is 18 hours. The extra two hours are allocated for a review session.

Please note that the above is an approximation and that the actual number of questions may vary slightly. However, it does provide a good indication of what a candidate can expect.

In addition the questions are classified in terms of their difficulty level. The difficulty levels are easy, moderate and difficult. The exact percentage for each level in any exam paper is know only to the EI but ,based on discussions with senior examiners, you should expect about a quarter of the questions to be easy, half to be moderate and the last quarter to be difficult.

Since everything is relative, two candidates sitting the same exam paper and obtaining the same score may find the examination very easy or very difficult. It is quite subjective.

Regardless of subjectivity, there are 40 questions, and a candidate needs a minimum of 26 correct answers to pass.

> *'Whether you agree or not with ITIL, during the examination you can disagree with ITIL up to 14 times and still pass the exam.'*
>
> Graham Price – Principal Consultant

Multiple-choice questions

The best way to approach a Foundation level exam is to know what is being examined. The ITIL Foundation level exam is NOT about any of the following:

- You
- Your organization
- How you execute your tasks
- How your organization is set-up

- Your practices
- Your organization's practices
- Anything about you
- Anything about your organization

The ITIL Foundation level exam is about your ability to know and comprehend (Bloom's levels 1 and 2) the basic concepts of the ITIL framework as listed in the official syllabus; no more, no less.

Think of a Foundation level exam as being able to demonstrate you know and comprehend the signs of the road and the rules of the road when driving. This is often a requirement in most countries as part of their driver licensing program.

Note from the author
This exam is not about how you drive. There is no practical test. For the duration of the exam you must answer the questions from the perspective I have dubbed 'ITIL-TOPIA'. This term is not derogatory in any way, shape, or form. It is meant to illustrate that the practices described is the core books can and should be (1) adopted and (2) adapted to your organization's reality.

Once you get your driver's license, do you really abide by all the rules and driving codes at all times?

Don't answer this question, it's rhetorical.

So what do you need to know?
The five core books cover a lot of topics. Is it realistic to learn about all of them over the course of 16 hours? The answer is no. It was decided to select key common topics and concepts which are familiar to most IT professionals.

Use the course syllabus to identify what you need to know. It is clearly indicated and cross-referenced to the official core books. However, as mentioned previously, there is no need to consult the core books. The course material from the ATO should be sufficient. In preparing for the exam, go through the topics and determine whether you know AND comprehend what they are, based on the practices described in the core books. Quite likely, the core terminology and concepts will be found in the ATO's course material.

About the Foundation syllabus

Since the content of the syllabus are subject to change, only the purpose of each section is covered here. The following information has been extracted un-amended from the ITIL Foundation Syllabus version 4.2 (2009).

Service Management as a practice

The purpose of this unit is to help the candidate to define Service Management and to comprehend and explain the concept of Service Management as a practice.

What does it mean?

This section covers important concepts used throughout the five core books.

The Service Lifecycle

The purpose of this unit is to help the candidate to understand the value of the Service Lifecycle, how the processes integrate with each other, throughout the Lifecycle and explain the objectives and business value for each phase in the Lifecycle.

What does it mean?

This section covers the goal, objectives and value to the business of each of the five stages in the lifecycle.

Generic concepts and definitions

The purpose of this unit is to help the candidate to define some of the key terminology and explain the key concepts of Service Management.

What does it mean?

This section covers important concepts found throughout the five core books. Although these concepts are explained as part of a particular process, they are used by many other processes.

Key Principles and Models

The purpose of this unit is to help the candidate to comprehend and account for the key principles and models of Service Management and to balance some of the opposing forces within Service Management.

What does it mean?

This section covers concepts such as value creation, the four Ps and the five aspects of Service Design, Deming's cycle, the Continual Service Improvement (CSI) model, definitions for baseline, key performance indicator and metric.

Processes

The purpose of this unit is to help the candidate understand how the Service Management processes contribute to the Service Lifecycle, to explain the high level objectives, scope, basic concepts, activities and challenges for five of the core processes, and to state the objectives and some of the basic concepts for thirteen of the remaining processes including how they relate to each other. The list of activities to be included from each process is the minimum required and should not be taken as an exhaustive list.

What does it mean?
The paragraph above speaks for itself. Please read the last sentence attentively. There are other terms and concepts covered but a candidate should already know about them or should be able to figure it out by using common sense.

Functions

The purpose of this unit is to help the candidate to explain the role, objectives and organizational structures of the Service Desk function, and to state the role, objectives and overlap of three other functions.

What does it mean?
This section covers the four Service Operation functions.

Roles

The purpose of this unit is to help the candidate to account for and to be aware of the responsibilities of some of the key roles in Service Management.

What does it mean?
This section covers only a few roles such as process owner, service owner and the concept of the authority matrix (RACI[24])

Technology and Architecture

The purpose of this unit is to help the candidate to understand how Service Automation assists with integrating Service Management processes.

What does it mean?
The paragraph above speaks for itself.

---

24 Responsible – Accountable – Consulted – Informed

Operational Support and Analysis Certificate

First section of interest

> The ITIL Intermediate Qualification: Operational Support and Analysis (OSA) Certificate is a freestanding qualification, but is also part of the ITIL Intermediate Capability stream, and one of the modules that leads to the ITIL Expert in IT Service Management Certificate. The purpose of this training module and the associated exam and certificate is, respectively, to impart, test, and validate the knowledge on industry practices in Service Management as documented in the ITIL Service Lifecycle core publications.

What does the above mean?
There are two primary reasons to pursue any of the Service Lifecycle and Service Capabilities qualifications. The first is to acquire the knowledge and to become more proficient at practicing the knowledge gained. The second reason is that an individual is seeking the ITIL Expert certification and has identified this particular course as part of their path toward it.

The syllabus for every qualification contains a similar section. This section is quite generic and the only differences are the name of the qualification and the stream. This means that every qualification is free-standing, so an individual may pursue that particular qualification only or as part of their route towards becoming an ITIL Expert.

Second section of interest

> The ITIL Certificate in Operational Support and Analysis is intended to enable the holders of the certificate to apply the practices in resolution and support of the Service Management Lifecycle and specifically in the following ITIL process, role and function areas:
> - Event Management
> - Incident Management
> - Request Fulfillment
> - Problem Management
> - Access Management
> - Service Desk
> - Technical Management

- IT Operations Management
- Application Management

It is also strongly recommended that candidates read the ITIL Service Management core publications in advance of attending training for the certification and specifically the Service Operation publication.

What does the above mean?
The syllabus for every qualification contains a similar section. This section is quite generic and the only differences are the name of the qualification and the list of topics covered. A candidate should pay close attention to this section to identify the main topics for the qualification being pursued.

A candidate should pay close attention to the last paragraph in the above section of interest. It means '**READ THE BOOKS BEFORE GETTING TO CLASS**'. It will make the learning experienced more interesting and the candidate will be able to ask clarification questions instead of focusing on the basic concepts. The Intermediate qualification is based on the assumption that candidates are professional enough to take their responsibilities seriously and be prepared when the course starts.

The above lists the major topics covered during the course. The list covers the five service operation processes and the four functions. It is important to note that the context and primary focus for this course are 'the practices in resolution and support of the Service Management Lifecycle'.

Hence, a candidate should look at the processes and functions from a resolution and support perspective. The resolution processes are primarily Incident and Problem Management while the support processes are Access Management, Event Management and Request Fulfillment.

It is important to remember that the activities of the processes will be performed by the individuals working in any of the four functions.

Although size and complexity will greatly influence how an IT organization is set up, it is possible to recognize every function, role and activity within the job descriptions of the IT personnel. The actual job title or departmental/group name is irrelevant. A candidate must be able to recognize the concepts provided by the practices described in the Service Operation book for this syllabus.

Here is an example of the primary set of activities performed by particular functions. Do not interpret Table 5.2 below as an absolute. It is simply an example. It is quite likely that all four functions will actually perform one or more activities of all five Service Operation processes.

For example, it is quite likely that Service Desk personnel will execute all of the activities of Incident Management but that the Technical and Application Management personnel will only be involved in Incident Management when a functional escalation is required.

Similarly, the Operations Control personnel are likely to perform all the activities of Event Management while the Service Desk may only be doing some of them. It is even possible that Technical Management and Application Management will not participate in any of the activities of Event Management. They would, however, use the information captured in various logs when investigating an incident or the root cause of a problem.

Function	Primary set of activities
Service Desk	Request Fulfillment Incident Management Event Management Access Management
Technical Management	Incident Management Problem Management Request fulfillment (such as some hardware installs)
Application management	Incident Management Problem Management Request fulfillment (such as some software installs)
IT Operations	
Operations control	Event Management Incident Management Access Management
Facilities Management	Incident Management Problem Management

Table 5.2 Functions and their primary activities

Third section of interest

Target Candidate

The target group of the ITIL Expert Qualification: Operational Support and Analysis includes but is not restricted to:

- IT professionals
- Business managers
- Business process owners
- Individuals who have attained the V3 ITIL Foundation certificate in Service Management, or the V2 Foundation plus the V3 Foundation Bridge certificate and who wish to advance to higher level ITIL certifications
- Individuals who require a deep understanding of ITIL Certificate in Operational Support and Analysis processes and how it may be used to enhance the quality of IT service support within an organization.
- IT professionals who are working within an organization that has adopted and adapted ITIL who need to be informed about and thereafter contribute to an ongoing service improvement program
- Operational staff involved in Event Management Process, Incident Management Process, Request Fulfillment Process, Problem Management Process, Access Management Process, Service Desk, Technical Management, IT Operations Management and Application Management

The above represent the potential candidates for this qualification. Of course, anyone with the Foundation certification is welcome to attend this course and pursue this qualification.

With the other qualifications, the primary audience targeted is more specific as a candidate moves into the Service Design and Service Strategy books. Additionally, the primary audience targeted for the Service Lifecycle qualifications is more for supervisory and managerial personnel.

Fourth section of interest

Prerequisite Entry Criteria

Candidates wishing to be trained and examined for this qualification must already hold the ITIL Foundation Certificate in IT Service Management (the V3 Foundation or V2 Foundation plus Bridge Certificate) which shall be presented as documentary evidence to gain admission.

It is strongly recommended that candidates:

- Can demonstrate familiarity with IT terminology and understand Operational Support and Analysis within the context of their own business environment
- Have exposure working in a service management capacity within a service provider environment, with responsibility emphasizing on at least one of the following management disciplines:
  - Event Management Process
  - Incident Management Process
  - Request Fulfillment Process
  - Problem Management Process
  - Access Management Process
  - Service Desk
  - Technical Management
  - IT Operations Management
  - Application Management

It is also strongly recommended that candidates read the ITIL Service Management core publications in advance of attending training for the certification and specifically the Service Operation publication.

What does the above mean?
A candidate MUST hold the foundation qualification before they can register and attend an intermediate level qualification. Additionally a candidate should be familiar with the topics covered in the qualification. With the discipline listed, it should not be inferred that you cannot pursue a certain qualification if you do not recognize your current role in the target audience or have not had the 'strongly recommended' exposure listed above. It is perfectly acceptable for someone aspiring to a particular role to pursue a qualification they are not yet practicing. However, if this is the case, then the candidate should prepare more diligently in advance of attending the qualification course.

Additionally, it should not be inferred that a candidate with years of experience in a particular domain does not need to prepare in advance for a qualification. Simply having experience and thinking that you only need to show up to be awarded the certification is utter nonsense. A candidate with a lot of experience needs to be prepared to have their established work habits challenged when attending any of the qualification courses. The examination is not about a candidate's own work habits but about how a candidate can apply the practices described in the core books in simulated situations known as scenarios.

Fifth section of interest

Eligibility for Examination

To be eligible for the examination leading to an accredited ITIL Certificate in Operational Support and Validation, the candidate must fill the following requirements:
- At least 30 contact hours (hours of instruction, excluding breaks, and not including summary review time, with an Accredited Training Organization (ATO) or an accredited e-learning solution) for this syllabus, as part of a formal, approved training course/scheme
- There is no minimum mandatory requirement but 2 to 4 years professional experience working in IT Service Management is highly desirable
- Hold the ITIL V3 Foundation Certificate in IT Service Management or ITIL V2 Foundation plus the bridging certificate
- It is also recommended that candidates should complete at a minimum 12 hours of personal study by reviewing the syllabus and the pertinent areas of the ITIL Service Management Practice core guidance publications and in particular, the Service Operation publication

What does the above mean?
The syllabus for every qualification contains a similar section. This section is quite generic and the only differences are the name of the qualification and the recommended books to read.

A candidate MUST attend a course. The course can be in a classroom, instructor-led online, self-paced online (computer-based or web-based) or a blended approach of the previous methods. The training organization must be accredited by one of the examination institutes. Such accredited training organizations are known by the acronym ATO. It is possible for an ATO to use an accredited training provider (ATP). The ATP can be a partner organization or a free-lance instructor. As the name implies, both need to be accredited in good standing.

The duration of a Service Capabilities course is 30 hours of contact time as is the Managing across the Lifecycle course while the Service Lifecycle courses are 21 hours. Contact time includes the face to face time with the instructor, whether in person or virtual.

However, the contact time does not include the following:
- Break periods
- Lunch periods
- Evening assignments and homework
- Pre-course reading assignment and homework
- Recommended personal study before attending the course
- The exam itself

Here is an example of a daily schedule to illustrate the contact time versus the non-contact time.

Start time	End Time	Duration	Session Description	Counts as contact time?
09:00	10:00	1:00	Session one	Yes
10:00	10:15	0:15	Break	No
10:15	11:15	1:00	Session 2	Yes
11:15	11:30	0:15	Break	No
11:30	12:30	1:00	Session 3	Yes
12:30	13:30	1:00	Lunch period	No
13:30	14:30	1:00	Session 4	Yes
14:30	14:45	0:15	Break	No
14:45	15:45	1:00	Session 5	Yes
15:45	16:00	0:15	Break	No
16:00	17:00	1:00	Session 6	Yes

Table 5.3 Example of valid contact hours

In the above example, although the course starts at 09:00 am and ends at 17:00 pm which represents eight (8) hours the actual contact time is six hours. Only the gray background sessions can be counted. Additionally, any study done by a candidate after the end of the day until the start of the next day cannot count as part of the 30 hours of contact time.

Syllabus at a glance

Learning Unit OSA01: Introduction to Operational Support and Analysis

Bloom's Level 2 Objectives – Full understanding of Operational Support and Analysis (OSA) terms and core concepts

1. The concept of Service Management as a practice
2. How it delivers value to customers and the business
3. The underpinning processes and functions that support the Service Lifecycle
4. Which stages of the Service Lifecycle contribute to Operational Support and Analysis how they interact

What does the above mean?
This is a rather generic section for all qualifications. Candidates should be familiar with this. This section is set at Bloom's level 2. This means that a candidate must (1) know the concept and (2) understand what it means.

1st bullet	a candidate should know what service management is all about.
2nd bullet	a candidate should know that value is a combination of utility and warranty. The candidate should also know what utility and warranty are
3rd bullet	a candidate should have a good understanding of the five stages of the lifecycle as well as a good understanding of the 26 processes and the four (4) functions.
4th bullet	a candidate should have a good understanding of the relationship (what a phase expects from another and what it will return back) between the four other phases and the ones discussed in the course.

Learning Unit OSA02: Event Management
Bloom's Level 4 Objectives – Support problem solving by putting theory into practice, interpret principles and relationships

1. The Event Management process inclusive of its design strategy, components, activities, roles and operation including its organizational structure as well as any interfaces with other processes
2. Efficient Event Management and provide examples of how it is used to ensure Quality Service within OSA
3. The benefits and business value that can be gained from Event Management

Learning Unit OSA03: Incident Management

Bloom's Level 4 Objectives – Support problem solving by putting theory into practice, interpret principles and relationships

1. The Incident Management process inclusive of its design strategy, components, activities, roles and operation including its organizational structure as well as any interfaces with other processes
2. The measurement model and the metrics that would be used to support Incident Management within OSA practices
3. The benefits and business value that can be gained from Incident Management

Learning Unit OSA04: Request Fulfillment

Bloom's Level 4 Objectives – Support problem solving by putting theory into practice, interpret principles and relationships

1. The Request Fulfillment process inclusive of its design strategy, components, activities, roles and operation including its organizational structure as well as any interfaces with other processes
2. The measurement model and the metrics that would be used to support Incident Management within OSA practices
3. The Benefits and business value that can be gained from Request Fulfillment as related to OSA

Learning Unit OSA05: Problem Management

Bloom's Level 4 Objectives – Support problem solving by putting theory into practice, interpret principles and relationships

1. The end-to-end process flow for Problem Management inclusive of design strategy, components, activities, roles and operation including its organizational structure as well as any interfaces with other processes
2. A measurement model and the metrics that would be used to support Problem Management within OSA practices
3. The benefits and business value that can be gained from Problem Management

Learning Unit OSA06: Access Management

Bloom's Level 4 Objectives – Support problem solving by putting theory into practice, interpret principles and relationships

1. The end-to-end process flow for Access Management process inclusive of design strategy, components, activities, roles and operation including its organizational structure as well as any interfaces with other processes
2. A measurement model and the metrics that would be used to support Access Management within OSA practices
3. The benefits and business value that can be gained from Access Management as related to OSA

What does the above mean?
In the above section, all five processes are grouped together as the explanation is the same for all five.

First, the above sections are set at Bloom's Level 4. The Level 4 implies that a candidate has mastered the previous three levels of knowing, understanding, and applying. Here a candidate is expected to support problem solving (in the form of a scenario) by putting theory (from the books) into practice (coming up with the best solution for the scenario being used), interpret principles (which means analysis), and relationships (which inputs are required, how to use them properly, and coming up with the appropriate output – in this case the best solution).

1st bullet:
Process flow inclusive of design strategy
- A candidate should be able to analyze the process flow from trigger to end
- A candidate should be able to analyze the reasons why the process was developed in the first place or why it needs to be designed now or what is not working well

Components
- A candidate should be able to know, understand and use (explain) all of the concepts that make up the process
- A candidate should be able to apply the concept in a given situation based on good practice and not based on how they presently do it

Activities and operation
- A candidate should be able to know, understand and use (explain) all of the activities that make up the process. The activities include the ones in the process flow as well as all activities such as managing, reporting and improving the process. Please refer to the process model in the Service Design book or consult Appendix <X>.
- A candidate should be able to apply the activities in a given situation based on good practice and not based on how they presently do it

Interfaces with other processes or lifecycle phases
- A candidate should be able to identify which inputs are required from which Lifecycle stage (and their respective processes)
- A candidate should be able to identify which outputs are required to be handed back to the other Lifecycle stage (and their respective processes)
- A candidate should be able to identify which triggers will start a particular process flow, management, reporting or improving activity.

2nd bullet
Measurement model
- A candidate should be able to differentiate between metrics, key performance indicators (KPIs), critical success factors (CSFs)
- A candidate should be able to identify the metrics, KPIs and CSFs related to a specific process or Lifecycle stage.

3rd bullet
Benefits and business value
- A candidate should be able to determine the contribution (benefit, business value) of a particular Lifecycle stage or of a process to the organization
- A candidate should also be able to determine the potential challenges and risks in some of the following situations:
  - The process is not in place
  - The process is in place and working well
  - The process is in place but not working well
  - The process is being implemented
  - The process is being outsourced
  - The process is outsourced
  - The process is being compared to one from an acquired organization
  - Etc.

Learning Unit OSA07: The Service Desk

Bloom's Level 4 Objectives – Support problem solving by putting theory into practice, interpret principles and relationships
- The complete end-to-end process flow for the Service Desk function inclusive of design strategy, components, activities and operation as well as any interfaces with other processes or lifecycle phases
- The Service Desk validation components and activities (e.g. Service Desk role, organizational structures, challenges, issues safeguards, etc.) and how these test components are used to ensure Quality Service within OSA
- A measurement model and the metrics that would be used to support the Service Desk function within OSA practices

What does the above mean?

First, the above section is set at Bloom's Level 4. This implies that a candidate has mastered the previous three levels of knowing, understanding, and applying. Here a candidate is expected to support problem solving (in the form of a scenario) by putting theory (from the books) into practice (coming up with the best solution for the scenario being used), interpret principles (which means analysis), and relationships (which inputs are required, how to use them properly, and coming up with the appropriate output – in this case the best solution).

1st bullet:

Process flow inclusive of design strategy

- A candidate should be able to analyze the process flow from trigger to end
- A candidate should be able to analyze the reasons why the process was developed in the first place or why it needs to be designed now or what is not working well

Components

- A candidate should be able to know, understand and use (explain) all of the concepts that make up the process
- A candidate should be able to apply the concept in a given situation based on good practice and not based on how they presently do it

Activities and operation

- A candidate should be able to know, understand and use (explain) all of the activities that make up the process. The activities include the ones in the process flow as well as all activities such as managing, reporting and improving the process. Please refer to the process model in the Service Design book or consult Appendix <X>.
- A candidate should be able to apply the activities in a given situation based on good practice and not based on how they presently do it

Interfaces with other processes or lifecycle phases

- A candidate should be able to identify which inputs are required from which Lifecycle stage (and their respective processes)
- A candidate should be able to identify which outputs are required to be handed back to the other Lifecycle stage (and their respective processes)
- A candidate should be able to identify which triggers will start a particular process flow, management, reporting or improving activity.

2nd bullet
Validation components and activities
- A candidate should be able to analyze the role of the Service Desk in a particular situation
- *A candidate should be able to determine the validity of a particular organizational structure and provide a recommendation based on that analysis*
- A candidate should be able to analyze the challenges facing, and raised by, a Service Desk
- A candidate should be able to analyze the safeguards as they relate to the issues at hand (from the scenario)

3rd bullet
Measurement model
- A candidate should be able to differentiate between metrics, key performance indicators (KPIs), critical success factors (CSFs)
- A candidate should be able to identify the metrics, KPIs and CSFs related to a specific process or Lifecycle stage.

Learning Unit OSA08: Functions

Bloom's Level 4 Objectives – Support problem solving by putting theory into practice, interpret principles and relationships
- The end-to-end process flow for OSA Functions (i.e. Technical Management, IT Operations Management, and Applications Management) inclusive of design strategy, objectives, components, activities, roles and operation including its organizational structure as well as any interfaces with other processes
- The benefits and business value that can be gained from functions as related to OSA

What does the above mean?
First, the above section is set at Bloom's Level 4. This implies that a candidate has mastered the previous three levels of knowing, understanding, and applying. Here a candidate is expected to support problem solving (in the form of a scenario) by putting theory (from the books) into practice (coming up with the best solution for the scenario being used), interpret principles (which means analysis), and relationships (which inputs are required, how to use them properly, and coming up with the appropriate output – in this case the best solution).

1st bullet:
Function flow inclusive of design strategy
- A candidate should be able to analyze the function flow from trigger to end
- A candidate should be able to analyze the reasons why the function was developed in the first place or why it needs to be designed now or what is not working well

Components
- A candidate should be able to know, understand and use (explain) all of the concepts that make up the function
- A candidate should be able to apply the concept in a given situation based on good practice and not based on how they presently do it

Activities, role and operation
- A candidate should be able to know, understand and use (explain) all of the activities that make up the function. The activities include the ones in the function flow as well as all activities such as managing, reporting and improving the function.
- A candidate should be able to apply the activities in a given situation based on good practice and not based on how they presently do it
- A candidate should be able to determine the validity of a particular organizational structure and provide a recommendation based on that analysis

Interfaces with other functions, processes or lifecycle phases
- A candidate should be able to identify which inputs are required from which Lifecycle stage (and their respective processes)
- A candidate should be able to identify which outputs are required to be handed back to the other Lifecycle stage (and their respective processes)
- A candidate should be able to identify which triggers will start a particular activity, management, reporting or improving activity.

2nd bullet
Benefits and business value
- A candidate should be able to determine the contribution (benefit, business value) of a function to the organization
- A candidate should also be able to determine the potential challenges and risks in some of the following situations:
    - The function is not in place
    - The function is in place and working well
    - The function is in place but not working well
    - The function is being implemented

- The function is being outsourced
- The function is outsourced
- The function is being compared to one from an acquired organization
- Etc.

Learning Unit OSA09: Technology and Implementation considerations

Bloom's Level 4 Objectives – Support problem solving by putting theory into practice, interpret principles and relationships

- Technology requirements for Service Management tools and where/how they would be used within OSA for process implementation
- What best practices should be used in order to alleviate challenges and risks when implementing
- Service Management technologies

What does the above mean?

First, the sections above are set at Bloom's Level 4. This implies that a candidate has mastered the previous three levels of knowing, understanding, and applying. Here a candidate is expected to support problem solving (in the form of a scenario) by putting theory (from the books) into practice (coming up with the best solution for the scenario being used), interpret principles (which means analysis), and relationships (which inputs are required, how to use them properly, and coming up with the appropriate output – in this case the best solution).

1st bullet:

Technology requirements

- A candidate should be able to analyze the mandatory requirements for a tool or set of tools as it relates to a particular process, a group of processes or to the entire Lifecycle stage.

2nd bullet:

Benefits and business value

- A candidate should be able to determine the contribution (benefit, business value) of a particular tool or set of tools, particularly the implementation of OSA processes.
- A candidate should also be able to determine the potential challenges and risks in some of the following situations:
  - The tool is not in place
  - The tool is in place and working well

- The tool is in place but not working well
- The tool is being implemented
- The tool is being compared to one from an acquired organization
- A third party vendor is using or needs to use the tool
- Etc.

3rd bullet:

Service Management technologies

- A candidate should know and understand the various Service Management technologies from a high level concept. The concepts centre on the modules for each process, monitoring tool, implementation tools, design tools, communication tools, various databases, the configuration management system (CMS), and the service knowledge management system (SKMS).

Qualification Learning Objectives

Candidates can expect to gain competence in the following areas upon successful completion of the education and examination components related to this certification:

- Service Management as a Practice
- Service Operation Principles
- The Processes pertaining to Operational Support and Analysis across the Service
- Lifecycle
- How all processes in ITIL Operational Support and Analysis interact with other Service Lifecycle processes
- How to use the ITIL Operational Support and Analysis processes, activities and functions to achieve operational excellence
- How to measure ITIL Operational Support and Analysis
- The importance of IT Security and its contributions to ITIL Operational Support and Analysis
- Understanding the technology and implementation considerations surrounding ITIL Operational Support and Analysis
- The challenges, Critical Success Factors and risks associated with ITIL Operational Support and Analysis
- Specific emphasis on the Service Operation Lifecycle processes &roles included in:

- Event Management which defines any detectable or discernible occurrence that has significance for the management of the IT Infrastructure or the delivery of an IT service
- Incident Management which has the capability to bring services back to normal operations as soon as possible, according to agreed service levels
- Request Fulfillment which fulfils a request providing quick and effective access to standard services which business staff can use to improve their productivity or the quality of business services and products
- Problem Management which prevents problems and resulting Incidents from happening, to eliminate recurring Incidents and to minimize the impact of Incidents that cannot be prevented
- Access Management which grants authorized users the right to use a service, while preventing access to non-authorized users

Operational activities of processes covered in other Lifecycle stages such as:
- Change Management
- Service Asset and Configuration Management
- Release and Deployment Management
- Capacity Management
- Availability Management
- Knowledge Management
- Financial Management for IT Services, and
- IT Service Continuity Management
- Organizing for Service Operation which describe functions to be performed within the Service Operation and Support such as Service Desk, Technical Management, IT Operations Management and Application Management

What does the above mean?
The syllabus of every qualification contains the first paragraph in the above section.

'Candidates can expect to gain competence in the following areas upon successful completion of the education and examination components related to this certification.'

The paragraph hints that what follow may be related to exam topics. This is not to say that a candidate should expect the bullets to be exam topics. However, a candidate should pay attention to the bullets in the list as they provide a good sample of exam preparation topics, or sub-topics.

Looking at the sample papers, a candidate can easily recognize the following topics in the various qualifications.

1st bulleted list
- Service Management as a Practice
- Principles
- The Processes pertaining to…
- How all processes in <…> interact with other Service Lifecycle processes
- How to use <…> to achieve operational excellence
- How to measure…
- The importance of IT Security…
- Understanding the technology and implementation considerations…
- The challenges, Critical Success Factors and risks…

2nd bulleted list
- This list provides a great summary of what the OSA processes are all about.
- A candidate should pay close attention to these summaries as well as recognizing roles mentioned in a scenario

3rd bulleted list
- A candidate should play close attention to this list. It provides an indication of which processes to pay particular attention to in the other stages
- A candidate should not avoid the other processes
- The processes in the other four stages all have operational activities
- In particular a candidate should identify the methods and techniques from the other processes and identify how they can be used in certain situations

The third bulleted list is not always present but a candidate should always analyze the relationships between processes. The relationships are at a high level and involve the use of methods, techniques, plans, and tools primarily found in a process and how it can be used by another process. In addition the activities of a process may generate triggers to start the activities of another process. An easy relationship is that every process will use information found in the Configuration Management System (CMS) and will provide feedback in the form of new or modified information

Here are a few examples using the third bulleted list provided above.

Change Management

- Standard changes can be used to resolve incidents, problems and fulfill service requests
- Incidents and problems may arise after a change

Service Asset and Configuration Management

- Anyone using the CMDB or the CMS can identify various issues with the information. This is part of the ongoing verification.
- Information found in the CMDB or CMS can be used by all processes for any activity

Release and Deployment Management

- Known errors identified in development, test and validation need to be provided to the known error database to be used by incident and Problem Management

Capacity Management

- Many of the techniques can be used by Event Management to monitor and address various capacity issues, within pre-defined parameters
- Many of the techniques can be used by Incident and Problem Management to investigate the cause of incidents and problems
- Problem management requires information about business, service and component capacity

Availability Management

- Many of the techniques can be used by Incident and Problem Management to investigate the cause of incidents and problems
- Access Management requires information about confidentiality, integrity and availability

Knowledge Management

- All processes will contribute to building the Service Knowledge Management System as well as use it

Financial Management for IT Services

- Every process must understand the financial impact of their activities
- Incident Management should track time and material to determine cost of an incident
- Problem Management needs to determine which is more economical, the work-around or fixing the problem permanently

- Access Management needs to understand the cost of the security measures
- Event management must understand the cost of monitoring events
- Request fulfillment should have identified the cost of fulfilling the various requests

IT Service Continuity Management (ITSCM)
- A crisis or a disaster can start its life as an incident
- Major problem reviews can be conducted to provide feedback to ITSCM
- Access management can provide feedback to ITSCM about security issues
- Service desk can act as the crisis center for ITSCM

Operational Support and Analysis Syllabus

The ITIL Intermediate Qualification: Operational Support and Analysis (OSA) is awarded to those who complete the following ten units of study and successfully pass the relevant examination.

Core guidance references with publication reference (SS- Service Strategy, SD – Service Design, ST – Service Transition, SO – Service Operation, CSI – Continual Service Improvement) and section numbers are included along with indicative contact study hours.

The contact hours are shown in each learning unit and are suggested to provide adequate time to cover the core guidance content however, Accredited Training Organizations (ATOs) are encouraged to combine or reorder the learning units in any way that suits the flow of their courseware content delivery. All ATO's must ensure however, the minimum contact hours for eligibility for examination are met.

Section numbers are indicated as 'chapter.section.subsection' (X.X.X). Unless otherwise indicated instructional coverage of the content of the entire section referenced is assumed.

What does the above mean?
The above section is mostly for training organizations but a candidate should pay very close attention to the last paragraph. As you can clearly see, a candidate must read the entire section even if the syllabus mentions, for example, section 7.1. Section 7.1 may contain many sub-sections.

The Operational Support & Analysis syllabus

Learning Unit ITIL SC: OSA01 Introduction

Curriculum subjects covered	Level of Difficulty
This learning unit of this course provides an introduction to the Core Concepts and terminology of the Service Lifecycle, and the role that OSA plays within the Lifecycle. An overview of Service Management is presented along with defining Service as a value proposition, the difference between functions and processes as well as how to create business value. The processes within Operational Support and Analysis practices and how these processes support the Service Lifecycle, inclusive of their roles and responsibilities are identified in the lifecycle stages of Service Transition, Service Operations and Service Design.	Up to Bloom level 2 Knowing and Comprehending The ability to recall, recite, name and understand the meaning of ITIL terminology and basic practice fundamentals.
To meet the learning outcomes and examination level of difficulty, the candidates must be able to understand and describe: • The concept of Service Management as a practice Core Guidance References – SS 2.1, SO 2.1 • The concept of Service, its value proposition and composition Core Guidance References – SS 2.2 , SO 2.2 • The functions and processes across the Lifecycle Core Guidance References – SS 2.6, SO 2.3 • The role of processes in the Service Lifecycle Core Guidance References – SS 2.6.2, 2.6.3 • How Service Management creates business value Core Guidance References – SS 3.1, ST 2.4.3, SO 2.4.3, SO 2.4.4, CSI 3.7.2 • How Operational Support and Analysis supports the Service Lifecycle Core Guidance References – SO 2.4	
Contact hours recommended – 1.5	

Table 5.4 ITIL SC: OSA01 Introduction

Sections to read and concepts to understand

SS 2.1 SO 2.1	Service Management as a practice 2.1 What is Service Management? 2.1 What is Service Management?
SS 2.2 SO 2.2	Service, its value proposition and composition 2.2 What are services? 2.2.1 The value proposition 2.2.2 Value composition 2.2 What are services? 2.2.1 The value proposition
SS 2.6 SO 2.3	Functions and processes across the Lifecycle 2.6 Functions and processes across the lifecycle 2.6.1 Functions 2.6.2 Processes 2.6.2 Specialization and coordination across the lifecycle 2.3 Functions and processes across the lifecycle 2.3.1 Functions 2.3.2 Processes 2.3.2 Specialization and coordination across the lifecycle
SS 2.6.2 SS 2.6.3	Role of processes in the Service Lifecycle 2.6.2 Processes 2.6.3 Specialization and coordination across the lifecycle
SS 3.1 ST 2.4.3 SO 2.4.3 SO 2.4.4 CSI 3.7.2	How Service Management creates business value 3.1.1 Mind the gap 3.1.2 Marketing mindset 3.1.3 Framing the value of services 3.1.4 Communicating utility 3.1.4.1 In terms of outcomes supported 3.1.4.2 In terms of ownership costs and risks avoided 3.1.5 Communicating warranty 3.1.5.1 Availability 3.1.5.2 Capacity 3.1.5.3 Continuity 3.1.5.4 Security 3.1.6 Combined effect of utility and warranty Value to business Value to business Optimizing Service Operation performance Value to business

SO 2.4	How OSA supports the Service Lifecycle
	2.4 Service Operation fundamentals 2.4.1 Purpose/goal/objective 2.4.2 Scope 2.4.3 Value to business 2.4.4 Optimizing Service Operation performance 2.4.5 Processes within Service Operation 2.4.5.1 Event Management 2.4.5.2 Incident and Problem Management 2.4.5.3 Request Fulfillment 2.4.5.4 Access Management 2.4.6 Functions within Service Operation 2.4.6.1 Service Desk 2.4.6.2 Technical Management 2.4.6.3 IT Operations Management 2.4.6.4 Application Management 2.4.6.5 Interfaces to other Service Management Lifecycle stages

Table 5.5 Suggested reading

LEARNING UNIT: ITIL SC: OSA02 Event Management

Curriculum subjects covered	Level of Difficulty
This learning unit covers how the process of Event Management contributes to OSA practices. A complete overview of the objectives, scope and importance of Event Management as a process to generate business value are explored. Event Management policies, principles, concepts, design, activities, methods and techniques are explained in relationship to OSA practices as well as to Information Management. Efficient use of Event Management metrics are reviewed in this unit. To meet the learning outcomes and examination level of difficulty, the candidates must be able to understand, describe, identify, demonstrate, apply, distinguish, produce, decide or analyze: • The purpose, goal and objectives of the Event Management process Core Guidance References – SO 4.1.1 • The scope of the Event Management process Core Guidance References – SO 4.1.2 • The value to business and to the Service Lifecycle Core Guidance References – SO 4.1.3 • The policies, principles and basic concepts Core Guidance References – SO 4.1.4 • The process activities, methods and techniques that enable this process and how it relates to the Service Lifecycle Core Guidance References – SO 4.1.5 • The triggers, inputs and outputs and the process interfaces Core Guidance References – SO 4.1.6 • Event Management involvement in Information Management Core Guidance References – SO 4.1.7 • How metrics can be used to check effectiveness and efficiency of the Event Management process Core Guidance References – SO 4.1.8, CSI 4.3, CSI 7.1.3 (CSI reference within the context of Event Management) • The challenges, Critical Success Factors and risks associated with the Event Management process Core Guidance References – SO 4.1.9 • How to design for Event Management Core Guidance References – SO 4.1.10	Up to Bloom level 4 Applying and Analyzing The candidate should reach a level of competence that supports problem solving, putting theory into practice, interpreting principles and relationships related to Event Management.
Contact hours recommended – 2.5	

Table 5.6 ITIL SC: OSA02 Event Management

Sections to read and concepts to understand

SO 4.1.1	The purpose, goal and objectives
SO 4.1.2	The scope
SO 4.1.3	The value to business
SO 4.1.4	The policies, principles and basic concepts
SO 4.1.5	The process activities, methods and techniques and how they relate 4.1.5.1 Event occurs 4.1.5.2 Event notification 4.1.5.3 Event detection 4.1.5.4 Event filtering 4.1.5.5 Significance of events 4.1.5.6 Event correlation 4.1.5.7 Trigger 4.1.5.8 Response selection 4.1.5.9 Review actions 4.1.5.10 Close event
SO 4.1.6	The triggers, inputs and outputs and the process interfaces
SO 4.1.7	Information Management
SO 4.1.8 CSI 4.3 CSI 7.1.3	Metrics CSI within the context of Event Management 4.3.1 Objective 4.3.2 Developing a Service Measurement Framework 4.3.3 Different levels of measurement and reporting 4.3.4 Defining what to measure 4.3.5 Setting targets 4.3.6 Service Management process measurement 4.3.7 Creating a measurement framework grid 4.3.8 Interpreting and using metrics 4.3.9 Interpreting metrics 4.3.10 Using measurement and metrics 4.3.11 Creating scorecards and reports 4.3.12 CSI Policies 7.1.3 Event management
SO 4.1.9	The challenges, Critical Success Factors and risks 4.1.9.1 Challenges 4.1.9.2 Critical Success Factors 4.1.9.3 Risks
SO 4.1.10	How to design for Event Management 4.1.10.1 Instrumentation 4.1.10.2 Error messaging 4.1.10.3 Event Detection and Alert Mechanisms

Table 5.7 Suggested reading

LEARNING UNIT: ITIL SC: OSA03 Incident Management

Curriculum subjects covered	Level of Difficulty
This learning unit covers how the process of Incident Management contributes to OSA practices. A complete overview of the objectives, scope and importance of Incident Management as a process to generate business value are explored. Incident Management policies, principles, concepts, activities, methods and techniques are explained in relationship to OSA practices. Efficient use of Incident Management metrics are reviewed in this unit. To meet the learning outcomes and examination level of difficulty, the candidates must be able to understand, describe, identify, demonstrate, apply, distinguish, produce, decide or analyze: • The purpose, goal and objectives of the Incident Management process Core Guidance References – SO 4.2.1 • The scope of the Incident Management process Core Guidance References – SO 4.2.2 • The value to business and to the Service Lifecycle Core Guidance References – SO 4.2.3 • The policies, principles and all basic concepts Core Guidance References – SO 4.2.4 • The process activities, methods and techniques and how they relate to the Service Lifecycle Core Guidance References – SO 4.2.5 • The triggers, inputs and outputs and the process interfaces Core Guidance References – SO 4.2.6 • Incident Management involvement in Information Management Core Guidance References – SO 4.2.7 • How metrics can be used to check effectiveness and efficiency of the Incident Management process Core Guidance References – SO 4.2.8, CSI 4.1, CSI 4.3, CSI 4.5 (CSI references within the context of Incident Management) • The challenges, Critical Success Factors and risks associated with the Incident Management process Core Guidance References – SO 4.2.9, CSI 4.5, CSI 9 (CSI references within the context of Incident Management)	Up to Bloom level 4 Applying and Analyzing The candidate should reach a level of competence that supports problem solving, putting theory into practice, interpreting principles and relationships related to Incident Management.
Contact hours recommended – 5.0	

Table 5.8 ITIL SC: OSA03 Incident Management

Sections to read and concepts to understand

SO 4.2.1	The purpose, goal and objectives
SO 4.2.2	The scope
SO 4.2.3	The value to business
SO 4.2.4	The policies, principles and basic concepts 4.2.4.1 Timescales 4.2.4.2 Incident Models 4.2.4.3 Major incidents
SO 4.2.5	The process activities, methods and techniques and how they relate 4.2.5.1 Incident identification 4.2.5.2 Incident logging 4.2.5.3 Incident categorization 4.2.5.4 Incident prioritization 4.2.5.5 Initial diagnosis 4.2.5.6 Incident escalation 4.2.5.7 Investigation and diagnosis 4.2.5.8 Resolution and Recovery 4.2.5.9 Incident closure
SO 4.2.6	The triggers, inputs and outputs and the process interfaces
SO 4.2.7	Information Management
SO 4.2.8	Metrics
CSI 4.1	CSI within the context of Incident Management
CSI 4.3 CSI 4.5	4.1 The 7-step improvement process 4.1.1 Integration with the rest of the lifecycle stages and Service Management processes 4.3.1 Objective 4.3.2 Developing a Service Measurement Framework 4.3.3 Different levels of measurement and reporting 4.3.4 Defining what to measure 4.3.5 Setting targets 4.3.6 Service Management process measurement 4.3.7 Creating a measurement framework grid 4.3.8 Interpreting and using metrics 4.3.9 Interpreting metrics 4.3.10 Using measurement and metrics 4.3.11 Creating scorecards and reports 4.3.12 CSI Policies 4.5 Business questions for CSI

SO 4.2.9	The challenges, Critical Success Factors and risks
	4.2.9.1 Challenges
CSI 4.5	4.2.9.2 Critical Success Factors
	4.2.9.3 Risks
CSI 9	
	CSI within the context of Incident Management
	4.5 Business questions for CSI
	9.1 Challenges
	9.2 Critical Success Factors
	9.3 Risks

Table 5.9 Suggested reading

LEARNING UNIT: ITIL SC: OSA04 Request Fulfillment

Curriculum subjects covered	Level of Difficulty
This unit covers the Request Fulfillment process and how it contributes to OSA. A complete overview of the objectives, scope and importance of Request Fulfillment as a process to generate business value are explored. Request Fulfillment policies, principles, concepts, activities, methods, request models and techniques are explained in relationship to OSA practices as well as to Information Management. Efficient use of Request Fulfillment metrics are reviewed in this unit. To meet the learning outcomes and examination level of difficulty, the candidates must be able to understand, describe, identify, demonstrate, apply, distinguish, produce, decide or analyze: • The purpose, goal and objectives of the Request Fulfillment process Core Guidance References – SO 4.3.1 • The scope of the Request Fulfillment process Core Guidance References – SO 4.3.2 • The value to business and to the Service Lifecycle Core Guidance References – SO 4.3.3 • The policies, principles and the request model concept Core Guidance References – SO 4.3.4 • The process activities, methods and techniques and how they relate to the Service Lifecycle Core Guidance References – SO 4.3.5 • The triggers, inputs and outputs and the process interfaces Core Guidance References – SO 4.3.6 • Request Fulfillment involvement in Information Management Core Guidance References – SO 4.3.7 • How metrics can be used to check effectiveness and efficiency of the Request Fulfillment process Core Guidance References – SO 4.3.8, CSI 7.1.6 • The challenges, Critical Success Factors and risks associated with the Request Fulfillment process Core Guidance References – SO 4.3.9, CSI 9 (CSI references within the context of Request Fulfillment)	Up to Bloom level 4 Applying and Analyzing The candidate should reach a level of competence that supports problem solving, putting theory into practice, interpreting principles and relationships related to Request Fulfillment.
Contact hours recommended – 4.0	

Table 5.10 ITIL SC: OSA04 Request Fulfillment

Sections to read and concepts to understand

SO 4.3.1	The purpose, goal and objectives
SO 4.3.2	The scope
SO 4.3.3	The value to business
SO 4.3.4	The policies, principles and basic concepts 4.3.4.1 Request Models
SO 4.3.5	The process activities, methods and techniques and how they relate 4.3.5.1 Menu Selection 4.3.5.2 Financial approval 4.3.5.3 Other approval 4.3.5.4 Fulfillment 4.3.5.5 Closure
SO 4.3.6	The triggers, inputs and outputs and the process interfaces
SO 4.3.7	Information Management
SO 4.3.8 CSI 7.1.6	Metrics CSI within the context of Access Management 7.1.6 Service Request and fulfillment (Service Catalogue and workflow)
SO 4.3.9 CSI 9	The challenges, Critical Success Factors and risks 4.3.9.1 Challenges 4.3.9.2 Critical Success Factors 4.3.9.3 Risks CSI within the context of Incident Management 9.1 Challenges 9.2 Critical Success Factors 9.3 Risks

Table 5.11 Suggested reading

LEARNING UNIT: ITIL SC: OSA05 Problem Management

Curriculum subjects covered	Level of Difficulty
This unit covers how Problem Management process contributes to OSA practices. A complete overview of the objectives, scope and importance of Problem Management as a process to generate business value is explored. Problem Management policies, principles, concepts, activities, methods, problem models and techniques are explained in relationship to OSA practices as well as to Information Management. Efficient use of Problem Management metrics are reviewed in this unit. To meet the learning outcomes and examination level of difficulty, the candidates must be able to understand, describe, identify, demonstrate, apply, distinguish, produce, decide or analyze: • The purpose, goal and objectives of the Problem Management process Core Guidance References – SO 4.4.1 • The scope of the Problem Management process Core Guidance References – SO 4.4.2 • The value to business and Service Lifecycle Core Guidance References – SO 4.4.3 • The policies, principles and the problem model concept Core Guidance References – SO 4.4.4 • The process activities, methods and techniques and how they relate to the Service Lifecycle Core Guidance References – SO 4.4.5 • The triggers, inputs and outputs and the process interfaces Core Guidance References – SO 4.4.6 • Problem Management involvement in Information Management Core Guidance References – SO 4.4.7 • How metrics can be used to check effectiveness and efficiency of the Problem Management process Core Guidance References – SO 4.4.8, CSI 4.1, CSI 4.6 (CSI references within the context of Problem Management) • The challenges, Critical Success Factors and risks associated with the Problem Management process Core Guidance References – SO 4.4.9, CSI 4.5, CSI 9 (CSI references within the context of Problem Management)	Up to Bloom level 4 Applying and Analyzing The candidate should reach a level of competence that supports problem solving, putting theory into practice, interpreting principles and relationships related to Problem Management.
Contact hours recommended – 5.0	

Table 5.12 ITIL SC: OSA05 Problem Management

Sections to read and concepts to understand

SO 4.4.1	The purpose, goal and objectives
SO 4.4.2	The scope
SO 4.4.3	The value to business
SO 4.4.4	The policies, principles and basic concepts 4.4.4.1 Problem Models
SO 4.4.5	The process activities, methods and techniques and how they relate 4.4.5.1 Problem detection 4.4.5.2 Problem logging 4.4.5.3 Problem Categorization 4.4.5.4 Problem Prioritization 4.4.5.5 Problem Investigation and Diagnosis 4.4.5.6 Workarounds 4.4.5.7 Raising a Known Error Record 4.4.5.8 Problem resolution 4.4.5.9 Problem Closure 4.4.5.10 Major Problem Review 4.4.5.11 Errors detected in the development environment
SO 4.4.6	The triggers, inputs and outputs and the process interfaces
SO 4.4.7	Information Management 4.4.7.1 CMS 4.4.7.2 Known Error Database
SO 4.4.8	Metrics
CSI 4.1	CSI within the context of Incident Management
CSI 4.6	4.1 The 7-step improvement process 4.1.1 Integration with the rest of the lifecycle stages and Service Management processes 4.6 Service Level management 4.6.1 Goal for SLM 4.6.2 Service improvement plan
SO 4.4.9	The challenges, Critical Success Factors and risks
CSI 4.5	CSI within the context of Incident Management
CSI 9	4.5 Business questions for CSI 9.1 Challenges 9.2 Critical Success Factors 9.3 Risks

Table 5.13 Suggested reading

LEARNING UNIT: ITIL SC: OSA06 Access Management

Curriculum subjects covered	Level of Difficulty
This learning unit covers how the Access Management process contributes to Operational Support and Analysis practices. A complete overview of the objectives, scope and importance of Access Management as a process to generate business value are explored. Access Management policies, principles, concepts, activities, methods and techniques are explained in relationship to OSA practices as well as to Information Management. Efficient use of Access Management metrics are reviewed in this unit. To meet the learning outcomes and examination level of difficulty, the candidates must be able to understand, describe, identify, demonstrate, apply, distinguish, produce, decide or analyze: • The purpose, goal and objectives of the Access Management process Core Guidance References – SO 4.5.1 • The scope of the Access Management process Core Guidance References – SO 4.5.2 • The value to business and Service Lifecycle Core Guidance References – SO 4.5.3 • The policies, principles and basic concepts Core Guidance References – SO 4.5.4 • The process activities, methods and techniques and how they relate with the Service Lifecycle Core Guidance References – SO 4.5.5 • The triggers, inputs and outputs and the process interfaces Core Guidance References – SO 4.5.6 • Access Management involvement in Information Management Core Guidance References – SO 4.5.7 • How metrics can be used to check effectiveness and efficiency of the Access Management process Core Guidance References – SO 4.5.8 • The challenges, Critical Success Factors and risks associated with the Access Management process Core Guidance References – SO 4.5.9, CSI 9 (CSI references within the context of Access Management)	Up to Bloom level 4 Applying and Analyzing The candidate should reach a level of competence that supports problem solving, putting theory into practice, interpreting principles and relationships related to Access Management.
Contact hours recommended – 2.5	

Table 5.14 ITIL SC: OSA06 Access Management

Sections to read and concepts to understand

SO 4.5.1	The purpose, goal and objectives
SO 4.5.2	The scope
SO 4.5.3	The value to business
SO 4.5.4	The policies, principles and basic concepts
SO 4.5.5	The process activities, methods and techniques 4.5.5.1 Requesting access 4.5.5.2 Verification 4.5.5.3 Providing rights 4.5.5.4 Monitoring identity status 4.5.5.5 Logging and tracking access 4.5.5.6 Removing or restricting rights
SO 4.5.6	The triggers, inputs and outputs and the process interfaces
SO 4.5.7	Information Management 4.5.7.1 Identity 4.5.7.2 Users, groups, roles and service groups
SO 4.5.8	Metrics
SO 4.5.9	The challenges, Critical Success Factors and risks
CSI 9	CSI within the context of Incident Management 9.1 Challenges 9.2 Critical Success Factors 9.3 Risks

Table 5.15 Suggested reading

LEARNING UNIT: ITIL SC: OSA07 The Service Desk

Curriculum subjects covered	Level of Difficulty
This learning unit covers the Service Desk function and how it contributes to OSA. A complete overview of the objectives, scope and importance of the Service Desk as a function to generate business value are explored. Service Desk policies, principles, concepts, activities, methods and techniques are explained in relationship to OSA. Also covered, is the Service Desk role, organizational structures, staffing options and outsourcing strategies. Efficient use of Service Desk metrics are reviewed in this unit. This unit covers the Service Desk and how it contributes to Service Operation and Analysis. To meet the learning outcomes and examination level of difficulty, the candidates must be able to understand, describe, identify, demonstrate, apply, distinguish, produce, decide or analyze: • The Service Desk role Core Guidance References – SO 6.2.1 • The Service Desk objectives Core Guidance References – SO 6.2.2 • Different Service Desk organizational structures Core Guidance References – SO 6.2.3 • Different Service Desk staffing options Core Guidance References – SO 6.2.4 • Different Service Desk metrics that can be used to measure its effectiveness and efficiency Core Guidance References – SO 6.2.5 • Issues and safeguards to consider when outsourcing the Service Desk Core Guidance References – SO 6.2.6	Up to Bloom level 4 Applying and Analyzing The candidate should reach a level of competence that supports problem solving, putting theory into practice, interpreting principles and relationships related to the Service Desk.
Contact hours recommended – 3.5	

Table 5.16 ITIL SC: OSA07 The Service Desk

Sections to read and concepts to understand

SO 6.2.1	Service Desk role
SO 6.2.2	Service Desk objectives
SO 6.2.3	Service Desk organizational structures 6.2.3.1 Local Service Desk 6.2.3.2 Centralized Service Desk 6.2.3.3 Virtual Service Desk 6.2.3.4 Follow the Sun 6.2.3.5 Specialized Service Desk groups 6.2.3.6 Environment 6.2.3.7 Building a single point of contact
SO 6.2.4	Service Desk staffing options 6.2.4.1 Staffing levels 6.2.4.2 Skills levels 6.2.4.3 Training 6.2.4.4 Staff retention 6.2.4.5 Super users Customer/user satisfaction surveys
SO 6.2.5	Service Desk metrics
SO 6.2.6	Issues and safeguards to consider when outsourcing 6.2.6.1 Common tools and processes 6.2.6.2 SLA targets 6.2.6.3 Good communications 6.2.6.4 Ownership of data

Table 5.17 Suggested reading

LEARNING UNIT: ITIL SC: OSA08 Common OSA Functions

Curriculum subjects covered	Level of Difficulty
This learning unit deals with how the Service Operation Functions of Technical Management, IT Operations Management, and Applications Management contribute to OSA practices. For each function, the roles are defined along with the objectives, scope, importance, policies, principles, concepts, activities, methods and techniques in relationship to OSA. To meet the learning outcomes and examination level of difficulty, the candidates must be able to understand, describe, identify, demonstrate, apply, distinguish, produce, decide or analyze: • The roles of each function Core Guidance References – SO 6.3.1, 6.4.1, 6.5.1 • Their objectives Core Guidance References – SO 6.3.2, 6.4.2, 6.5.2 • Each function's activities Core Guidance References – SO 6.3.3, 6.4.3, 6.5.5	Up to Bloom level 4 Applying and Analyzing The candidate should reach a level of competence that supports problem solving, putting theory into practice, interpreting principles and relationships related to each of the common functions.
Contact hours recommended – 4.0	

Table 5.18 ITIL SC: OSA08 Common OSA Functions

SECTIONS TO READ AND CONCEPTS TO UNDERSTAND

SO 6.3.1	Technical Management role
SO 6.3.2	Technical Management Objectives
SO 6.3.3	Generic Technical Management activities
SO 6.4.1	IT Operations Management role
SO 6.4.2	IT Operations Management objectives
SO 6.4.3	IT Operations Management organization
SO 6.5.1	Application Management role
SO 6.5.2	Application Management objectives
SO 6.5.5	Application Management generic activities

Table 5.19 Suggested reading

LEARNING UNIT: ITIL SC: OSA9 Technology and Implementation considerations

Curriculum subjects covered	Level of Difficulty
This unit covers technology implementation as part of implementing Service Management process capabilities. It also covers the special technology functions and features that are related to OSA practices. To meet the learning outcomes and examination level of difficulty, the candidates must be able to understand, describe, identify, demonstrate, apply, distinguish, produce, decide or analyze: • The generic requirements for technology to support process capability Core Guidance References – SO 7.1 • The evaluation criteria for technology and tools for process implementation Core Guidance References – SD 7.2 • Project, risk and staffing practices for process implementation Core Guidance References – SO 8.2, 8.3, 8.4 • The challenges, Critical Success Factors and risks related to implementing practices and processes Core Guidance References – ST 9.1, 9.2, 9.3, SD 9.1, 9.2, 9.2, SO 9.1, 9.2, 9.3 • How to plan and implement Service Management technologies Core Guidance References – SO 8.5	Up to Bloom level 4 Applying and Analyzing The candidate should reach a level of competence that supports problem solving, putting theory into practice, interpreting principles and relationships related to OSA Technology and implementation.
Contact hours recommended – 2.0	

Table 5.20 ITIL SC: OSA9 Technology and Implementation considerations

Sections to read and concepts to understand

SO 7.1	Generic requirements 7.1.1 Self-Help 7.1.2 Workflow or process engine 7.1.3 Integrated CMS 7.1.4 Discovery/Deployment/Licensing technology 7.1.5 Remote control 7.1.6 Diagnostic utilities 7.1.7 Reporting 7.1.8 Dashboards 7.1.9 Integration with Business Service Management
SD 7.2	7.2 Service Management tools
SO 8.2 SO 8.3 SO 8.4	Project, risk and staffing practices for process implementation 8.2 Service Operation and project management 8.3 Assessing and managing risk in Service Operation 8.4 Operational staff in Service Design and Transition
ST 9.1 ST 9.2 ST 9.3 SD 9.1 SD 9.2 SD 9.2 SO 9.1 SO 9.2 SO 9.3	Challenges, Critical Success Factors and risks related to implementing practices and processes 9.1 Challenges 9.2 Critical Success Factors 9.3 Risks 9.1 Challenges 9.2 Critical Success Factors 9.3 Risks 9.1 Challenges 9.2 Critical Success Factors 9.3 Risks
SO 8.5	Plan and implement Service Management technologies

Table 5.21 Suggested reading

LEARNING UNIT: ITIL SC: OSA10 Summary, Exam Preparation and Directed Studies

Curriculum subjects covered	Level of Difficulty
This unit summarizes the material covered in the previous units and prepares candidates for the examination. It is likely that most course providers will wish to offer, and review, at least one mock examination opportunity.	
Contact hours recommended – 2.0	

Table 5.22 ITIL SC: OSA10 Summary, Exam Preparation and Directed Studies

Terminology list

A candidate is expected to understand the following terms after completing an OSA course.

*-Denotes the term is covered at the Foundation level and should be covered in this module within the module's context.

Access Management	Monitoring and Control
Achieving Balance (in Service Operations)	Network Management
Alert*	Operational Health
Applications Management	Operational Level Agreement (OLA)*
Business Case*	Problem*
Configuration Item*	Organizational Structures
Configuration Management System*	Problem Management
Continual Service Improvement	Project Management
Database Management	Request Fulfillment
Desktop Support	Risk Management
Directory Services Management	Server Management and Support
Event*	Service Catalogue*
Event Management	Service Desk
Facilities and Data centre Management	Service Design
Functions	Service Knowledge Management System (SKMS)*
Incident*	Service Level Agreement*
Incident Management	Service Operation
Internet/Web Management	Service Provider*
IT Operations	Service Request*
IT Operations Management	Service Strategy
IT Security Management	Service Transition
Known Error Database (KEDB)*	Storage and Archive
Known Error*	Technical Management
Lifecycle	Telephony
Mainframe Management	Value to Business
Middleware Management	

Table 5.23 Terminology list

During the course delivery

Here are some important aspects to consider during the course delivery.

Things to do

Regardless of the delivery method for a course a candidate should always pay attention to the instructor, as the material may not always be present on the slide of the accompanying text.

Ask questions. The only so-called 'stupid question' is the one that a candidate does not ask.

Focus on the practices describes by the framework. The exam is about the practices, not those of a candidate or their organization.

Read the course workbook and the core book sections in the evening or early morning. Remember that the core books are reference material; therefore, the writing style is not the same as a novel or a biography.

Take notes. This involves Bloom's psychomotor domain and is has been demonstrated numerous times that people who involve this domain have a higher level of retention than those who don't.

Unless you are taking notes, leave your laptop turned off. Reading email during a course is disrespectful to the instructor, bad manners and is a major irritant to the other attendees. Additionally, it is a significant distractor for the candidate.

Complete your evening assignment or homework if the instructor mentions it.

Clear your calendar as much as possible for the duration of the course.

Things not to do

Read email. – See above

Leave your mobile phone on; for the same reasons as email above

Be late to class. Don't be disrespectful to the instructors and to the other candidates; show up on time at the beginning of class, after breaks and after lunch periods

Monopolize the discussions. Although you may have valid questions and valid comments, so do the other candidates.

Disagree and get frustrated with the framework. Although the framework is not perfect and some concepts may seem to go against what you have learned and done in the past, you are attending the course to learn about some aspects of the framework. Make the most of it; frustration only leads to distractions and distractions often lead a candidate to fail the exam.

Wait till the last minute to start preparing for the course.

Burn the 'midnight oil', pull an 'all nighter' – staying up late all night to work or study is not a good idea. Get a good night sleep instead

Don't prepare for the course. Relying on your experience, knowledge and your exam's 'good luck charm' does not work.

Put in a full day's worth of office work in the evening or the following morning or during the course. If your organization cannot afford to have you away for a few days to attend a course, it is sadly mistaken and certainly does not believe in education and training.

If you think you can step away for long stretches of course time; think again. Experience has shown, time and time again that people who miss large course portions to attend meetings physically or by conference call have a much lower success rate in the exam.

Note from the author – OK I am ranting here.
I have conducted hundreds of courses around the world and I have seen each and every item in the above list being done. I warned the candidates at the beginning of each class and, in many cases, weeks before the class and still many do not prepare, do not pay attention, step away from the classroom and conduct more office work during the course than paying attention during the course.

Personally, I would love to have a 100% success rate for every course I teach. However, there comes a time when enough is enough. I don't care about the culture of your organization which forces you to read email all day long. I don't care if you spend more time working than paying attention to me as an instructor.

The above is disrespectful. Don't waste the time of the instructor and that of the other candidates in the course. You can't be there physically or mentally? That's fine. Just don't complain about the exam at any level if you fail. Don't complain about the way the exam is structured or written. It is the way it is.

As an instructor I do not criticize the way you do your job or your organization's values and culture. As a candidate, don't criticize the instructor, the framework or the exam.

It is all so very simple.
You prepare, you read, you pay attention, you participate, you concentrate, you do your homework, you avoid distractions, and you focus on the framework, then your probabilities of passing the exam are very high.

Do none of the above and your probabilities of passing the exam are very low.

It is what it is; period.

Reading the material

As mentioned already, the core books form a frame or reference about good Service Management practices. These books are not novels. They are rather dry to read.

Read only a few sections at a time and don't read more than 12 to 15 pages at a time.

Read each section two or three times to ensure understanding and take notes.

There is no need to learn everything by rote. This is a major waste of time and it is utterly useless. There is a need to know and understand the concepts.

A good exercise is to try to identify where a particular concept or topic exists in your organization. It may not be called the same. It may not be exactly the same but it does exist in your organization.

Another good exercise is to use analogies. All the practices described in the core books exist outside of IT. They are usually called by different names and may not be exactly the same but the similarities are there. Look around your home, the shopping mall, or any other business. Look for the concepts. Identifying them outside of IT makes it easier to remember them and to apply them.

Application is Bloom's level 3. If you try to analyze them for effectiveness and efficiency and to identify areas for improvement for example, you are practicing Bloom's level 4.

The Service Capabilities syllabuses recommend 12 hours of self-study time while the Service Lifecycle syllabuses recommend 21 hours. Use your time wisely.

Before the course, and starting early, read the books, take notes, write down your questions, and bring them to the course.

While you attend the course, do some light preparation reading, take notes, write down your questions, and bring them to the course the next day.

Understanding the material

As previously mentioned, there is no need to learn everything by rote. However, it is expected that a candidate is able to recall the purpose of each lifecycle stage, the names of the processes in each stage, the goals of processes covered in the syllabus, the definitions of the various terms covered in the syllabus and the high level relationships between processes.

Looking back to Bloom's levels, Levels 1 and 2 are about knowledge and comprehension which means a candidate has read the material a few times, can remember the concepts and can explain them in their own words.

In order to understand the material, a candidate should use the core books and the syllabus to determine if they can apply the concepts in the context provided in the *Syllabus at a Glance* and the *Qualification Learning Objectives* section of the syllabus.

Let us be honest here. It is not expected of any candidate to know the contents of every book, to be able to recall verbatim the goals, the objectives, and the definitions. What is expected is that a candidate understands and recalls some key concepts.

Here is a breakdown of the key concepts to know and understand for any qualification (Table 5.13).

It is up to the candidate to look up these terms in the core books, including the glossary at the end of each book. This is a good way to practice learning, using the reference books. The more you do, the better your probability of passing the examination. Additionally, the more you consult the books, the more you will learn and the more people will look up to you as a source of knowledge.

Note from the author
Why are the definitions not provided in the following list of key concepts?

You are taking the exam, not me. Therefore, you do the research and you learn about the terms. Hint: Look the terms up in the glossary provided at the end of this book.

As we often say in English 'Been there, done that'.

In my particular case, this is true; I possess the following ITIL certifications.

- *The Foundation certificate; v1, v2, and v3*
- *Three of the four v2 Practitioners*
- *The Service Manager (thrice – v1, v2(twice) – just for fun)*
- *All ten V3 Intermediate certificates and the ITIL Expert certificate*

However, there is a glossary of terms provided at the end of this book.

7-step improvement process	Four reasons to measure	Restore
Access	Goal	Return on Investment
Access Management	Governance	Review
Accounting	Impact	Role
Alert	Incident	Service
Application Management	Incident Management	Service Asset & Configuration Management
Audit	Information Security Management	Service capacity
Availability	Integrity	Service catalog
Availability Management	IT Infrastructure	Service Catalog Management
Baseline	IT Operations Management	Service Design
Benchmark	IT Service Continuity Management	Service Knowledge Management System
Budget	Key Performance Indicator	Service Level Agreement
Business capacity	Knowledge Management	Service Level Management
Business case	Known Error	Service Management
Business outcomes	Known Error database	Service Manager
Capabilities	Maturity	Service measurement
Capacity	Metric	Service Operation
Capacity Management	Mission	Service owner

Categorization	Model	Service pipeline
Change	Objective	Service portfolio
Change advisory board	Operational	Service Portfolio Management
Change Management	Operational Level Agreement	Service reporting
Charging	Operations Control	Service request
Compliance	Plan	Service Strategy
Component capacity	Priority	Service Transition
Confidentiality	Problem	Service Validation and Testing
Configuration Management database	Problem Management	Standard change
Configuration Management system	Procedure	Strategic
Continual service improvement	Process	Supplier
Continuous improvement model	Process Control	Supplier categories
Critical Success Factor	Process Manager	Supplier Contract Database
Customer	Process Owner	Supplier Management
Demand	Project	System
Demand Management	Project Management	Tactical
Deming cycle	Provider	Technical Management
DIKW model	Quality	Third party
Downtime	Recover	Transition Planning and Support
Effectiveness	Release	Underpinning Contract
Efficiency	Release and Deployment Management	Urgency
Emergency Change Advisory Board	Release options	User
Evaluation	Release policy	Utility
Event	Repair	Value creation
Event Management	Report	Value on Investment
Facilities Management	Request Fulfillment	Vendor
Five aspects of Service Design	Resolve	Vision
Four Ps of Service Design	Resources	Warranty

Table 5.24 List of key concepts in ITIL V3

Summary

A candidate can look at a qualification course from one of two perspectives. The first is to acquire new knowledge and the second is to confirm the knowledge already acquired through experience.

In both instances there are basically three scenarios. One, a candidate is usually assigned to a new role and needs to rapidly acquire a certain level of familiarity with the new role or job function. This often happens when an organization has decided or already adopted and adapted good practices. Two, this is also a familiar path for an instructor who will soon be delivering this course. Finally the third scenario involves a consultant attending such courses to fulfill a customer's requirement or as a refresher for an upcoming assignment.

Regardless of the reason for attending a qualification course, a candidate should acquire the syllabus and the appropriate core books. The candidate should then identify the appropriate reading sections and actually do the reading before attending the course. This cannot be stressed often or strongly enough.

Note from the author

It is easy to recognize someone who has read the material before getting to class when you are an instructor. During a discussion at a client site, a conference or during a job interview, it is just as easy to recognize someone who, although they possess the certification, has not read the literature or applied any of the concepts.

Here is a bit of small free advice.

Do yourself and your career a major service, take qualifications and certifications seriously and do what we call the 'heavy lifting'. READ THE SYLLABUS! READ THE BOOKS! Again, and again, and again...

CHAPTER 6

Understanding the exam paper

Before you start the examination

The examination is about to start. The person invigilating (or proctoring) the examination has just completed the registration process and is about to instruct the candidates to open the envelope containing the examination paper. The candidates are prepared, they are anxious to get this over with.

	**Make sure this is the correct paper first!**

As part of an exam paper, important standard information is always provided. The information is a useful reminder to read before going to the first question.

There are two primary reasons to do this. The first reason is quite obvious: instructions may change as part of regular examination maintenance or as part of a significant change in exam format or philosophy. Although minor, there were indeed some changes to the instructions between 2007 and the end of 2010.

The second reason is that mistakes do happen. You may be looking at the wrong exam paper. Although it is quite unlikely, an incorrect exam paper – other topic or other language – may have been shipped by the EI and received by the ATO. It is also possible the ATO may have ordered the incorrect exam paper. This is more likely to happen for paper-based exams than electronic-based.

This does not mean that electronic-based exam papers are free of such logistical errors. It is possible the candidate may have registered for another paper inadvertently. It is also possible that someone from the EI may have uploaded an exam paper under an incorrect name.

However, there is no need to worry too much about the above or to lose any sleep over it for these mistakes are rather rare. The quality controls of ATOs and EIs usually guard against such occurrences.

This being said, what does this standard information look like?

The following information about the scenario booklet is the standard text for each paper as provided by the Accreditor.

	The following shaded text comes from the Accreditor and is found in every exam paper (sample or live)

SCENARIO BOOKLET

This booklet contains the scenarios upon which the 8 examination questions will be based. All questions are contained within the Question Booklet and each question will clearly state the scenario to which the question relates. In order to answer each of the 8 questions, you will need to read the related scenario carefully.

On the basis of the information provided in the scenario, you will be required to select which of the four answer options provided (A, B, C or D) you believe to be the optimum answer. You may choose ONE answer only, and the Gradient Scoring system works as follows:

- If you select the CORRECT answer, you will be awarded 5 marks for the question
- If you select the SECOND BEST answer, you will be awarded 3 marks for the question
- If you select the THIRD BEST answer, you will be awarded 1 mark for the question
- If you select the DISTRACTER (the incorrect answer), you will receive no marks for the question

In order to pass this examination, you must achieve a total of 28 marks or more out of a maximum of 40 marks (70%).

Characteristics of scenarios

As mentioned previously, an exam paper consists of three major parts, the scenario – known as the scenario booklet – the question and the possible answers – known as the question booklet.

In this chapter the scenario booklet is explored in more detail. The following points are covered:
- How to read a scenario
- How much time to spend on reading a scenario
- Sifting through the information
- Identifying the relevant material
- Identifying the distractions

A scenario has the following characteristics:
- The length of any scenario should not exceed 400 words
  - This is a guideline only; there are exceptions. For example, there are five scenarios in the sample papers exceeding this guideline[25]
- Together with the question and answers, the total number of words making up one 'question' should not exceed 600 words
  - Again, this is a guideline only; there are exceptions. For example, there are 64 questions with a total word count in the sample papers exceeding this guideline[26]
- The information contained in the scenario is useful in selecting the best answer available
- A scenario can be used for one or two questions
  - Please read the question carefully to know which is the correct scenario to use for the question you are attempting
  - Underneath the question number, a statement indicates which scenario to refer to for this question.
  - This means that an exam paper may contain anywhere between four and eight scenarios

---

25   See Tables 6.3 and 6.4
26   See Tables 6.5 and 6.6

How to read a scenario

Before going any further, it is important to define what a scenario[27] is. Of course, in the dictionary, the word has many meanings. The one which is of particular interest to us is provided here.

Definition of a scenario

sce•nar•io   *noun*   \,in-fər-'mā-shən\
\sə-'ner-ē-,ō, USA also and especially British -'när-\

Definition of SCENARIO

3: a sequence of events especially when imagined;
   especially: an account or synopsis of a possible course
   of action or events

Figure 6.1 Definition of a scenario

It is important to note that for the purpose of the exams, certain conditions had to be imposed on the examiners. Here are some of them.

- They cannot use the name of a real or fictitious company. Examiners are encouraged to use the type of organization as opposed to using a fictitious company name. This being said, a candidate may face a question where a company is given a name.

Example:

Not recommended: The CIO of the High-Fees Bank wants to ...

Recommended: The CIO of a financial institution wants to...

- They cannot use the name of real products. Examiners are encouraged to use the type of product as opposed to a fictitious product name. This being said, a candidate may face a question where a product is given a name.

---

27   Merriam-Webster dictionary

Example:

Not recommended: The organization is using the Not-so-Intuitive CMDB (Configuration Management Database) tool...

Recommended: The organization is using a CMDB (Configuration Management Database) tool...

- They should avoid specific city or geographical areas. Examiners are encouraged to avoid naming specific cities, countries or continents unless it is required to identified the best answer. The reason is to avoid providing too much distracting information. A candidate should focus on the specific ITIL topic and not worry about geography. This being said, a candidate may face a question where a geographical area is named.

Example:

Not recommended: The organization is located in the remote village of X in the country of Y...

Recommended: The organization, located in Asia...

- The examiners should aim for gender neutrality. Examiners are encouraged to avoid using genders. This is done to avoid being cultural and gender-bias. Additionally the use of 'he / she' is also discouraged as it makes the text more difficult to read and adds to the word count. This being said, a candidate may face a question where a character in a scenario is given a gender or a name.

Example:

Not recommended: The CIO of a financial institution wants to... He asked... He wants... He wants you to...
Recommended: The CIO of a financial institution wants to... The CIO asked... The CIO wants... The CIO wants you to...

Scenarios have been in used in many qualifications and in academia for a very long time. The scenario is used here to provide context for a particular topic being examined. A candidate is very likely to have faced or will face a similar situation in their career. The question is asking them what should be done according to ITIL. If there were no scenario the answer would be very simple.

A   ...
B   ...
C   ...
D It depends...

Length/size of scenarios

An exam is ninety (90) minutes. A candidate cannot – and should not – spend too much time on the scenario, nor should they ignore or skip the scenario. For the sake of simplicity in this book, scenarios are categorized into three categories: short, medium and large. The ranges are somewhat arbitrary and are not based on any science or statistical evidence. The categories are explained further in the following table.

Short scenario	Less than 200 words
Medium-sized scenario	201 to 300 words
Large scenario	301+ words

Table 6.1 Size categories for scenarios

Coming up with a size category is useless without providing further information. An analysis of the word count for each qualification for the sample papers used in the fall of 2010 is presented in the following tables. The reason for providing the word counts is to help a candidate make an approximate assessment of the relationship between the size of the scenario and the question itself.

- The larger the scenario, the more likely the question will be shorter and vice versa.
- The larger the scenario, the more likely a candidate will have to go back and forth between the scenario and the question.
- Regardless of the relative sizes, the answer to the question is always based on the scenario

A simple word count is provided in the following tables. Additional analysis is provided further in this chapter.

Table No.	The table represents the word count for...
Table 6.3	Scenarios sample paper 1
Table 6.4	Scenarios sample paper 2
Table 6.5	Questions sample paper 1
Table 6.6	Questions sample paper 2
Table 6.7	Totals sample paper 1

Table No.	The table represents the word count for...
Table 6.8	Totals sample paper 2
Table 6.9	Number of scenarios per category
Table 6.10	Number of questions per category
Table 6.11	Consolidated analysis for both sample papers

Table 6.2 Analysis of word counts

The following table provides the number of words per scenario only for sample paper 1 for each qualification.

QUALIFICATION		WORD COUNT FOR SCENARIO NUMBER							
		One	Two	Three	Four	Five	Six	Seven	Eight
Capabilities	OSA	196	331	158	159	268	220	175	193
	RCV	333	178	189	243	181	208	143	n/a
	PPO	330	406	389	301	n/a	n/a	n/a	n/a
	SOA	102	206	171	151	250	135	217	216
Lifecycle	SS	203	202	282	327	324	249	445	272
	SD	191	298	220	225	163	286	219	196
	ST	277	271	233	247	171	349	179	141
	SO	366	231	291	222	244	173	223	280
	CSI	447	211	187	205	73	174	138	n/a
Capstone	MALC	441	392	289	237	332	303	n/a	n/a

Table 6.3 Scenario word count for sample paper 1 by qualification

The following table provides the number of words per scenario only for sample paper 2 for each qualification.

QUALIFICATION		WORD COUNT FOR SCENARIO NUMBER							
		One	Two	Three	Four	Five	Six	Seven	Eight
Capabilities	OSA	230	342	199	191	285	335	290	403
	RCV	265	315	361	277	227	245	220	209
	PPO	267	396	141	302	287	199	n/a	n/a
	SOA	206	185	172	148	151	179	123	199
Lifecycle	SS	268	319	302	197	20	290	237	187
	SD	280	139	207	172	213	240	176	134
	ST	266	349	294	280	248	284	372	113
	SO	285	347	237	273	200	205	161	346
	CSI	227	182	143	144	398	313	324	231
Capstone	MALC	379	270	345	291	266	162	n/a	n/a

Table 6.4 Scenario word count for sample paper 2 by qualification

The following table provides the number of words by question only for sample paper 1 for each qualification.

QUALIFICATION		WORD COUNT FOR QUESTION NUMBER							
		One	Two	Three	Four	Five	Six	Seven	Eight
Capabilities	OSA	358	288	383	272	389	262	204	413
	RCV	203	267	318	255	177	390	244	300
	PPO	360	368	349	351	273	356	419	342
	SOA	249	183	330	388	583	312	446	258
Lifecycle	SS	417	359	324	278	281	337	318	344
	SD	420	381	342	385	212	384	371	359
	ST	349	409	451	380	239	342	318	137
	SO	181	319	319	368	381	367	366	331
	CSI	196	206	406	445	390	309	385	204
Capstone	MALC	352	246	263	430	133	264	363	102

Table 6.5 Question word counts for sample paper 1 by qualification

The following table provides the number of words by question only for sample paper 2 for each qualification.

QUALIFICATION		WORD COUNT FOR QUESTION NUMBER							
		One	Two	Three	Four	Five	Six	Seven	Eight
Capabilities	OSA	393	257	337	375	280	213	301	176
	RCV	258	284	37	318	368	213	344	345
	PPO	457	375	339	340	387	371	333	249
	SOA	358	334	371	226	92	281	439	409
Lifecycle	SS	306	222	402	403	233	305	447	508
	SD	185	388	370	402	387	297	382	310
	ST	330	272	289	481	333	328	352	276
	SO	410	258	396	331	382	373	311	234
	CSI	319	293	320	433	36	402	380	419
Capstone	MALC	282	249	206	253	245	245	231	213

Table 6.6 Question word counts for sample paper 2 by qualification

The following table provides the total number of words per question (scenario and question) for sample paper 1 for each qualification.

QUALIFICATION		TOTAL WORD COUNT (SCENARIO & QUESTION)							
		QUESTION NUMBER							
		One	Two	Three	Four	Five	Six	Seven	Eight
Capabilities	OSA	554	619	541	431	657	482	379	606
	RCV	536	600	496	444	420	571	452	443
	PPO	690	698	755	757	662	745	720	643
	SOA	351	389	501	539	833	447	663	474
Lifecycle	SS	620	561	606	605	605	586	763	616
	SD	611	679	562	610	375	670	590	555
	ST	626	680	684	627	410	691	497	278
	SO	547	550	610	590	625	540	589	611
	CSI	643	653	617	632	595	382	559	342
Capstone	MALC	793	687	655	719	370	501	695	405

Table 6.7 Total word count of entire question for sample paper 1 by qualification

The following table provides the total number of words in the question (scenario and question) for sample paper 2 for each qualification.

QUALIFICATION		TOTAL WORD COUNT (SCENARIO & QUESTION)							
		QUESTION NUMBER							
		One	Two	Three	Four	Five	Six	Seven	Eight
Capabilities	OSA	623	599	536	566	565	548	591	579
	RCV	523	599	398	595	595	458	564	554
	PPO	724	642	735	736	528	673	620	448
	SOA	564	519	543	374	243	460	562	608
Lifecycle	SS	574	541	704	600	253	595	684	695
	SD	465	527	577	574	600	537	558	444
	ST	596	621	583	761	581	612	724	389
	SO	695	605	633	604	582	578	472	580
	CSI	546	475	463	577	434	715	704	650
Capstone	MALC	661	628	476	523	590	536	497	375

Table 6.8 Total word count of entire question for sample paper 2 by qualification

The following table provides the number of scenarios (only) for all qualifications and for both sample papers within each word count category.

Short scenarios	Less than 200 words	49
Medium-sized scenarios	201 to 300 words	65
Large scenarios	301+ words	34
Total number of scenarios		148

Table 6.9 Number of scenarios by category

The following table provides the number of questions (only) for all qualifications and for both sample papers within each word count category.

Short question	Less than 200 words	12
Medium-sized question	201 to 300 words	47
Large question	301+ words	101
Total number of questions		160

Table 6.10 Number of questions by category

The following table provides the number of questions (scenario and question) for all qualifications and for both sample papers within each word count category.

Short question	Less than 400 words	14
Medium-sized question	401 to 600 words	82
Large question	601+ words	64
Total number of questions		160

Table 6.11 Number of questions (scenario and question) by category

The following table provides an 'at-a-glance' view of the average, median, lowest and highest total number of words in each question (scenario and question) for each qualification. The figures include both sample papers 1 and 2.

QUALIFICATION		Consolidated			
		Average	Median	Lowest	Highest
Capabilities	OSA	555	566	379	657
	RCV	516	530	398	600
	PPO	674	694	448	757
	SOA	504	510	243	833
Lifecycle	SS	601	605	253	763
	SD	558	568	375	679
	ST	585	617	278	761
	SO	588	590	472	695
	CSI	562	586	342	715
Capstone	MALC	569	563	370	793

Table 6.12 A consolidated analysis for both sample papers

The following are three examples of various lengths. The classification used here is somewhat arbitrary. Examining the sample papers available at the time of publication, scenarios can be broken down into three categories.

Example of a short scenario[28] – 161 words

A Government Department is preparing to outsource its IT Operations Management to a private company, which will be responsible for delivering to a set of contractual service levels and satisfying several key performance indicators. One of these key performance indicators needs to represent the end-to-end 'customer experience'. The service provider has been asked to recommend realistic metrics, propose a means of measuring the 'customer experience,' and identify a system that will satisfy these reporting requirements.

It is well understood within the Department that simply measuring the availability of single components within the infrastructure, such as central servers, will not truly represent the end-to-end service being provided by the service provider to the end users. It is also understood that the end user perception of service quality may not necessarily portray a realistic picture. The Department is therefore keen to ensure that there is an objective meaningful measurement that accurately represents the quality of service being delivered to the end user.

---

28   Service Strategy – Sample Paper 2 – version 4.0 – Scenario Seven

Example of a medium-sized scenario[29] – 203 words
A large IT training provider has a training centre containing twenty classrooms fully equipped with PCs and servers for delivering technical training courses. The building also contains the organization's administrative offices. A wireless network serving the administrative areas was installed about two years ago.

The wireless network can be accessed from the training area. Management decided to allow students who bring their own laptops to access the internet via the wireless network as a free 'value-added' service. Students appreciate this additional service.

Over time, usage of the wireless network by both the administrative staff and students has increased. This is affecting the availability and performance of the administrative systems, therefore it is occasionally necessary to restrict and prevent student access.

The availability and performance issues continue to increase in frequency, and the training center staff is overwhelmed with complaints from students when the network is not available to them. The management team is very concerned as the course evaluation forms show increasing student dissatisfaction.

The decision has been taken to withdraw the wireless network access service from students immediately and notices have been posted in the training areas informing students of the decision.

Management must now consider what further action should be taken.

Example of a large scenario[30] – 324 words
An organization makes car parts in four factories in Europe. The Head Office is based in a large city close to one of the factories. All four factories have small administrative offices supporting local purchasing, sales and distribution. Shared Services such as Finance and Human Resources are based at the Head Office.

The customers are mainly comprised of the following three types:
- Large car manufacturers who have an ongoing requirement for standard parts, which are planned a long time in advance. This business is fairly secure, based upon relatively long term contracts, and brings in steady, low margin income.

---

29   Service Strategy – Sample Paper 1 – version 4.0 – Scenario One
30   Service Strategy – Sample Paper 1 – version 4.0 – Scenario Five

- *Car repairers who have a mixture of steady requirements and ad hoc requirements, and require parts at relatively short notice. This type of business is based upon a mix of medium and short term contracts. There is strong competition for this business, and the level of service and responsiveness is seen as a differentiator.*
- *Development units of car manufacturers and car specialists who have specific one-off requirements for which they are willing to pay a high premium and to wait for delivery. Sometimes these arrangements lead to lucrative long term manufacturing contracts.*

Customers are supplied by their local factory and the larger customers may be served by more than one factory.

Most of the organization's IT services are managed from the Head Office by a central IT unit. However smaller local IT units serve each of the factories with infrastructure management and support. The IT services for the factories and sales run on distributed IT infrastructure and are supported locally.

The Chief Information Officer (CIO) has been asked by the Chief Executive Officer (CEO) to reduce the cost of IT across the whole organization, as part of an overall cost-cutting initiative. The CIO has decided to investigate a strategy of consolidation and centralization of the local IT infrastructure and IT services into the central IT unit to provide savings through economies of scale.

How much time to spend on a scenario

As mentioned previously, an examination is ninety (90) minutes. A candidate cannot and should not spend too much time on the scenario, nor should they ignore or skip the scenario.

The escapist answer to the above question would be to say: 'It depends'. Other than not providing any assistance whatsoever, such an answer is actually an easy way out for many instructors.

The duration of the examination is 90 minutes. There are eight questions. It is relatively easy to determine that you can spend an average of eleven minutes on each question. However, in order to build a safety cushion, a candidate should spend no more than ten minutes on a question. This approach provides a candidate time to revisit a question for which the answer is in doubt.

To come up with an approximation of the word count for a scenario and a question, look at both but don't read them. Look at the relative size of both. According to most serious websites, an adult should be able to easily read 250 words per minute (wpm). Many instructors, as well as the guidance provided by the EIs, recommend to their students to take their time when reading. This is excellent advice. By slowing the speed of reading to approximately 180 wpm, a candidate would normally need about three to four minutes for the average overall question size of approximately 570 words. Even considering the largest sample question at 833 words, it would take a reader less than five minutes to read the whole question, leaving about five minutes to think about and come up with the best answer. It is important to remember that it is very unlikely for an exam paper to have all eight questions above the recommended maximum of 600 words. Additionally, most candidates will not require the full ten minutes per question, leaving ample time to properly address a very large question.

English Second Language (ESL) candidates

The syllabuses are quite clear on the language requirements for individuals whose mother tongue is not English.

Candidates completing an exam have a maximum of 120 minutes to complete the exam and are allowed the use of a dictionary *if*:

* The exam is in a language that is not their mother tongue, and
* The candidate is in a country where the language of the exam is not a business language in that country

For such individuals, the average time per question goes up to 15 minutes. However, in order to build some buffer time, an ESL candidate should aim to spend about thirteen minutes per question, which provides a time buffer of sixteen minutes. Assuming, without being discriminatory to anyone, than an ESL candidate can comfortably read at a speed of 120 wpm, then an 800+ words question is still feasible within the allotted time. Taking the above question at 833 words as a reference, an ESL student should be able to read it in about 6½ minutes leaving that same amount to analyze the question and come up with the best available answer.

Without rushing the reading, a candidate should spend no more than one-third of the allotted time per question on the scenario. Of course, some scenarios are quite long and may require more time. However, the question is likely to be shorter and thus take less time to read and interpret.

Identifying the relevant information

Myth: 'There are trick questions in the exams'

Reality: *'There are no traps in the scenario.'*

The reality statement above is a true statement. However, a good examiner may provide information which does not affect the outcome of the question. Additional information may be provided in an attempt to mislead the candidate to a 'common practice' answer. In other words, the examiner provides information that leads a careless candidate to select the answer which most resembles the way their organization behaves instead of selecting the *'proven practice'* answer.

Scenario lengths and styles vary tremendously from one question to the next, from one paper to the next and certainly between the various qualifications. This is intentional and is also a result of the team approach used by the examination panel.

Additionally, writing a scenario is both an art and a science. The 'art' part is the literary aptitudes of the examiner; the 'science' part is application of the appropriate Bloom's levels to the question.

Tip[31]:
Visualizing the scenario often helps clarifying relationships between businesses, services, people, organizations, parties involved, etc. For some people, drawing those relationships and interfaces helps them to better approach the scenario.

It is understood that this is easier to do using a paper-based exam as opposed to a web-based exam.

Note from the author
Before you are too quick at judging the quality or the validity of a question or scenario, try walking in the examiner's shoes first.

Almost every time I challenge someone complaining too much about the questions to do something constructive instead, such as becoming an examiner or a reviewer, the answer is 'no'.

If anyone thinks they can do a better job they are welcome to apply to APMG to become an examiner.

---

31   With thanks to Mart Rovers

Adopting and adapting services and processes within an organization are no easy tasks. It takes time and effort. As mentioned previously, no one can become an expert overnight.

That being said, a candidate may be very good at what they do within their organization but it may not necessarily be the good practices described in the literature. It does not mean that what is being done is incorrect; simply that it is not the same as in the core books.

Exams need to have a certain degree of difficulty to be recognized by the industry. This is why the intermediate level exams are written at Bloom's levels 3 and 4.

This qualification scheme does not ask questions on topics such as grammar, spelling, mathematics, logic, history, astronomy, etc. It is about the application of good practice in a very specific situation. The answer will, therefore, be quite specific.

OSA Sample Paper 1 – Scenario Two

Here is an example of a scenario. It is taken from the Operational Support and Analysis Sample Paper 1, version 4.1 from July 2010.

1	*In an effort to reduce costs and avoid expanding its corporate Headquarters, a large*
2	*company has made the decision to launch a telecommuting program. Participants in this*
3	*program will work at home using corporate laptops and will access corporate systems via*
4	*the Internet. Participants will commute to the corporate Headquarters no more than once*
5	*a month and will utilize designated work areas that will be reserved in advance, much like*
6	*a hotel room.*
7	
8	*An initial pilot of the program is in the planning stage and will involve 100 senior*
9	*employees. No more than five employees per department may participate in the program*
10	*and participants must have at least five years of service with the Company. It is expected*
11	*that in time the program will be expanded considerably and may grow to include*
12	*thousands of employees.*
13	
14	*The corporate Headquarters is comprised of three large buildings. Open work areas are*
15	*available in each of these buildings. Optimally, telecommuters will reserve a work area*
16	*in the building where the telecommuter's Supervisor and team members reside. However,*
17	*telecommuters may at times have to walk from one building to another to attend*
18	*meetings, participate in training classes, and other activities. Telecommuters will scan*
19	*their corporate badge to gain access to the buildings. They will proceed to the reserved*
20	*cubicle and 'check-in' using an online reservation system called 'TOffice.'*
21	
22	*You represent the Service Desk and are participating on a team that is determining*
23	*what changes must be made to the Access Management process to accommodate this*
24	*new program. The Access Management process is working well and is based on ITIL*
25	*best practices. The organization adopted ITIL more than 10 years ago and its IT Service*
26	*Management practices in general are quite mature.*
27	

28	*The team working on this project includes representatives from Human Resources,*
29	*Information Security Management, and all of the Service Operation functions. Following*
30	*a revision of the new Information Security Policy and an initial brainstorming session, the*
	team is preparing to present a recommendation to Management.

Let us take a closer look

The word count for this scenario is 331 words and there are five paragraphs. Of course, during an exam the word count is not provided, nor is it recommended for a candidate to count the number of words manually. Suffice to say that looking at the scenario then at the relevant question will provide an approximation of the relative sizes of both elements.

The numbers on the left hand side are line numbers to help with the analysis.

Paragraph 1

1	In an effort to reduce costs and avoid expanding its corporate Headquarters, a large
2	company has made the decision to launch a telecommuting program. Participants in this
3	program will work at home using corporate laptops and will access corporate systems via
4	the Internet. Participants will commute to the corporate Headquarters no more than once
5	a month and will utilize designated work areas that will be reserved in advance, much like
6	a hotel room.

Highlights
- Large organization
- Reduce cost
- Launch telecommuting program
- Connect via the internet

What does it mean?
- Issues to anticipate include slow response (capacity), connectivity (availability), service requests
- A potential question about any of the five processes in Service Operation
- Event Management for monitoring. It the fault with the user's Internet provider, a supplier or internal to the organization
- Access Management for user access
- Incident Management for slow response and connectivity
- Request Management for questions, enquiries and everything else

Paragraph 2

7	An initial pilot of the program is in the planning stage and will involve 100 senior
8	employees. No more than five employees per department may participate in the program
9	and participants must have at least five years of service with the Company. It is expected
10	that in time the program will be expanded considerably and may grow to include
11	thousands of employees.

Highlights
- Initial pilot in planning stage
- 100 senior employees
- May grow to include thousands of employees

What does it mean?
- Already in place, therefore all previous phases are either completed (Strategy and Design) or in progress (Transition)
- Known errors from development to transition and from there to operation (known error database)

Paragraph 3

12	The corporate Headquarters is comprised of three large buildings. Open work areas are
13	available in each of these buildings. Optimally, telecommuters will reserve a work area in
14	the building where the telecommuter's Supervisor and team members reside. However,
15	telecommuters may at times have to walk from one building to another to attend
16	meetings, participate in training classes, and other activities. Telecommuters will scan their
17	corporate badge to gain access to the buildings. They will proceed to the reserved cubicle
18	and 'check-in' using an online reservation system called 'TOffice.'

Highlights
- Three large buildings
- Reserve a work area
- Walk from one building to the next
- Scan their corporate badge
- 'TOffice' is the online reservation system

What does it mean?

- Access Management because of movement between buildings
- Request Management for online reservation
- Incident Management for overbooking or lack of available cubicles

Paragraph 4

20	You represent the Service Desk and are participating on a team that is determining
21	what changes must be made to the Access Management process to accommodate this
22	new program. The Access Management process is working well and is based on ITIL
23	best practices. The organization adopted ITIL more than 10 years ago and its IT Service
24	Management practices in general are quite mature.

Highlights

- You represent the Service Desk
- Team member
- Determining changes to be made to the Access Management
- Access Management working well, based on ITIL
- ITSM practices are quite mature

What does it mean?

- Everything is already in place
- Looking specifically at improving Access Management process if it is required
- Look at the activities of the process
- Not looking at improving the technology
- Think about the relationships between the Service Operation processes
- Think about knowledge transfer from Technical and Application management
- IT Operations will be doing a lot of monitoring of TOffice
- Don't assume there is a group dedicated to deal with access requests
- Event logs about tracking reservations

Paragraph 5

26	The team working on this project includes representatives from Human Resources,
27	Information Security Management, and all of the Service Operation functions. Following
28	a revision of the new Information Security Policy and an initial brainstorming session, the
29	team is preparing to present a recommendation to Management.

Highlights
- Team includes Human Resources, Information Security Management, and Service Operation functions
- New Information Security Policy
- Team preparing to present recommendation to Management

What does it mean?
- Communication of the new release policy through Human Resources
- Logistics of deployment will affect volume of activities for Access Management
- Need to have access to user profiles through Information Security Management
- Confidentiality issues
- Identifying remote users

Having stripped out the superfluous verbiage, about one third of the information is relevant. The following table represents the number of highlighted words per paragraph.

Paragraph 1	15 words
Paragraph 2	18 words
Paragraph 3	29 words
Paragraph 4	33 words
Paragraph 5	25 words
Total	**120 words**

Table 6.13 Number of highlighted words per paragraph

Arguably, someone may consider some of the information highlighted to be superfluous and may consider other information to be important. The learning point here is that the important information is not always obvious. The advantage that experienced instructors and examiners have over a practitioner candidate is that they see a wide variety of scenarios; with practice, it will become easier to identify the important information. There are many available scenarios in the sample papers. As identified earlier there are, at the time of publication of this book, 148 scenarios to practice with.

Although this represents a lot of reading, candidates are not expected to read all the scenarios and identify the key elements for each. What is expected of any candidate is to put in a real effort and actually do some research on their own, read on their own and practice on their own. As already mentioned numerous times already, no one can become an expert in any field without working hard for it. In other words, one has to earn it.

SO Sample Paper 1 – Scenario Six

Here is a second scenario, this time much shorter. It is from the Service Operation lifecycle qualification, Sample Paper 1, version 4.0, Scenario 6, from July 2010.

1	A regional utility company has a five year strategy to grow the business and better serve
2	its customers. In support of that strategy, it has acquired two local companies. One is a
3	gas provider, the other an electricity provider. A part of the strategy is to quickly assess
4	the Technical Management function in place at each company and determine how to best
5	integrate the two companies.
6	
7	You are a consultant and have been asked to develop a plan aimed at evaluating each
8	acquired company's Technical Management function and assessing its abilities. Your plan is
9	to benchmark each function against ITIL best practices in an effort to determine its current
10	capabilities and level of maturity.
11	
12	Your aim is to:
13	• Ensure the function is providing the organization with the technical knowledge and
14	expertise needed to manage the IT infrastructure
15	• Determine if the function is supporting the Service Lifecycle
16	
17	Your first step is to collect and review the documentation being produced in an effort to
18	determine how effectively Technical Management is performing its role.

The word count for this scenario is 173 words and there are four paragraphs. The numbers on the left hand side again are line numbers to help with the analysis.

Paragraph 1

1	A regional utility company has a five year strategy to grow the business and better serve
2	its customers. In support of that strategy, it has acquired two local companies. One is a
3	gas provider, the other an electricity provider. A part of the strategy is to quickly assess
4	the Technical Management function in place at each company and determine how to best
5	integrate the two companies.

Highlights
• Grow the business and better serve its customers
• Acquired two local companies
• Quickly assess the Technical Management function
• Integrate the two companies

What does it mean?
- Technical management is about being custodian of technical knowledge and supplying resources for various technical activities

Paragraph 2

7	You are a consultant and have been asked to develop a plan aimed at evaluating each
8	acquired company's Technical Management function and assessing its abilities. Your plan is
9	to benchmark each function against ITIL best practices in an effort to determine its current
10	capabilities and level of maturity.

Highlights
- You are a consultant
- Develop a plan
- Benchmark each function against ITIL

What does it mean?
- You are a consultant, therefore think like one. You do not work full time for this organization.
- Benchmark is a snapshot in time

Paragraph 3

12	Your aim is to:
13	
14	Ensure the function is providing the organization with the technical knowledge and
15	expertise needed to manage the IT infrastructure
16	Determine if the function is supporting the Service Lifecycle

Highlights
- Providing technical knowledge and expertise
- Is it supporting the Service Lifecycle?

What does it mean?
- Is the function in the first company doing its job as described in ITIL?
- Is the function in the second company doing its job as described in ITIL?
- Does the function in the first company understand they should participate in all five phases of the lifecycle?

- Does the function in the second company understand they should participate in all five phases of the lifecycle?

Paragraph 4

18	Your first step is to collect and review the documentation being produced in an effort to
19	determine how effectively Technical Management is performing its role.

Highlights
- Step 1 = Collect and review the documentation

What does it mean?
- Which information do you need?
- People information such as job description
- Looking for evidence of a service approach
- Looking for evidence of participating through the Service Lifecycle
- Looking for evidence of plans that cover all five phases
- Looking for partnerships that can participate throughout the lifecycle

Having stripped out the superfluous verbiage, about one third of the information is relevant. The following table represents the number of highlighted words per paragraph.

Paragraph 1	16 words
Paragraph 2	15 words
Paragraph 3	13 words
Paragraph 4	9 words
Total	**53 words**

Table 6.14 Number of highlighted words per paragraph

Again it can be noted that the word count for important information is about one-third that of the original word count.

This exercise can be repeated ad nauseum in this book. This is not the intent. In order to explain the validity of stripping away the superfluous information, a context must be introduced, the question itself.

Author's recommendation
Go to your EI's website and download all the sample papers for all ten qualifications.

Practice the following:
1. *Let us assume that you are taking the OSA qualification course and exam. Put aside the OSA sample papers.*
2. *Select one scenario from any other sample paper*
3. *Read the scenario – do not look at the time it takes to read it*
4. *Read the scenario – look at the time it takes to read it*
5. *Read the scenario – identify and highlight the key points*
6. *Understand the scenario*
7. *Put the scenario aside for a few days*
8. *Repeat steps 2 to 7 a few days later with the same scenario*
9. *Repeat steps 1 to 7 with another scenario*

Rule number ONE of reading the scenario – READ THE SCENARIO!

Rule number TWO of reading the scenario – RE-READ THE SCENARIO!

Rule number THREE of reading the scenario – DON'T MAKE ASSUMPTIONS!
If it is not mentioned, then it does not exist.

Summary

Analyzing a scenario does not take very long. As part of the preparation for the exam, sample papers are provided. Take them seriously. Take your time with them, practice analyzing them. Analyze them properly.

Acquire the sample papers from the other qualifications and practice with those as well. The more you practice, the better you will become at it. This will also ensure less valuable time is spend on the scenario analysis and more quality time is spend on identifying the best answer.

Before the exam, come up with a plan for approaching a question. Decide ahead of time how much time to spend on reading the scenario vs. reading the question. The exam lasts 90 minutes. It is 120 minutes for English Second Language candidates under certain conditions but for the purpose of the example we'll use the former.

So, you have 90 minutes and eight questions. Set aside ten minutes as a buffer. Allocate ten minutes per question. Decide how much time to spend on reading and re-reading the scenario. Do the same for the question.

Here is an example: two minutes for the scenario, three minutes for the question, four minutes for the analysis and one minute to review. This should be more than ample time to address one question.

With exam preparation, of course time is precious. Work, family, friends, home, and social activities will take up a lot of your available time. However, a qualification and a certification is an investment in your career. Set time aside for preparation.

Work and life balance is important. Don't ignore it.

When practicing for the examination, use some of the practice tips provided in the following chapters: Using scenarios for practice, Using exam questions for practice and Using answers and rationales for practice.

CHAPTER 7

Understanding the question

Before starting the discussion on questions, it must be noted that a reference to the appropriate scenario is always present. Therefore, it is very important to identify which scenario to use for a particular question. Do not make the mistake of assuming that question three necessarily refers to scenario three. As seen in ***Table 6.3 Scenario word count for sample paper 1 by qualification***, the PPO Sample Paper 1 only has four scenarios, while the CSI Sample Paper 1 has seven scenarios.

Note from the author
During the exam review/preparation sessions of many courses, I have seen people make the above mistake many times. Of course many start arguing, some with vigorous passion, the validity of the answer provided, pointing out that the scenario does not relate to the question at all and vice versa. It is only when someone pointed out the relevant scenario number that these people realize their error. Most people apologize for any outburst and vow never to make this mistake again. This is usually an important lesson learned for everyone in the group at the time.

A question is made of three parts. The first part, which is optional from an examiner's perspective, is referred to as additional information. This is sometimes done when a particular scenario is used for two separate questions. Additional information may also be provided even if the scenario is only used once.

The second part of the question is the question itself. More often than not, the question asks specifically which is the BEST answer based on the information provided in the scenario and, possibly, in the additional information.

The third part of the question is the four possible choices provided. Please note that all four choices have about the same word count. The reason for this is simple. It usually takes more words to properly provide the best possible answer to a question in day-to-day conversations. This is normal and it is easy to observe. People have a tendency to add more details to support their argument.

Therefore, in order to avoid making it too obvious, the examiners are asked to ensure the number of words for each of the four choices is about the same. Please note that is only a guideline and that in some rare cases there may be answers that are much longer than others. This does not mean that the longest answer is either the best answer or the distracter.

Rule number ONE of any examination: READ THE QUESTION!

Rule number TWO of any examination: RE-READ THE QUESTION!

Before we look at whole questions and answers, let us explore some examples of questions and how to properly identify what the question is really asking.

About a few sample questions

Here are a few sample questions. They are taken from the Service Operation lifecycle qualification, Sample Paper 1, version 4.0, Scenario 6, from July 2010.

Question One

Refer to Scenario One
Which one of the following sets of metrics can BEST be used to determine the cause of poor support levels and plan improvements?

What is the question asking?
Select the BEST set of ITIL-based practices to help you determine
A. The cause of the poor customer service scores
    AND
B. How to start planning for improvements

What do you look for in the answers?
- Look for metrics, not CSFs or KPIs.
- Look for metrics related to poor customer service
- Look for metrics related to establishing a baseline or benchmark
- Look for metrics related to the desired end state

Question Two

Refer to Scenario Two
Which one of the following options is the BEST set of Access Management-related activities that must be undertaken to accommodate the telecommuter program?

What is the question asking?

Select the BEST set of ITIL-based practices to help you determine

- Access Management-related activities that must be undertaken to accommodate the telecommuter program

What do you look for in the answers?

- Look for activities related to Access Management
- Look for activities which tie in with other Service Operation processes
- Ignore activities from the strategy phase
- Ignore activities from the design phase
- Ignore activities that are project management related

Question Three

Refer to Scenario Three

Which one of the following options BEST reflects how ITIL best practices and Problem Management can be used to determine a resolution of this Problem?

What is the question asking?

Select the BEST set of ITIL-based practices and from Problem Management which

- Can be used to determine a resolution

What do you look for in the answers?

- Look for activities related to Problem Management
- Look for key relationships such as consulting the Incident Management database or the Configuration Management System
- Look for identification of appropriate personnel from the Operational functions
- Look for generic activities and process activities
- Look for trending activities
- Ignore activities with specific values such as priorities
- Ignore how your organization currently performs Problem Management

Question Four

Refer to Scenario Four

As the Data Center Manager, which one of the following options BEST describes your requirements of the Service Desk software?

What is the question asking?

Select the BEST set of ITIL-based practices to help you describe the

- Requirements for Service Desk software that your Data Center personnel will be asked to use

What do you look for in the answers?

- Look for business requirements
- Look for activities related to the Service Desk
- Look for relationship between IT Operations and the Service Desk, i.e. Event Management
- Look for compliance to your mandatory requirements
- An obvious flaw in the above analysis is the lack of knowledge about the scenario. This omission is intentional. The purpose of the analysis of the question is to make sure that the intent of the question is properly understood. For example, a candidate should always look at a question and determine the number of key elements to identify.

In Question 1 above, there are two distinct key elements. They are the cause of the poor customer service scores and how to plan improving the situation. Therefore, the answer which best covers the two key elements will be the best answer to select.

Of course the nuances between the best and the second best answers will not be so easy to identify unless a candidate always keeps in mind that the examination is about ITIL-based practices and not the candidate's or the candidate's organization practices.

In the next section, one sample exam question and its scenario from each of the ten qualifications will be analyzed in detail.

For simplicity reasons, such as not making this book too large or too boring, only one example is provided. Question One from Sample Paper 1 will be used for all ten examples.

Operational Support and Analysis – OSA

Scenario One

A large travel agency has several locations delivering travel services which include flights, accommodations and special package deals. In addition to visiting the agency Branch locations, customers can book travel online or by telephone.

Both Branch and Call Center staff rely on IT services for booking flights, accommodation, printing tickets, itineraries and invoices. The Head Office deals with corporate and administrative activities.

A year ago, in an attempt to improve IT services, the IT Department introduced ITIL Service Management processes and practices. Most of the Service Management processes have been in place for six months and there have been some perceived improvements in the level of service.

During the last two months, however, some complaints have been received regarding poor levels of service from the Service Desk. These include telephone calls not answered quickly enough and analysts taking too long to provide first-line support. The number of complaints seems to increase whenever a new release of the main booking system TravelBook is deployed.

A major release of TravelBook is planned for next month. The Service Desk Manager is working with the Release and Deployment Manager to improve the support from the Service Desk during this deployment.

In order to plan this support, the Release and Deployment Manager has suggested that the Service Desk Manager reviews reports of the relevant metrics used by the Service Desk.

Scenario analysis

Paragraph 1

1	A large travel agency has several locations delivering travel services which include flights,
2	accommodations and special package deals. In addition to visiting the agency Branch
3	locations, customers can book travel online or by telephone.

Highlights
- Large travel agency
- Several locations
- Customers can book at branch, online or by telephone

What does it mean?
- A large organization has many branches and customers can purchase products at branch, online or by phone

Paragraph 2

5	Both Branch and Call Center staff rely on IT services for booking flights, accommodations,
6	printing tickets, itineraries and invoices. The Head Office deals with corporate and
7	administrative activities.

Highlights
- Branch and Call Center rely on IT services when dealing with customers
- Head office is corporate and administration

What does it mean?
- Customer interactions are at Branches or at call center. Both rely heavily on computerized services. Head office does administrative functions. This means Head Office does not deal with customers.

Paragraph 3

8	A year ago, in an attempt to improve IT services, the IT Department introduced ITIL
9	Service Management processes and practices. Most of the Service Management processes
10	have been in place for six months and there have been some perceived improvements in
11	the level of service.

Highlights
- Introduced service management a year ago
- Some perceived improvements

What does it mean?
- Most Service Management practices adopted about a year ago with some success. We don't know what was not adopted and we don't know what exactly has improved.

Paragraph 4

12	During the last two months, however, some complaints have been received regarding
13	poor levels of service from the Service Desk. These include telephone calls not answered
14	quickly enough and analysts taking too long to provide first-line support. The number
15	of complaints seems to increase whenever a new release of the main booking system
16	TravelBook is deployed.

Highlights
- Increase in complaints over last two months
- Poor service
- Calls not answered quickly
- First level takes too long
- Apparent link between increase in complaints and release of TravelBook

What does it mean?
- There seems to be a link between a new release of TravelBook and rise in complaints. Two main complaints are 'slow to answer phone' and 'slow to resolve calls'.

Paragraph 5

17	A major release of TravelBook is planned for next month. The Service Desk Manager is
18	working with the Release and Deployment Manager to improve the support from the
19	Service Desk during this deployment.

Highlights
- Upcoming release of TravelBook
- Working with Release and Deployment Manager to improve support

What does it mean?
- There seems to be some cooperation between Service Desk Manager and Release and Deployment Manager

Paragraph 6

20	In order to plan this support, the Release and Deployment Manager has suggested that the
21	Service Desk Manager reviews reports of the relevant metrics used by the Service Desk.

Highlights
• Reviews reports of the relevant metrics

What does it mean?
• Service Desk manager should review the existing metrics and reports. It is possible the current service measuring is driving inappropriate behavior.

Question One

Refer to Scenario One
Which one of the following sets of metrics can BEST be used to determine the cause of poor support levels and plan improvements?

A.	Metric	Description of usage
	Percentage of Changes responded to within the target time	Identifies which requests take the longest to handle, particularly TravelBook
	Incident first-line support fix rate per IT service	Identifies whether Service Desk agents have appropriate technical knowledge
	Breakdown of telephone calls by travel type, e.g. flight, accommodation, package	Identifies which systems cause the most problems.
	Number of voicemail messages received	Identifies if user training is required for voicemail usage
B.	Metric	Description of usage
	Volume of telephone calls per IT Service, per hour of the day, by day	Identifies patterns in call volume, staff numbers and shift patterns
	Average duration of telephone calls broken down by IT service and Service Desk agent	Indicates time spent on each call, possibly indicating weak areas
	Number of Incidents logged by IT Service, type and by user department	Identifies trends by Incident type and source of call and to establish issues with TravelBook
	Incident first-line support fix rate per IT Service	Identifies whether Service Desk agents have appropriate technical knowledge and information
C.	Metric	Description of usage
	Number of telephone calls to the Service Desk	To indicate if target number of calls is achieved
	Number of Incidents closed	To indicate trends in call closure
	Number of Changes raised	To identify which requests take longest to handle
	Number of telephone calls not answered	May indicate errors in the telephone system

D.	Metric	Description of usage
	Percentage of telephone calls answered within target time	May indicate staff or shift pattern problems.
	Percentage of Changes responded to within target time	To identify which requests take longest to handle, particularly TravelBook
	Number of TravelBook calls as a percentage of all calls by day	To identify increases in TravelBook calls during deployments
	Number of telephone calls received within Service Desk hours compared with calls received outside Service Desk hours	To identify if Service Desk hours are well known, or if longer support hours are required

Question analysis

What is the question asking?
Select the BEST sets of metrics
1. To determine the cause of poor support levels
   AND
2. To plan improvements

What do you look for in the answers?
- Metrics, not KPIs or CSFs
- Metrics to identify issues
- Customer service metrics
- Metrics to plan improvements
- Metrics over time

A.	Metric	Description of usage	
	Percentage of Changes responded to within the target time	Identifies which requests take the longest to handle, particularly TravelBook	*Only one metric could be useful*
	Incident first-line support fix rate per IT service	Identifies whether Service Desk agents have appropriate technical knowledge	
	Breakdown of telephone calls by travel type, e.g. flight, accommodation, package	Identifies which systems cause the most problems.	
	Number of voicemail messages received	Identifies if user training is required for voicemail usage	

B.	Metric	Description of usage	
	Volume of telephone calls per IT Service, per hour of the day, by day	Identifies patterns in call volume, staff numbers and shift patterns	*All four metrics have merit and could be useful*
	Average duration of telephone calls broken down by IT service and Service Desk agent	Indicates time spent on each call, possibly indicating weak areas	
	Number of Incidents logged by IT Service, type and by user department	Identifies trends by Incident type and source of call and to establish issues with TravelBook	
	Incident first-line support fix rate per IT Service	Identifies whether Service Desk agents have appropriate technical knowledge and information	
C.	Metric	Description of usage	
	Number of telephone calls to the Service Desk	To indicate if target number of calls is achieved	*Numbers don't mean much unless compared over time for trends*
	Number of Incidents closed	To indicate trends in call closure	
	Number of Changes raised	To identify which requests take longest to handle	
	Number of telephone calls not answered	May indicate errors in the telephone system	
D.	Metric	Description of usage	
	Percentage of telephone calls answered within target time	May indicate staff or shift pattern problems.	*Only two metrics could be useful*
	Percentage of Changes responded to within target time	To identify which requests take longest to handle, particularly TravelBook	
	Number of TravelBook calls as a percentage of all calls by day	To identify increases in TravelBook calls during deployments	
	Number of telephone calls received within Service Desk hours compared with calls received outside Service Desk hours	To identify if Service Desk hours are well known, or if longer support hours are required	

Based on the above breakdown, the best answer is B, second best is D, third best should be C and the distractor should be A.

The rationale for this answer follows.

Answer and rationale

How to use the rationale

First   look at the syllabus unit which in this case is Learning Unit 7.

Second   the subject covered is Service Desk metrics that can be used to measure its effectiveness and efficiency, which is bullet 5 in that section

Third   the book references section SO 6.2.5 Service Desk Metrics

This section points to some suggested metrics for the Service Desk which are provided below

For further details, please refer to the Service Operation book.

The bullets in **bold** can be found in answer B.

- The first-line resolution rate:
  - **The percentage of calls resolved during the first contact with the Service Desk**
  - The percentage of calls resolved by the Service Desk staff themselves without having to seek deeper support from other groups
- **Average time to resolve an incident (when resolved at first line)**
- Average time to escalate an incident (where first-line resolution is not possible)
- Average Service Desk cost of handling an incident
  - Total cost of the Service Desk divided by the number of calls
  - By calculating the percentage of call duration time on the desk overall and working out a cost per minute
- Percentage of customer or user updates conducted within target times, as defined in SLA targets
- Average time to review and close a resolved call
- **The number of calls broken down by time of day and day of week**

QUESTION	One		Scenario	One
Question Rationale	This question focuses on the different Service Desk metrics that may be used to measure its effectiveness.			
MOST CORRECT (5)	B	These are all well-described objective metrics with plausible rationales. They allow the Service Desk Manager to extract the right information to address the complaints of fix time, fix rates and unanswered calls to the SD.		
SECOND BEST (3)	D	This set of metrics is missing some obvious metrics which link in with the current complaints, like call answer time. Also time to respond to changes is not something over which the Service Desk has control.		
THIRD BEST (1)	C	The metrics are in the right area, but are very subjective, i.e. they are not broken down in a way that allows information to be extracted. Also the rationales are vague and in some cases wrong.		

QUESTION	One		Scenario	One
DISTRACTER (0)	A	Most of these metrics indicate nothing of use to the Service Desk Manager to identify poor support levels.		
Syllabus Unit / Module supported	ITIL SC: OSA07 – Service Desk			
Bloom's Taxonomy Testing Level	Level 3 Applying – Use ideas, principles and theories in new, particular and concrete situations. Behavioral tasks at this level involve both knowing and comprehension and might include choosing appropriate procedures, applying principles, using an approach or identifying the selection of options. Application – The candidate must apply their knowledge of Service Design metrics to determine which of them can identify the issued described in the scenario.			
Subjects covered	Service Desk metrics that can be used to measure its effectiveness and efficiency			
Book Section Refs	SO 6.2.5 – Organizing for Service Operation – Service Desk – Service Desk metrics			
Difficulty	Moderate			

Release Control and Validation – RCV

Scenario One

You are the Release and Deployment Manager for a food manufacturer experiencing rapid sales growth in a competitive market. The busiest sales period of the year starts in four weeks.

The organization uses an application known as FMX that is developed and hosted in-house. This is integrated with a Word Processing package and a supporting Java application. These are installed on all PCs and laptops. All PCs have the same configuration. According to the configuration records a large number of laptops have not received a Java upgrade for two years. Half of the users in the Sales Department use laptops.

Some users are complaining that the performance of FMX is slow, and at peak times this makes the application unusable.

There is a Release Policy in the company containing the following key statements:

- All software should be tested before deployment.
- Releases must meet business requirements.
- Risks to the business should be minimized.
- Releases will be deployed every three months.

A Release Package, RP1, has been created containing the following release units:

Release unit description	Release unit No.	Reason for change
FMX performance improvement	RU1	Improve performance for Sales and Manufacturing
FMX quarterly upgrade	RU2	Resolves twelve low impact problems
Java upgrade for PCs and laptops	RU3	Six monthly service packs from the supplier containing support for more languages. The currently deployed version will no longer be supported by the manufacturer in six months time
Word processing quarterly upgrade	RU4	Quarterly service pack from the supplier. No critical fixes.

RP1 is scheduled to be deployed in four week's time on 01 December.

Testing the Release Package took two weeks. Tests executed using PCs were successful. However, two tests executed using laptops failed. The symptom is that the laptop sometimes freezes and must be rebooted, with a five minute loss of service. The root cause has been identified as an error in the RU3 Java upgrade. The software team has advised that a permanent resolution may take three weeks to develop.

Scenario analysis

Paragraph 1

1	You are the Release and Deployment Manager for a food manufacturer experiencing rapid
2	sales growth in a competitive market. The busiest sales period of the year starts in four
3	weeks.
4	
5	The organization uses an application known as FMX that is developed and hosted
6	in-house. This is integrated with a Word Processing package and a supporting
7	Java application. These are installed on all PCs and laptops. All PCs have the same
8	configuration. According to the configuration records a large number of laptops have
9	not received a Java upgrade for two years. Half of the users in the Sales Department use
10	laptops.

Highlights
• You are the Release and Deployment Manager
• According to the configuration records a large number of laptops have not received a Java upgrade for two years

What does it mean?

- You are the Release and Deployment Manager and many laptops are not up-to-date regarding a specific upgrade

Paragraph 2

10 11 12	Some users are complaining that the performance of FMX is slow, and at peak times this makes the application unusable.
13 14	There is a Release Policy in the company containing the following key statements:
15	All software should be tested before deployment.
16	Releases must meet business requirements.
17	Risks to the business should be minimized.
18 19	Releases will be deployed every three months.
20	A Release Package, RP1, has been created containing the following release units:

Highlights

- Performance of FMX is slow, and at peak times this makes the application unusable.
- There is a Release Policy

What does it mean?

- Performance issues can get so bad that the application is unusable

Paragraph 3

22	Release unit description	Release unit No.	Reason for change
23 24	FMX performance improvement	RU1	Improve performance for Sales and Manufacturing
25 26	FMX quarterly upgrade	RU2	Resolves twelve low impact problems
27 28 29 30	Java upgrade for PCs and laptops	RU3	Six monthly service packs from the supplier containing support for more languages. The currently deployed version will no longer be supported by the manufacturer in six months time
31 32	Word processing quarterly upgrade	RU4	Quarterly service pack from the supplier. No critical fixes.

Highlights

- Each of the four elements listed above

What does it mean?
- Release RP1 is about
  - Improved performance for Sales and Manufacturing
  - Resolves twelve low impact problems
  - Six monthly service packs from the supplier containing support for more languages
  - Quarterly service pack from the supplier but it contains no critical fixes

Paragraph 4

33	
34	RP1 is scheduled to be deployed in four week's time on 01 December.
35	
36	Testing the Release Package took two weeks. Tests executed using PCs were successful.
37	However, two tests executed using laptops failed. The symptom is that the laptop
38	sometimes freezes and must be rebooted, with a five minute loss of service. The root cause
39	has been identified as an error in the RU3 Java upgrade. The software team has advised
40	that a permanent resolution may take three weeks to develop.

Highlights
- RP1 is scheduled to be deployed in four weeks time
- Symptom is that the laptop sometimes freezes
- Root cause has been identified as an error in the RU3 Java upgrade
- Permanent resolution may take three weeks to develop

What does it mean?
- The root cause of the laptop freezing is an error in the RU3 Java upgrade
- Development of solution may take three weeks but release is scheduled in four weeks
- Retesting the release may take weeks again which means not enough time

Question One

Refer to Scenario One
You have been asked by the Chief Information Officer to recommend the approach that should be taken to deploy the release units, taking into account business requirements and the Release Policy. Which one of the following four recommendations is the BEST approach?

A:	Deploy the original Release Package RP1 on 1st December, and establish Early Life Support to manage any issues. Once the fix is available to RU3, immediately deploy it as an Emergency Release.
B:	B: Re-assemble the release units into the following Release Packages: • RP2: Release units RU1, RU2 and RU4 • RP3: Release unit RU3 Once the fix is available to RU3, test it, and immediately deploy both RP3 and RP2.
C:	C: Re-assemble the release units into the following Release Packages: • RP2: Release units RU1, RU2 and RU4 • RP3: Release unit RU3 Test RP2 and plan to deploy it on 01 December. Once the fix is available to RU3, test it, and plan to include in the March release
D:	D: Deploy the original Release Package RP1 on 1st December, but do not deploy release unit RU3 to the laptops. Once the fix is available to RU3, test it, and then immediately deploy release unit RU3 to the laptops.

Question analysis

What is the question asking?
Select the BEST
- Approach
  AND
- Take into account business requirements
  AND
- Take into account the Release Policy

What do you look for in the answers?
- Business requirements…
- The busiest sales period of the year starts in four weeks
- The release policy is…
  - All software should be tested before deployment.
  - Releases must meet business requirements.
  - Risks to the business should be minimized.
  - Releases will be deployed every three months.

A:	Deploy the original Release Package RP1 on 1st December, and establish Early Life Support to manage any issues. Once the fix is available to RU3, immediately deploy it as an Emergency Release.	*Two tests executed using laptops failed. The root cause has been identified as an error in the RU3 Java upgrade. Permanent resolution may take three weeks to develop. Waiting for the fix brings the scenario to December 08. Three weeks to get the fix plus two weeks, why deploy something defective (this is best practice not common practice situation)*
B:	B: Re-assemble the release units into the following Release Packages: • RP2: Release units RU1, RU2 and RU4 • RP3: Release unit RU3 Once the fix is available to RU3, test it, and immediately deploy both RP3 and RP2.	*This is not much different than option A.*
C:	C: Re-assemble the release units into the following Release Packages: • RP2: Release units RU1, RU2 and RU4 • RP3: Release unit RU3 Test RP2 and plan to deploy it on 01 December. Once the fix is available to RU3, test it, and plan to include in the March release	*This is a much better approach. Removing the faulty component may provide something that works. RU1 is important to deploy. RU3 is not that critical since it relates to something that will no longer be supported in six months, which means May 01 of the following year.*
D:	D: Deploy the original Release Package RP1 on 1st December, but do not deploy release unit RU3 to the laptops. Once the fix is available to RU3, test it, and then immediately deploy release unit RU3 to the laptops.	*This is a more sensible approach than A or B however; there is no mention of testing the new release package made up of RU1, RU2 and RU4 for the laptops. RU3 is not that critical since it relates to something that will no longer be supported in six months which means May 01 of the following year.*

Based on the above breakdown, the best answer is C, second best is D, third best should be B and the distracter should be A.

The rationale for this answer follows.

Answer and rationale

How to use the rationale

First look at the syllabus unit, which in this case is Learning Unit 5.

Second the subject covered is Release Unit, which is bullet 3 in that section

Third the book references

    ST 4.4.4.1 Release unit and identification

    ST 4.4.4.2 Release design options and considerations

    For further details, please refer to the Service Transition book.

QUESTION	One		Scenario	One
Question Rationale	Explain the concept of Release Unit, and differentiate various Release Design options and considerations. Check that the candidate can apply ITIL practices to review a set of required changes and construct a valid approach to release units and release packages. Test that the candidate can analyze which option best meets business requirements with manageable risk.			
MOST CORRECT (5)	C	This is the right answer. This approach most closely aligns to the guidance on Release Units and Release Packages, by linking together release units that have dependencies into Release Packages, and having separate Release Packages for unconnected components, and deploys the needed performance improvements in time for the busiest sales period. The revised FMX and office tools Release Package will be tested before deployment. The timescales are likely to be met because the release units have already been tested together when testing the original release package. The Java upgrade has IT but not business drivers for deployment, and can be safely delayed with no impact until after the busiest sales period to minimize the risk to the business. Including it and the fix with the next FMX quarterly upgrade in a new Release Package minimizes the work needed to release it.		
SECOND BEST (3)	B	There is some merit in this answer. Separating RP1 into two new release units is the correct approach. However, immediately deploying once the fix is available breaches release policy that releases should be deployed every three months. Waiting until the fix is available to the Java problem before deploying RP2 risks adversely affecting the business, as RU1 and RU2 are the performance upgrades that are needed to the busy sales period. Delaying RU4 is acceptable as it has no crucial fixes.		

QUESTION	One		Scenario	One
THIRD BEST (1)	D	There is little merit in this answer. Deploying RP1 together with RU3 to the business environment is very risky, and it breaches the Release Policy that: 'All software should be tested before deployment.' 'Risks to the business should be minimized.' Immediately deploying RU3 once the fix is available and tested also breaches release policy that releases should be deployed every 3 months. Delaying RU4 is acceptable as it has no crucial fixes.		
DISTRACTER (0)	A	This is the wrong answer. The testing failed, and there is a high risk that the sales laptops will experience the problem leading to repeated loss of service in the busiest sales period of the year. The root cause is already known, and Early Life Support will not assist in developing the fix. Deploying the fix as an Emergency Release with no testing breaches the Release Policy.		
Syllabus Unit / Module supported	ITIL SC: RCV05 Release and Deployment Management			
Bloom's Taxonomy Testing Level	Level 4 – Analysis. The ability to use the practices and concepts in a situation or unprompted use of an abstraction. Can apply what is learned in the classroom, in workplace situations. Can separate concepts into component parts to understand structure and can distinguish between facts and inferences. Application – The candidate must apply their knowledge of Release and Deployment Management to the issues described in the scenario to determine the correct approach.			
Subjects covered	Categories covered: Release Package			
Book Section Refs	ST 4.4 – Service Transition processes – Release and Deployment Management ST 4.4.4.1 – Service Transition processes – Release and Deployment Management – Policies, principles and basic concepts – Release unit and identification ST 4.4.4.2 – Service Transition processes – Release and Deployment Management – Policies, principles and basic concepts – Release design options and considerations			
Difficulty	Easy			

Planning, Protection and Optimization – PPO

Scenario One

SC is a subsidiary of a major bank. SC provides mortgage loans for high-earning clients and has a reputation for responding to mortgage requests quickly. SC offers a service called Mortgage Express which guarantees that mortgage proposals will be issued to clients within two days.

Three months ago, SC launched a new service providing mortgages for the purchase of holiday [vacation][32] homes and has since seen a 19% increase in mortgage requests.

All of SC's IT services are provided by the parent bank's Central Technology Group (CTG), and Service Level Agreements (SLAs) are in place for each service.

The main IT service supporting Mortgage Express is the Premier Loan Application System (PLAS). PLAS collects and validates client data and performs risk assessments. PLAS also interfaces with an external service called V-FACT. V-FACT provides details of a client's credit rating which is used in the risk assessment.

The PLAS service has a target availability of 99% during the agreed service hours of 08:00 to 20:00, seven days a week. Availability reports for the PLAS service are produced monthly.

Three months ago there were a number of short periods of unavailability which did not have an impact on the business. At the beginning of this month there was a major Incident that resulted in PLAS being unavailable for 3 hours, 18 minutes. Two weeks later, PLAS performance was severely degraded for 5 hours 45 minutes. During that time, very slow responses were experienced and many of the mortgage requests had to be re-processed due to system timeouts. Both of this month's Incidents caused mortgage requests to be delayed and the 2-day guarantee target was missed.

The CTG service report for this month shows PLAS availability of 99.09%, which includes the downtime from the first Incident. The second incident did not affect the availability figure, because although PLAS had been slow, it had still been available for use.

---

32   [Vacation] added by the author for clarification

SC's Business Manager has raised concerns about the availability of the PLAS service provided by CTG.

Scenario analysis

Paragraph 1

1	SC is a subsidiary of a major bank. SC provides mortgage loans for high-earning clients and
2	has a reputation for responding to mortgage requests quickly. SC offers a service called
3	Mortgage Express which guarantees that mortgage proposals will be issued to clients
4	within two days.
5	
6	Three months ago, SC launched a new service providing mortgages for the purchase of
7	holiday homes and has since seen a 19% increase in mortgage requests.

Highlights
- SC is a subsidiary of a major bank
- Mortgage Express which guarantees that mortgage proposals will be issued to clients within two days

What does it mean?
- Business has guaranteed customers that mortgage proposals will be issued within two days

Paragraph 2

8	All of SC's IT services are provided by the parent bank's Central Technology Group (CTG),
9	and Service Level Agreements (SLAs) are in place for each service.
10	
11	The main IT service supporting Mortgage Express is the Premier Loan Application System
12	(PLAS). PLAS collects and validates client data and performs risk assessments. PLAS also
13	interfaces with an external service called V-FACT. V-FACT provides details of a client's
14	credit rating which is used in the risk assessment.

Highlights
- All of SC's IT services are provided by the parent bank's Central Technology Group (CTG), and Service Level Agreements (SLAs) are in place for each service
- The main IT service supporting Mortgage Express is the Premier Loan Application System (PLAS)

What does it mean?
- Parent company is the IT supplier, there are SLAs in place. Primary service is called PLAS

Paragraph 3

16	Three months ago there were a number of short periods of unavailability which did not
17	have an impact on the business. At the beginning of this month there was a major Incident
18	that resulted in PLAS being unavailable for 3 hours, 18 minutes. Two weeks later, PLAS
19	performance was severely degraded for 5 hours 45 minutes. During that time, very slow
20	responses were experienced and many of the mortgage requests had to be re-processed
21	due to system timeouts. Both of this month's Incidents caused mortgage requests to be
22	delayed and the 2-day guarantee target was missed.

Highlights
- Both of this month's Incidents caused mortgage requests to be delayed and the 2-day guarantee target was missed

What does it mean?
- The business could not meet its guarantee that mortgage proposals be issued within 2 days
- One incident caused outright unavailability
- One incident caused performance issues

Paragraph 4

23	The CTG service report for this month shows PLAS availability of 99.09%, which includes
24	the downtime from the first Incident. The second incident did not affect the availability
25	figure, because although PLAS had been slow, it had still been available for use.
26	
27	SC's Business Manager has raised concerns about the availability of the PLAS service
28	provided by CTG.

Highlights
- This month shows PLAS availability of 99.09%, which includes the downtime from the first Incident
- The second incident did not affect the availability figure

What does it mean?
- Although only one incident directly affected availability target, both incidents caused the business to miss its 2 day target

Question One

Refer to Scenario One
You are the Central Technology Group's (CTG's) Availability Manager and have been asked to respond to SC's concerns.

Which one of the following options is the BEST approach to take to respond to SC's concerns about the Premier Loan Application System (PLAS) service?

A:	Liaise with CTG's application support teams to review the design of the PLAS application and establish a mechanism for measuring the availability of each component. The contract with V-FACT should be reviewed to ensure this supports the PLAS availability requirement. The Service Level Agreement (SLA) should be amended to include targets for each component, such as application and telephony, to ensure SC have greater visibility of the underlying causes of unavailability.
B:	As the two-day guarantee target has been missed, you should recommend an increased target of 99.9% availability for the PLAS service. The CTG application development team should be asked to create a proposal for re-designing PLAS to provide continuous availability with a 99.9% availability target. The SLA and associated service level monitoring should be amended to reflect this change, and you should ensure that this new target is fully understood by CTG staff and SC.
C:	Determine the impact of the outages and understand the availability required to satisfy the two-day guarantee. You should investigate and agree the maximum time that PLAS can be unavailable before the two-day guarantee target is jeopardized. This timescale should be used to determine a target for Mean Time to Restore Service (MTRS), and this should be included in the SLA. You should also agree the minimum performance requirements for PLAS, including a threshold at which loss of performance will be considered as unavailability.
D:	You should liaise with the CTG application support team to review the PLAS design and ascertain whether the current availability target is appropriate. You should also propose that maintainability and serviceability targets are added to the SLA. In addition, the SLA should contain a separate measurement of degraded PLAS performance. As a gesture of goodwill, you should ask the Service Level Manager to amend the availability figure for the previous month to 97.51%, in order to include the business impact of the second Incident.

Question analysis

What is the question asking?
Select the BEST
• Approach to respond to SC's concerns about the Premier Loan Application System (PLAS) service

What do you look for in the answers?
- Business perspective regarding availability
- Real and perceived availability
- Analysis of the facts

A:	Liaise with CTG's application support teams to review the design of the PLAS application and establish a mechanism for measuring the availability of each component. The contract with V-FACT should be reviewed to ensure this supports the PLAS availability requirement. The Service Level Agreement (SLA) should be amended to include targets for each component, such as application and telephony, to ensure SC have greater visibility of the underlying causes of unavailability.	*Measuring component availability will eventually have to be done. However, this is not an end-to-end service perspective. The SLA should stick to service availability, not component availability.*
B:	As the two-day guarantee target has been missed, you should recommend an increased target of 99.9% availability for the PLAS service. The CTG application development team should be asked to create a proposal for re-designing PLAS to provide continuous availability with a 99.9% availability target. The SLA and associated service level monitoring should be amended to reflect this change, and you should ensure that this new target is fully understood by CTG staff and SC.	*This is an IT centric perspective. The service is not the only the application but all components from an end-to-end perspective. This answer is weaker than A*
C:	Determine the impact of the outages and understand the availability required to satisfy the two-day guarantee. You should investigate and agree the maximum time that PLAS can be unavailable before the two-day guarantee target is jeopardized. This timescale should be used to determine a target for Mean Time to Restore Service (MTRS), and this should be included in the SLA. You should also agree the minimum performance requirements for PLAS, including a threshold at which loss of performance will be considered as unavailability.	*This answer analyzes the business requirements and determines the availability targets based on business requirements. Adding the MTRS in the SLA is a good idea. Finally, this answer recognizes that degraded performance can be perceived as unavailability.*
D:	You should liaise with the CTG application support team to review the PLAS design and ascertain whether the current availability target is appropriate. You should also propose that maintainability and serviceability targets are added to the SLA. In addition, the SLA should contain a separate measurement of degraded PLAS performance. As a gesture of goodwill, you should ask the Service Level Manager to amend the availability figure for the previous month to 97.51%, in order to include the business impact of the second Incident.	*The business is not involved here in the review of the PLAS design. Adding serviceability and maintainability targets to a SLA is valid. The goodwill gesture is nice touch as it involves both real and perceived availability; however, this is only a temporary measure which is unlikely to satisfy the business.*

Based on the above breakdown, the best answer is C, second best is D, third best should be A and the distracter should be B.

The rationale for this answer follows.

Answer and rationale

How to use the rationale

First   Look at the syllabus unit which in this case is Learning Unit 3.

Second   The subject covered is Availability Management, which is bullet 3 in that section

Third   The book references sections

SD 4.4.4 –Policies/principles/basic concepts

SD 4.4.5 –Process activities, methods and techniques

For further details, please refer to the Service Design book.

QUESTION	One		Scenario		One
Question Rationale	This question focuses on how availability requirements are determined and how to construct an approach to a review of availability requirements against the scenario given. Also to demonstrate an understanding of activities that would follow a review of availability requirements.				
MOST CORRECT (5)	C	This is the most correct answer as it starts with an assessment of the impact of the incident on SC's business targets. This answer recognizes that the duration of the outage is a significant factor, rather than the frequency of outages, hence the proposal that an additional target is added for MTRS. The answer also recognizes that, from a business perspective, slow performance can have the same impact as unavailability.			
SECOND BEST (3)	D	This is the second best answer, as it recognizes the need to review the availability design and considers additional targets that may be meaningful to the customer. Though it may be valid to amend the availability figure for the previous month, this answer isn't as good as answer C because it suggests that the review of the availability design should be with the CTG support team, and does not mention involvement of the business			
THIRD BEST (1)	A	This is the third best answer, as it focuses on a technical review of impact, rather than a review with the business. Whilst component availability measures would be of use to CTG in understanding trends and underlying causes of incidents, the suggestion is not customer focused, as SC would be interested in the overall service availability, not component availability .			
DISTRACTER (0)	B	This answer is the distracter as it suggests that the target should be determined by the Availability Manager, not by the business. It also states that a continuous availability solution should be implemented, but there is no evidence this would be cost-justified and there is no mention of undertaking cost-benefit analysis. Continuous availability is expensive and this level of availability may not be needed by the business to achieve its target.			

QUESTION	One	Scenario	One
Syllabus Unit / Module supported	ITIL SC: PPO03 Availability Management		
Bloom's Taxonomy Testing Level	Level 4 Analysis – The ability to use the practices and concepts in a situation or unprompted use of an abstraction. Can apply what is learned in the classroom, in workplace situations. Can separate concepts into component parts to understand structure and can distinguish between facts and inferences. Application – The candidate must apply their knowledge of Availability Management and analyze the needs described in the scenario. Use of knowledge related to the approach for reviewing availability and the business implications of unavailability and degraded availability within the context of the scenario must be considered to select the correct answer option.		
Subjects covered	Categories covered: Availability Requirements		
Book Section Refs	SD 4.4.4 – Service Design processes – Availability Management – Policies/ principles/basic concepts SD 4.4.5 – Service Design processes – Availability Management – Process activities, methods and techniques		
Difficulty	Moderate		

Service Offerings and Agreements – SOA

Scenario One

A retail organization has enjoyed significant growth in revenue and profit due to an aggressive marketing campaign over the past year. This growth has enabled the company to fund a program of Change to utilize the internet more extensively to market and sell its products, and to enhance their email system which is used to communicate with their customers and retail partners across the globe.

The Board wants to conduct a financial review of the service provision model options for utilizing the internet and enhancing the email system. Both internal support teams and external suppliers are currently responsible for providing these systems.

Scenario analysis

Paragraph 1

1	A retail organization has enjoyed significant growth in revenue and profit due to an
2	aggressive marketing campaign over the past year. This growth has enabled the company
3	to fund a program of Change to utilize the internet more extensively to market and sell
4	its products, and to enhance their email system which is used to communicate with their
5	customers and retail partners across the globe.

Highlights
- A retail organization
- Utilize the internet more extensively

What does it mean?
- A retail organization has been successful enough to look into utilizing the internet more extensively to serve its customers and partners around the world

Paragraph 2

6	The Board wants to conduct a financial review of the service provision model options for
7	utilizing the internet and enhancing the email system. Both internal support teams and
8	external suppliers are currently responsible for providing these systems.

Highlights
- The Board wants to conduct a financial review of the service provision model options for utilizing the internet and enhancing the email system

What does it mean?
- Business wants to review the various options from a financial perspective

Question One

Refer to Scenario One

Which one of the following options is the BEST approach to perform the financial assessment for service provisioning to be able to calculate the potential Return on Investment (ROI)?

A:	Review the current total internal expenditure, apportioning each cost directly to the appropriate service. The organization's network infrastructure and team costs are shared equally between these two systems. This creates an internal baseline for comparison with the anticipated Business outcomes and ROI that can be presented to the Board for review.
B:	Produce a summary of current costs, noting that some resources are utilized for other services. Therefore, by looking at the Service Catalogue, a service cost model for the systems is created with the costs shared appropriately. These costs can then be compared with outsourced service provisioning costs and the anticipated Business revenue.
C:	Produce a summary of current costs, understanding that the resources are shared across all services and calculate a unit cost per transaction. The costs for each system can then be calculated using the cost per transaction and the Service Catalogue. These costs can then be compared with an outsourced service cost and the anticipated Business outcomes.
D:	Produce a summary of current costs, understanding that the resources are shared across all services, and calculate a unit cost per transaction. The costs for each system can then be calculated using the cost per transaction and the Service Catalogue. These costs can then be compared with alternative service provisioning model costs and the anticipated Business revenues.

Question analysis

What is the question asking?

Select the BEST

- approach to conduct a financial assessment for service provisioning AND
- be able to calculate the potential Return on Investment (ROI)

What do you look for in the answers?

- End to end service provisioning
- Mentions of people, process, partners, and products
- Focus on business perspective and outcomes
- Considerations for various options

A:	Review the current total internal expenditure, apportioning each cost directly to the appropriate service. The organization's network infrastructure and team costs are shared equally between these two systems. This creates an internal baseline for comparison with the anticipated Business outcomes and ROI that can be presented to the Board for review.	*This answer looks at internal costs only and at one service only. It does not provide options.*

B:	Produce a summary of current costs, noting that some resources are utilized for other services. Therefore, by looking at the Service Catalogue, a service cost model for the systems is created with the costs shared appropriately. These costs can then be compared with outsourced service provisioning costs and the anticipated Business revenue.	*This answer looks at the costs for the systems not the services. It does suggest comparing with an outsourced option.*
C:	Produce a summary of current costs, understanding that the resources are shared across all services and calculate a unit cost per transaction. The costs for each system can then be calculated using the cost per transaction and the Service Catalogue. These costs can then be compared with an outsourced service cost and the anticipated Business outcomes.	*This answer looks at the costs the services as well as unit costs per transaction. It does suggest comparing with an outsourced option.*
D:	Produce a summary of current costs, understanding that the resources are shared across all services, and calculate a unit cost per transaction. The costs for each system can then be calculated using the cost per transaction and the Service Catalogue. These costs can then be compared with alternative service provisioning model costs and the anticipated Business revenues.	*Like answer C, this answer looks at the costs of the services as well as unit costs per transaction. However, it suggests comparing with various service provisioning models instead of just one.*

Based on the above breakdown, the best answer is D, second best is C, third best should be B and the distracter should be A.

The rationale for this answer follows.

Answer and rationale

How to use the rationale

First   Look at the syllabus unit which in this case is Learning Unit 7.

Second   The subject covered is Financial Management, which is bullet 7 in that section

Third   The book references sections

SS 5.1.3 – Methods, models, activities and techniques

SS 5.1.3.2 – Service provisioning models and analysis

For further details, please refer to the Service Strategy book.

In this scenario, the best answer is about end-to-end service costs and compares the finding with alternate provisioning models – unlike the other answers, which all focus on only one or two models.

QUESTION	One		Scenario	One
Question Rationale	The question focuses on the correct activities involved in determining Service Provisioning costs, the associated models available and the basic Financial Management activities to determine investment ROI.			
MOST CORRECT (5)	d.	This is the best answer since it takes the best from all possible answers, allows for any comparisons with all Service Provisioning options.		
SECOND BEST (3)	c.	This is the next best answer, but only compares the costs with an outsourced solution and does not include all services		
THIRD BEST (1)	b.	This is the next best solution and is like option C, but it is not usage based.		
DISTRACTER (0)	a.	This is wrong because it has all of the issues associated with option B but only analyzes internal costs		
Syllabus Unit / Module supported	ITIL SC: SOA07 Financial Management			
Bloom's Taxonomy Testing Level	Level 3 Applying – Use ideas, principles and theories in new, particular and concrete situations. Behavioral tasks at this level involve both knowing and comprehension and might include choosing appropriate procedures, applying principles, using an approach or identifying the selection of options. Level 4 Analysis – The ability to use the practices and concepts in a situation or unprompted use of an abstraction. Can apply what is learned in the classroom, in workplace situations. Can separate concepts into component parts to understand structure and can distinguish between facts and inferences. Application – The candidate must apply their knowledge of the Financial Management process and the various methods and model for service valuation. The candidate must analyze and then select the method and activities that will produce the desired result described in the scenario.			
Subjects covered	Concepts of Service Valuation The main activities, methods and techniques of Financial Management			
Book Section Refs	SS 5.1.3 – Service Economics – Financial Management – Methods, models, activities and techniques SS 5.1.3.2 – Service Economics – Financial Management – Methods, models, activities and techniques – Service provisioning models and analysis			
Difficulty	Easy			

Service Strategy

Scenario One

A large IT training provider has a training centre containing twenty classrooms fully equipped with PCs and servers for delivering technical training courses. The building also contains the organization's administrative offices. A wireless network serving the administrative areas was installed about two years ago.

The wireless network can be accessed from the training area. Management decided to allow students who bring their own laptops to access the internet via the wireless network as a free 'value-added' service. Students appreciate this additional service.

Over time, usage of the wireless network by both the administrative staff and students has increased. This is affecting the availability and performance of the administrative systems, therefore it is occasionally necessary to restrict and prevent student access.

The availability and performance issues continue to increase in frequency, and the training centre staff is overwhelmed with complaints from students when the network is not available to them. The management team is very concerned as the course evaluation forms show increasing student dissatisfaction.

The decision has been taken to withdraw the wireless network access service from students immediately and notices have been posted in the training areas informing students of the decision.

Management must now consider what further action should be taken.

Scenario analysis

Paragraph 1

1	A large IT training provider has a training centre containing twenty classrooms fully
2	equipped with PCs and servers for delivering technical training courses. The building
3	also contains the organization's administrative offices. A wireless network serving the
4	administrative areas was installed about two years ago.
5	

Highlights
- Large IT training provider
- A wireless network serving the administrative areas was installed about two years ago

What does it mean?
- The administrative areas of a large IT training provider are using a wireless network installed about two years ago

Paragraph 2

6	The wireless network can be accessed from the training area. Management decided to
7	allow students who bring their own laptops to access the internet via the wireless network
8	as a free 'value-added' service. Students appreciate this additional service.
9	

Highlights
- Management decided to allow students who bring their own laptops to access the internet via the wireless network as a free 'value-added' service

What does it mean?
- Without assessing anything, the organization allowed students to use the wireless network for free

Paragraph 3

10	Over time, usage of the wireless network by both the administrative staff and students has
11	increased. This is affecting the availability and performance of the administrative systems,
12	therefore it is occasionally necessary to restrict and prevent student access.
13	

Highlights
- Usage of the wireless network by both the administrative staff and students has increased

What does it mean?
- More and more people are using the wireless network

Paragraph 4

14	The availability and performance issues continue to increase in frequency, and the training
15	centre staff is overwhelmed with complaints from students when the network is not
16	available to them. The management team is very concerned as the course evaluation forms
17	show increasing student dissatisfaction.

Highlights
• The availability and performance issues continue to increase in frequency, and the training centre staff is overwhelmed with complaints from students

What does it mean?
• Because more and more people are using the wireless network, there are more and more issues, especially from the students although this is a 'free' service

Paragraph 5

18	The decision has been taken to withdraw the wireless network access service from students
19	immediately and notices have been posted in the training areas informing students of the
20	decision.
21	Management must now consider what further action should be taken.

Highlights
• The decision has been taken to withdraw the wireless network access service from students immediately
• What further action should be taken

What does it mean?
• The students will be unhappy but the personnel should now be able to use the wireless

Question One

Refer to Scenario One

What is the BEST action for the IT training provider to take in this situation?

A:	The wireless network should be seen as a customer asset, which is used to provide connectivity service to two market spaces – the administrative team and the students. Denying service to the students will improve service to the administrative team, but will impact the level of customer satisfaction with the training courses, possibly resulting in lost revenue. In this situation, the minimum level of service should be defined according to the external customer. The wireless network capacity should be upgraded immediately to allow for use by both students and administrative staff. This will create time to plan for a more satisfactory solution in the next financial year.
B:	The wireless network is a service asset, which allows the administrative team to access internal services, and should not have been made available to the students. This service is not required to deliver training, and is outside of the core business of the training company. Making corporate IT services available to students dilutes the strength of the company's offering and represents a significant security risk. Notices should be published within the classrooms to explain why internet access is not available, so as to reduce the pressure on the training reception staff and set student expectations appropriately.
C:	Internet access is clearly an important service for the students. If planned and implemented appropriately, it could increase customer satisfaction and retention. The decision to terminate the service was misguided, and internet access should be restored as soon as possible. However, to manage demand and increase security, an 'Internet café' approach should be adopted whereby students can use a small number of dedicated desktop PCs located in the public areas of the training rooms. This should restore student satisfaction levels at an acceptable and quantifiable cost, while allowing the company to focus on its core competency – training.
D:	The wireless network provides a clearly defined market space, with opportunities to improve competitive advantage through improved administrative services and connectivity for students. However, there are two distinct types of customer and service, each with different requirements. An assessment should be conducted to quantify and cost the additional capacity, security and availability resources necessary to allow student access to the wireless network; and proposals should be made to implement enhancements. Wireless access should be re-launched as a formalized service. Training marketing material should be revised to publicize the availability of internet access so as to set student expectations.

Question analysis

What is the question asking?
Select the BEST
- Action to take

What do you look for in the answers?
- Market spaces – different customers means different requirements
- Assessment and analysis of the situation
- Suggestions / recommendation
- Communication

A:	The wireless network should be seen as a customer asset, which is used to provide connectivity service to two market spaces – the administrative team and the students. Denying service to the students will improve service to the administrative team, but will impact the level of customer satisfaction with the training courses, possibly resulting in lost revenue. In this situation, the minimum level of service should be defined according to the external customer. The wireless network capacity should be upgraded immediately to allow for use by both students and administrative staff. This will create time to plan for a more satisfactory solution in the next financial year.	*Although this answer seems to make sense, it only focuses on meeting the needs of the students and totally disregards the financial impact of providing the service.*
B:	The wireless network is a service asset, which allows the administrative team to access internal services, and should not have been made available to the students. This service is not required to deliver training, and is outside of the core business of the training company. Making corporate IT services available to students dilutes the strength of the company's offering and represents a significant security risk. Notices should be published within the classrooms to explain why internet access is not available, so as to reduce the pressure on the training reception staff and set student expectations appropriately.	*This answer seems to make sense from an internal customer perspective but disregards the possible income from providing the service to the students.*

C:	Internet access is clearly an important service for the students. If planned and implemented appropriately, it could increase customer satisfaction and retention. The decision to terminate the service was misguided, and internet access should be restored as soon as possible. However, to manage demand and increase security, an 'Internet café' approach should be adopted whereby students can use a small number of dedicated desktop PCs located in the public areas of the training rooms. This should restore student satisfaction levels at an acceptable and quantifiable cost, while allowing the company to focus on its core competency – training. This answer makes more sense than the previous two however; it only considers satisfying a few customers at a time. There are many who cannot access their organization's email and intranet accounts from a public terminal. The decision to terminate access was not misguided but there was no communication. This answer does not consider communication about explaining the 'internet café' approach.	
D:	The wireless network provides a clearly defined market space, with opportunities to improve competitive advantage through improved administrative services and connectivity for students. However, there are two distinct types of customer and service, each with different requirements. An assessment should be conducted to quantify and cost the additional capacity, security and availability resources necessary to allow student access to the wireless network; and proposals should be made to implement enhancements. Wireless access should be re-launched as a formalized service. Training marketing material should be revised to publicize the availability of internet access so as to set student expectations.	*This answer contains all the appropriate steps and considers the internet access as an additional revenue source. It also considers a cost-benefit analysis as well as communication to set expectations*

Based on the above breakdown, the best answer is D, second best is C, the third best answer and the distractor can either be A or B.

The rationale for this answer follows.

Answer and rationale

How to use the rationale

First Look at the syllabus unit which in this case is Learning Unit 3.

Second The subject covered is Conducting Strategic Assessments, which is bullet 1 in that section

Third The book references sections

SS 4.3 – Develop strategic assets

SS 4.4 – Prepare for Execution

For further details, please refer to the Service Strategy book.

QUESTION	One		SCENARIO	One
Question Rationale	This question focuses on the development of service potential and Service Management as a strategic asset by understanding market spaces and value creation principles.			
MOST CORRECT (5)	D	This answer is the most comprehensive as it recognizes the value that the internet access creates for students and also considers the cost justification of providing it. By treating internet access as a service in its own right, proper decisions can be made regarding costs and value creation. This answer also correctly identifies the relationship between market spaces, customers and services.		
SECOND BEST (3)	C	This is a reasonable answer as it recognizes the value potential of internet access for students. Providing an 'internet café' approach would enable better control over demand for the resources devoted to student internet access. It doesn't address the potential for developing the internet access facility as a service in its own right. Also the utility of wireless connectivity is taken away in the case of Internet access from the café. Students may be able to do quick references and download lecture slides while they are in class. Answer C therefore does not fully explore the nature of demand for wireless access.		
THIRD BEST (1)	B	This is a solution that lacks any consideration of the possibilities of developing internet access for students. It has merit in the sense that it would result in a clearer setting of student expectations, but fails to consider the value creation possibilities.		
DISTRACTER (0)	A	This is an incorrect answer as it incorrectly identifies the market spaces and fails to address any considerations of costs and risks. It also makes untested assumptions regarding the level of cost compared with customer satisfaction. Also the assumption that only the needs of external customers need to be taken into account is incorrect. Poorly performing administrative services can be just as damaging to the business (e.g. late billing)		
Syllabus Unit / Module supported	ITIL SL: SS03 Conducting Strategic Assessments			

QUESTION	One	SCENARIO	One
Bloom's Testing Level	Level 3 Applying – Use ideas, principles and theories in new, particular and concrete situations. Behavioral tasks at this level involve both knowing and comprehension and might include choosing appropriate procedures, applying principles, using an approach or identifying the selection of options. Application – The candidate must apply their knowledge of Demand Management and place this into the context of the scenario in order to determine the service potential and best choice for the organization depicted.		
Subjects covered	Categories covered: Strategic analysis Service potential Demand Management		
Book Section Refs	SS 4.3 – Service strategy – Develop strategic assets SS 4.4 – Service strategy – Prepare for Execution		
Difficulty	Moderate		

Service Design

Scenario One

An internet shopping company was set up two years ago and has been very successful. Much of its success can be attributed to frequent marketing campaigns with special offers.

The company develops its own website applications used by shoppers for browsing and ordering products. The website is hosted by a well known Internet Service Provider (ISP) who provides the infrastructure that supports live operations. The applications are developed and tested on the company's own infrastructure. Changes and upgrades are sent to the ISP via a Wide Area Network link. Relationships with the ISP are generally good, but there have been occasions when the ISP has charged high prices for last minute increases in capacity.

Some shoppers have reported unexpected errors when using the website, which resulted in lost or duplicate orders. It is not known how often this has happened as not all customers report errors. Also, when the Company launches new products, customers have complained of slow response times from the website.

Over the last six months the company has introduced an initiative to implement Service Management. The main purpose of this initiative is to streamline operations and reduce costs.

Scenario analysis

Paragraph 1

1	An internet shopping company was set up two years ago and has been very successful.
2	Much of its success can be attributed to frequent marketing campaigns with special offers.
3	

Highlights
- Internet shopping company

What does it mean?
- A successful organization will start to encounter various issues

Paragraph 1

4	The company develops its own website applications used by shoppers for browsing
5	and ordering products. The website is hosted by a well known Internet Service Provider
6	(ISP) who provides the infrastructure that supports live operations. The applications are
7	developed and tested on the company's own infrastructure. Changes and upgrades are
8	sent to the ISP via a Wide Area Network link. Relationships with the ISP are generally
9	good, but there have been occasions when the ISP has charged high prices for last minute
10	increases in capacity.

Highlights
- Occasions when the ISP has charged high prices for last minute increases in capacity

What does it mean?
- Lack of planning and understanding of business growth led to expensive out-of-contract demands

Paragraph 1

11	Some shoppers have reported unexpected errors when using the website, which resulted
12	in lost or duplicate orders. It is not known how often this has happened as not all
13	customers report errors. Also, when the Company launches new products, customers have
14	complained of slow response times from the website.
15	
16	Over the last six months the company has introduced an initiative to implement Service
17	Management. The main purpose of this initiative is to streamline operations and reduce
18	costs.

Highlights
- Reported unexpected errors
- Lost or duplicate orders
- Not known how often this has happened as not all customers report errors
- Launches new products, customers have complained of slow response times from the website
- Streamline operations and reduce costs

What does it mean?
- Customers are complaining as some of their orders are either lost of duplicated. Full impact is not known since not all customers report issues
- The launch of a new product results in more complaints regarding slow response.
- In response, the organization has decided to streamline operations by adopting Service Management.

Question One

Refer to Scenario One

You have been given the responsibility for solving the capacity issues and improving the management of capacity.

Which one of the following sets of actions is the BEST way to achieve this?

A.	• Modify the contract with the Internet Service Provider (ISP) so that they are required to seek approval for any increase in capacity resources prior to implementation, in order to reduce the number of 'panic' upgrades. • Implement capacity thresholds and automatic alerts to warn all customers when systems are slow. • Improve the Change Management processes of the company and the ISP, and establish interfaces between them to ensure that changes affecting capacity are assessed. • Agree with the ISP that they will set up a project to review their Capacity Management processes and align them with current Service Management practice.
B.	• Establish improved links with the Marketing department in order to get adequate warning of product launches and campaigns that may increase customer use of the website. • Work with the ISP to ensure that changes and updates to the web applications are tested and modeled on the ISP's infrastructure in addition to the company's infrastructure. • Agree with the ISP to introduce monitoring against predetermined thresholds that will give advance warning of capacity issues allowing action to be taken to avoid incidents. • Introduce a Capacity Plan such that longer term capacity changes based upon growth prediction can be planned and funded.
C.	• Establish improved links with the Marketing department in order to get adequate warning of product launches and campaigns that may increase customer use of the website. • Improve the testing of changes and updates to the website applications and ensure that modeling is included in the testing programs. • Perform usage growth predictions based on monitoring data, enabling accurate predictions of future demand to be made and the necessary resources to be provided. • Establish interfaces between the Capacity Management process and the Change Management processes of both the company and the ISP.
D.	• Introduce Business Capacity Management to identify any business changes that might alter the demand for the website applications. • Introduce Application Sizing so that accurate predictions of the resources required supporting the website applications can be predicted and provided. • Introduce modeling techniques to ensure that the performance of the website applications are tested under various workload scenarios. • Write a Capacity Plan to support the annual budget and ensure that adequate funds are available to buy additional capacity for the website applications.

Question analysis

What is the question asking?
Select the BEST set of actions for
- Solving the capacity issues
  AND
- Improving the management of capacity

What do you look for in the answers?
- Assessment and analysis of the situation
- Suggestions / recommendation in the form of an improvement plan
- Communication
- Implementing or improving the capacity process

A.	• Modify the contract with the Internet Service Provider (ISP) so that they are required to seek approval for any increase in capacity resources prior to implementation, in order to reduce the number of 'panic' upgrades. • Implement capacity thresholds and automatic alerts to warn all customers when systems are slow. • Improve the Change Management processes of the company and the ISP, and establish interfaces between them to ensure that changes affecting capacity are assessed. • Agree with the ISP that they will set up a project to review their Capacity Management processes and align them with current Service Management practice.	*This answer only focuses on the ISP and IT. It does not address the issue and does not address managing the capacity adequately as it only asks the ISPO to do so.*
B.	• Establish improved links with the Marketing department in order to get adequate warning of product launches and campaigns that may increase customer use of the website. • Work with the ISP to ensure that changes and updates to the web applications are tested and modeled on the ISP's infrastructure in addition to the company's infrastructure. • Agree with the ISP to introduce monitoring against predetermined thresholds that will give advance warning of capacity issues allowing action to be taken to avoid incidents. • Introduce a Capacity Plan such that longer term capacity changes based upon growth prediction can be planned and funded.	*This answers addresses communication with the business to plan better. It addresses the issues from both the organization and ISP perspective* *This answer looks at being proactive in terms on monitoring based on values determined by the business* *A capacity plan should help manage the capacity better*

C.	• Establish improved links with the Marketing department in order to get adequate warning of product launches and campaigns that may increase customer use of the website. • Improve the testing of changes and updates to the website applications and ensure that modeling is included in the testing programs. • Perform usage growth predictions based on monitoring data, enabling accurate predictions of future demand to be made and the necessary resources to be provided. • Establish interfaces between the Capacity Management process and the Change Management processes of both the company and the ISP.	*This answer addresses communication with the business to plan better. It addresses the issues from both the organization and ISP perspective* *Improving testing should help but not if done in isolation as is the case here. The business and the ISP are not involved.* *Predictions based on historical data ignore the future plans of the business* *Improving the relationship between change and capacity management processes is a good idea but does not go far enough to address better management of capacity*
D.	• Introduce Business Capacity Management to identify any business changes that might alter the demand for the website applications. • Introduce Application Sizing so that accurate predictions of the resources required supporting the website applications can be predicted and provided. • Introduce modeling techniques to ensure that the performance of the website applications are tested under various workload scenarios. • Write a Capacity Plan to support the annual budget and ensure that adequate funds are available to buy additional capacity for the website applications.	*This answer seems to make sense but does not mention including the business or the ISP.* *This answer focuses too much on IT.*

Based on the above breakdown, the best answer is B, second best is C, the third best should be D and the distracter should be A.

The rationale for this answer follows.

Answer and rationale

How to use the rationale

First　　　Look at the syllabus unit which in this case is Learning Unit 3.

Second　　The subject covered is Managerial and supervisory aspects of the Capacity Management process, which is bullet 1 in that section

Third　　　The book references sections

SD 4.3.3 – Value to business

SD 4.3.4 – Policies, principles and basic concepts

SD 4.3.5 – Process activities, methods and techniques

For further details, please refer to the Service Design book.

QUESTION	One	SCENARIO	One
Question Rationale	This question focuses on the managerial and supervisory aspects of the Capacity Management process. Main issues in the scenario are: Capacity issues possibly caused by marketing campaigns for which IT was not prepared. The scenario states that changes are tested on the company's infrastructure but not the live infrastructure that is owned by the ISP. The company is implementing Service Management and the question is about addressing the above issues and implementing capacity management.		
MOST CORRECT (5)	B.	This answer addresses the issues described in the scenario as well as basic activities enabling improved management of capacity. Improving links with the Marketing department will reduce surprises in the future. This will allow IT to predict and provide any increase in capacity. The scenario states that changes are tested on the company's infrastructure but not the live infrastructure that is owned by the ISP. This bullet addresses this point so that the ISP can ensure that adequate resources are predicted and provided. The third bullet is in general a good idea when establishing capacity management, enabling proactive actions to be taken to avoid incidents and therefore increase uptime. Introduce a Capacity Plan such that longer term capacity changes based upon growth prediction can be planned and funded. Buying new capacity in a timely manner will reduce performance related incidents and help avoid sudden expensive increases. This will increase customer satisfaction by ensuring the website is useable when required.		

QUESTION	One		SCENARIO	One
SECOND BEST (3)	C.	Good points here but does not address all the issues: Scenario indicates that a stronger link to the marketing department is needed. Bullet 2 suggests improving testing but does not mention the issue of testing on a more representative infrastructure. This will increase customer satisfaction by ensuring the website is useable when required. To establish interfaces with the Change Management processes of the company and the ISP will ensure that any relevant changes affecting capacity and performance are assessed, avoiding downtime due to capacity-related incidents.		
THIRD BEST (1)	D.	A very good theoretical answer but not adequately related to the scenario. Nor does it address the lack of testing on the ISP infrastructure.		
DISTRACTER (0)	A.	This answer shifts too much of the responsibility to the ISP, and is not a proactive approach to Capacity Management: The scenario did not state that the ISP was the reason for the panic upgrade. Better to improve own internal process to avoid asking for last minute changes. It will not help much to warn the customers about slow systems. They'll find another shop. Normally it's outside your mandate to improve the change process of your ISP, but it's important to address the interface.		
Syllabus Unit / Module supported	ITIL SL: SD03 Service Design Processes			
Bloom's Testing Level	Level 4 Analysis – The ability to use the practices and concepts in a situation or unprompted use of an abstraction. Can apply what is learned in the classroom, in workplace situations. Can separate concepts into component parts to understand structure and can distinguish between facts and inferences. Application – Analyzing scenario for issues affecting capacity to decide best way to solve issues and improve management of capacity. The candidate must distinguish that best practice is not enough on its own, the solutions must address the issues in the scenario and so which practices will be chosen will be impacted by this			
Subjects covered	Categories Covered: Managerial and supervisory aspects of the Capacity Management process (SD 4.3)			
Book Section Refs	SD 4.3.3 – Service Design processes – Capacity Management – Value to business SD 4.3.4 – Service Design processes – Capacity Management – Policies, principles and basic concepts SD 4.3.5 – Service Design processes – Capacity Management – Process activities, methods and techniques			
Difficulty	Hard			

Service Transition

Scenario One

A Banking company has decided to use the ITIL guidance as a basis for its IT Service Management Framework. One of the first processes the Bank wants to work on is Change Management. The Bank currently has multiple Change Management processes in place and each is entirely based on the technical group performing the Change, i.e., the server group, the application group, etc. Within the different groups the Change activities are not consistently being followed. Change approvals are more ad hoc, based on the size of the Change, rather than being assessed on the risk of the Change.

The Bank recognizes that implementing consistent Change Management requires them to develop and implement a single process that will be followed across all of IT and that one of the keys to success will be consistent Change assessment and authorization.

During the awareness campaign there has been significant resistance from various stakeholders. The major concern is that putting in place a more formal Change Management process will increase the level of bureaucracy and decrease the IT organization's capability to respond quickly to new or changing business requirements. They fear this will result in IT service provision that falls further behind current requirements or that staff will try to bypass the new process.

One of the goals for the organization is to reduce the number of major Incidents that are Change-related. Currently about 70% of all major Incidents are caused by failed Changes. The Chief Information Officer at the Bank feels that the only way to reduce the number of failed Changes is to implement a single process that is documented with complete process workflows, procedures and roles and responsibilities.

Scenario analysis

Paragraph 1

1	A Banking company has decided to use the ITIL guidance as a basis for its IT Service
2	Management Framework. One of the first processes the Bank wants to work on is Change
3	Management. The Bank currently has multiple Change Management processes in place
4	and each are entirely based on the technical group performing the Change, i.e., the server
5	group, the application group, etc. Within the different groups the Change activities are not
6	consistently being followed. Change approvals are more ad-hoc, based on the size of the
7	Change, rather than being assessed on the risk of the Change.

Highlights
- Banking company
- Wants to work on Change Management
- Multiple Change Management processes
- Change activities are not consistently being followed

What does it mean?
- A bank with multiple change management processes wants to have only one as changes are out of control.

Paragraph 2

8	The Bank recognizes that implementing consistent Change Management requires them to
9	develop and implement a single process that will be followed across all of IT and that one
10	of the keys to success will be consistent Change assessment and authorization.
11	

Highlights
- One key to success will be consistent Change assessment and authorization.

What does it mean?
- Getting the buy-in for only one change process when groups were allowed free rein will be difficult

Paragraph 3

12	During the awareness campaign there has been significant resistance from various
13	stakeholders. The major concern is that putting in place a more formal Change
14	Management process will increase the level of bureaucracy and decrease the IT
15	organization's capability to respond quickly to new or changing business requirements.
16	They fear this will result in IT service provision that falls further behind current
17	requirements or that staff will try to bypass the new process.

Highlights
- Significant resistance from various stakeholders
- Will increase the level of bureaucracy
- Decrease the IT organization's capability to respond quickly to new or changing business requirements

What does it mean?

- Common issues and complaints about introduction of change management are voiced such as resistance to a new process, perception of increased bureaucracy and negatively impacting the responsiveness to business requirements.

Paragraph 4

18	One of the goals for the organization is to reduce the number of major Incidents that are
19	Change-related. Currently about 70% of all major Incidents are caused by failed Changes.
20	The Chief Information Officer at the Bank feels that the only way to reduce the number of
21	failed Changes is to implement a single process that is documented with complete process
	workflows, procedures and roles and responsibilities.

Highlights

- Reduce the number of major Incidents that are Change-related
- Implement a single process that is documented with complete process workflows, procedures and roles and responsibilities

What does it mean?

- Change the culture of the organization to use the same change process

Question One

Refer to Scenario One

You have been hired as an ITSM Consultant and have been asked to provide guidance on the development and implementation of Change Management within the Bank.

Which one of the following options is the BEST course of action for this organization?

A.	Develop a Change Management process that will be implemented across the entire IT organization and to address the specific issues ensure that the Process includes: A range of different Change Models matched to different types of Changes A Change Authorization Matrix indicating sign-off levels for the various types of Change A Risk Model to be used by all of IT to support the assessment and evaluation activities
B.	Develop a Change Management process that will be implemented across the entire IT organization and to address the specific issues ensure that the Process includes: A range of different Change Models to handle each different type of Change Establishing a single Change Advisory Board to handle the Change requests consistently across the organization A Risk Model to be used by the Change Management team to support the assessment and evaluation activities

C.	Develop Change Management processes matched to different business units that will cover the whole organization and to address the specific issues ensure that the Process includes: A range of different Change Models to handle each different type of Change An approval process signed off by a local Change Manager Regular audit for compliance and relevance by a central Change Manager role Detailed reporting of Change statistics to the central Change role
D.	Develop a Change Management process that will be implemented across the entire IT organization and to address the specific issues ensure that the Process includes: A range of different Change Models to handle each different type of Change. Establishing a single Change Advisory Board that considers all Change requests Central assessment of risk by the Change Management team to ensure Changes are as low risk as possible Escalation of all Change related Incidents to IT Services manager to ensure tight control

Question analysis

What is the question asking?
Select the BEST
- Course of action
  AND
- Guidance on the development of Change Management
  AND
- Guidance on the implementation of Change Management

What do you look for in the answers?
Nothing too specific at this time, you are looking for high level activities
- Cover whole organization
- Roles and responsibilities
- Change models
- Assessment guidelines

A.	• Develop a Change Management process that will be implemented across the entire IT organization and to address the specific issues ensure that the Process includes: • A range of different Change Models matched to different types of Changes • A Change Authorization Matrix indicating sign-off levels for the various types of Change • A Risk Model to be used by all of IT to support the assessment and evaluation activities	Nothing too specific at this time Does covers whole organization Has roles and responsibilities matrix Mentions change models Assessment guidelines in the form of risk model Meets all requirements

B.	• Develop a Change Management process that will be implemented across the entire IT organization and to address the specific issues ensure that the Process includes: • A range of different Change Models to handle each different type of Change • Establishing a single Change Advisory Board to handle the Change requests consistently across the organization • A Risk Model to be used by the Change Management team to support the assessment and evaluation activities	Nothing too specific at this time Does cover whole organization Roles and responsibilities too specific – one CAB Mentions change models Assessment guidelines of a risk model Misses on an important requirement, single process does not mean single CAB
C.	• Develop Change Management processes matched to different business units that will cover the whole organization and to address the specific issues ensure that the Process includes: • A range of different Change Models to handle each different type of Change • An approval process signed off by a local Change Manager • Regular audit for compliance and relevance by a central Change Manager role • Detailed reporting of Change statistics to the central Change role	Too specific at this time – change manager, local and central and reporting is too early at this time Cover whole organization Roles and responsibilities do not cover CAB membership Mentions change models Assessment guidelines Does cover local and central CAB but other items are too specific
D.	• Develop a Change Management process that will be implemented across the entire IT organization and to address the specific issues ensure that the Process includes: • A range of different Change Models to handle each different type of Change. • Establishing a single Change Advisory Board that considers all Change requests • Central assessment of risk by the Change Management team to ensure Changes are as low risk as possible • Escalation of all Change related Incidents to IT Services manager to ensure tight control	Too specific at this time changes as low risk as possible and integration with incident management is too early at this time Does cover whole organization Roles and responsibilities are too limited – single CAB and team Mentions change models Assessment guidelines are central not taking into account local requirements Misses on too many items. This is too specific at this time.

Please note that each of the answers contain two identical statements. When this happens, simply ignore them as they become irrelevant. The items in question are

- Develop a Change Management process that will be implemented across the entire IT organization and to address the specific issues ensure that the Process includes:
- A range of different Change Models to handle each different type of Change.

Based on the above breakdown, the best answer is A, second best is B, the third best should be C and the distracter should be D.

The rationale for this answer follows.

Answer and rationale

How to use the rationale

First   Look at the syllabus unit which in this case is Learning Unit 3.

Second   The subject covered is Change Process Models, Assess and evaluate the change, Risk categorization, authorizing the change, which is bullet 1 in that section

Third   The book references ST 4.2 – Change Management

For further details, please refer to the Service Transition book.

In this scenario, the best answer looks at business requirements and how the business perceives availability then analyzes them before making suggestions.

QUESTION	One		Scenario	One
Question Rationale	This question focuses on the need to develop a Change process that provides for effectiveness in assessing, evaluating and authorizing different types of Changes, as well as efficiencies in the handling of the Change volume. A relevant Change process also has to allow for appropriate risk, and must allow low risk Changes to proceed with minimal bureaucracy to allow available resource to concentrate where it will deliver the maximum benefit.			
MOST CORRECT (5)	A.	This solution provides a range of approaches – defined and maintained via Change Models -to address the different levels of risk and business areas etc. The Change Authorization Matrix will allow Changes to be authorized at the appropriate levels, speeding up lower risk and routine Changes, but ensuring appropriate attention is paid to potentially more dangerous Changes. The Risk Model will be used across the organization and help ensure that the right Changes are dealt with at the right levels.		
SECOND BEST (3)	B.	This is not a bad answer, but it does not address the need for efficiency. The CAB will be relevant, but not for every type of Change, and the need for Change Models matching Change type to specific procedures is lacking. Risk needs to be considered across the organization, reflecting business risk, not just focused on IT.		
THIRD BEST (1)	C.	The range of Change processes suggested here might be easier to sell within the organization, but ultimately this is likely to increase the level of bureaucracy and decrease the consistency across the organization. The lack of consistency will cost more staff resources due to the need to specialize and be aware of multiple approaches, and the extra reporting and central control will add a layer of cost and bureaucracy that is not necessary.		

QUESTION	One		Scenario	One
DISTRACTER (0)	D.	The degree of bureaucracy and control here would simply stop the Changes happening at all, or ensure they are not put through the process. The CAB will not have time or resource to consider every Change request, and the IT Services manager needs to concentrate on priorities, not receive blanket coverage of trivial Incidents. They need information, not raw data.		
Syllabus Unit / Module supported	ITIL SL: ST03 Service Transition Processes			
Bloom's Taxonomy Testing Level	Level 3 Applying – Use ideas, principles and theories in new, particular and concrete situations. Behavioral tasks at this level involve both knowing and comprehension and might include choosing appropriate procedures, applying principles, using an approach or identifying the selection of options. Application -The candidate must apply their knowledge of Change Models and assess the range of approaches sufficiently to determine which will meet the need described in the scenario. The key is detecting that there are different levels of risk which indicate a variety of models to address the needs.			
Subjects covered	Change Process Models • Assess and evaluate the change • Risk categorization • Authorizing the change			
Book Section Refs	ST 4.2 -Service Transitions processes – Change Management			
Difficulty	Hard			

Service Operation

Scenario One

A large financial institution relies on a number of IT services to support its business functions. Many of these are critical. Generally there is a good relationship between IT and the business that has resulted in a reliable set of IT services that are aligned with the business needs.

The IT department has adopted ITIL and is seen as an example of best practice. This has resulted in motivated IT staffs that are keen to adopt beneficial changes to working practices. The IT department has excellent Service Strategy and Service Design activities and processes in place. A well-managed Service Portfolio ensures that strong business cases are established for new and changed services with the result that funding and other resources are matched to business and IT needs. Service Level Agreements (SLAs) are in place for all services.

The Service Desk is well managed and uses established Incident Management and Problem Management processes which are supported by a mature Configuration Management System (CMS) which incorporates a Known Error Database (KEDB). These processes ensure that incidents and problems are escalated to the correct technical teams. This is essential as many services rely on specialist technology where only certain staffs have the required skill to resolve issues. In general the Service Desk is well liked; however there are some users who don't follow Service Desk procedures and attempt to contact support staff directly or resolve issues without contacting IT. Requests from IT Operations Managers to Business Managers to ask users to adhere to Service Desk procedures have failed to achieve any change in the situation.

The Technical Management function is organized into a number of technology teams. Each team is well-managed but Service Operation as a whole is a busy department. Staffs are employed for their specialist skill-sets, but due to the busy workload little time is available for cross-training of roles or sharing of knowledge.

Technical Management teams use established monitoring and Event Management supported by associated tools. This provides access to much of the information that is used by other Service Management processes to report on various service levels. Service level achievements are good with very few major incidents or outages. Service availability targets are always met.

Scenario analysis

Paragraph 1

1	A large financial institution relies on a number of IT services to support its business
2	functions. Many of these are critical. Generally there is a good relationship between IT
3	and the business that has resulted in a reliable set of IT services that are aligned with the
4	business needs.

Highlights
- Large financial institution
- Good relationship between IT and the business

What does it mean?
- There is a good relationship within a large financial institution between IT and the business
- IT and the business are aligned
- Business supports IT

Paragraph 2

5	The IT department has adopted ITIL and is seen as an example of best practice. This
6	has resulted in motivated IT staffs that are keen to adopt beneficial changes to working
7	practices. The IT department has excellent Service Strategy and Service Design activities
8	and processes in place. A well-managed Service Portfolio ensures that strong business
9	cases are established for new and changed services with the result that funding and other
10	resources are matched to business and IT needs. Service Level Agreements (SLAs) are in
11	place for all services.

Highlights
- Adopted ITIL
- Motivated IT staffs that are keen to adopt beneficial changes to working practices
- Strong business cases are established for new and changed services with the result that funding and other resources are matched to business and IT needs

What does it mean?
- ITIL practices are in place such as Strategy, Design and SLAs.
- No resistance to cultural change
- Funding provided as required

Paragraph 3

12	The Service Desk is well managed and uses established Incident Management and Problem
13	Management processes which are supported by a mature Configuration Management
14	System (CMS) which incorporates a Known Error Database (KEDB). These processes ensure
15	that incidents and problems are escalated to the correct technical teams. This is essential as
16	many services rely on specialist technology where only certain staffs have the required skill
17	to resolve issues. In general the Service Desk is well liked; however there are some users
18	who don't follow Service Desk procedures and attempt to contact support staff directly or
19	resolve issues without contacting IT. Requests from IT Operations Managers to Business
20	Managers to ask users to adhere to Service Desk procedures have failed to achieve any
21	change in the situation.

Highlights
- Only certain staffs have the required skill to resolve issues
- Some users don't follow Service Desk procedures and attempt to contact support staff directly or resolve issues without contacting IT
- Have failed to achieve any change in the situation

What does it mean?
- Lack of cross-training and people are too busy
- Although ITIL practices are in place, some users don't follow Service Desk procedures and attempt to contact support staff directly or resolve issues without contacting IT and attempts have failed to achieve any change in the situation

Paragraph 4

22	The Technical Management function is organized into a number of technology teams. Each
23	team is well-managed but Service Operation as a whole is a busy department. Staffs are
24	employed for their specialist skill-sets, but due to the busy workload little time is available
25	for cross-training of roles or sharing of knowledge.
25	

Highlights
- Service Operation as a whole is a busy department
- Little time is available for cross-training of roles or sharing of knowledge

What does it mean?
- Although ITIL practices are in place, Service Operation as a whole is a busy department and there is little time is available for cross-training of roles or sharing of knowledge

Paragraph 5

27	Technical Management teams use established monitoring and Event Management
28	supported by associated tools. This provides access to much of the information that is
29	used by other Service Management processes to report on various service levels. Service
30	level achievements are good with very few major incidents or outages. Service availability
	targets are always met.

Highlights
- Technical Management teams use established monitoring and Event Management
- Service availability targets are always met.

What does it mean?
- There is a Technical Management team, however, they do the monitoring when IT Operations Control should be doing it

Question One

Refer to Scenario One

Which one of the following options BEST summarizes the risks that the IT organization currently faces?

A.	• Resistance to change within IT is a risk • Differing customer and IT expectations is a risk • Lack of testing is NOT a risk • Lack of involvement of IT Operations staff in other lifecycle activities is NOT a risk
B.	• Reliance on key personnel along with their knowledge and skill is a risk • Lack of adequate tools is a risk • Lack of business support is NOT a risk • Inadequate funding is NOT a risk
C.	• Reliance on key personnel along with their knowledge and skill is a risk • Lack of business support is a risk • Resistance to change within IT is NOT a risk • Inadequate funding is NOT a risk
D.	• Resistance to change within IT is a risk • Inadequate funding is a risk • Alignment of IT with the business is NOT a risk • Lack of involvement of IT Operations staff in other lifecycle activities is NOT a risk

Question analysis

What is the question asking?

Select the BEST

• The set of options that summarizes the risks that the IT organization currently faces

What do you look for in the answers?

• Business perspective i.e. money
• People, process, partners and/or product perspectives
• Related to the scenario, not a theoretical answer

A.	• Resistance to change within IT is a risk • Differing customer and IT expectations is a risk • Lack of testing is NOT a risk • Lack of involvement of IT Operations staff in other lifecycle activities is NOT a risk	• *False* • *False* • *False* • *False*

B.	• Reliance on key personnel along with their knowledge and skill is a risk • Lack of adequate tools is a risk • Lack of business support is NOT a risk • Inadequate funding is NOT a risk	• *True – staff is very busy, no time for cross training* • *False* • *False* • *True – good business cases results in funds being allocated where needed*
C.	• Reliance on key personnel along with their knowledge and skill is a risk • Lack of business support is a risk • Resistance to change within IT is NOT a risk • Inadequate funding is NOT a risk	• *True – staff is very busy, no time for cross training* • *True, business is asking staff NOT to bypass Service Desk* • *True* • *True – good business cases results in funds being allocated where needed*
D.	• Resistance to change within IT is a risk • Inadequate funding is a risk • Alignment of IT with the business is NOT a risk • Lack of involvement of IT Operations staff in other lifecycle activities is NOT a risk	• *False* • *False* • *True – business cases, SLAS, strategy, etc.* • *False – staff is very busy, no time for cross training*

Looking at the number of True (or correct) statements) you can determine the best answer to be C.

A = 0 correct statements

B = 2 correct statements

C = 4 correct statements

D = 1 correct statement

Based on the above breakdown, the best answer is C, second best is B, the third best should be D and the distracter should be A.

The rationale for this answer follows.

Answer and rationale

How to use the rationale

First   Look at the syllabus unit which in this case is Learning Unit 8.

Second   The subject covered is Challenges, Critical Success Factors and Risks, which is bullet 1 in that section

Third   The book references SO 9 – Challenges, Critical Success Factors and risks; SO 9.2 – Critical Success Factors, SO 9.3 –Risks

    For further details, please refer to the Service Operation book.

QUESTION	One		Scenario	One
Question Rationale	This question focuses on risks to successful Service Operation. It also requires understanding of the point that risks are often the result of a failure to address challenges and critical success factors. It should be noted that all the issues stated in the answer options are generic risks as described in the ITIL books. The purpose of the question is for candidates to demonstrate that they can identify those that are relevant to the scenario.			
MOST CORRECT (5)	C.	Bullet 1 – Correct. The evidence for this is firstly the scenario refers to escalating incidents and problems to specialists. Secondly, staffs are too busy for cross-training. Bullet 2 – Correct. The evidence is in the reaction of business management to requests for staff to not bypass the Service Desk. Bullet 3 – Correct. The reference to motivated staff is evidence that this is not a risk. Bullet 4 – Correct. The second paragraph in the scenario refers to good portfolio management and good business cases.		
SECOND BEST (3)	B.	Bullet 1 – Correct. The evidence for this is firstly the scenario refers to escalating incidents and problems to specialists. Secondly, staffs are too busy for cross-training. Bullet 2 – Incorrect. This is often a risk, but not in this case as there is evidence in the scenario of a CMS, KEDB and Event Management tools. Bullet 3 – Incorrect. The evidence is in the reaction of business management to requests for staff to not bypass the Service Desk. Bullet 4 – Correct. The second paragraph in the scenario refers to good portfolio management and good business cases.		
THIRD BEST (1)	D.	Bullet 1 – Incorrect. The reference to motivated staff is evidence that this is not a risk. Bullet 2 – Incorrect. This is a risk for many organizations; however there is evidence in the scenario that it is not in this case. The second paragraph in the scenario refers to good portfolio management and good business cases. Bullet 3 – Correct. The excellent Service Strategy and Service Design processes along with the well-managed Service Portfolio are evidence. Bullet 4 – Incorrect. The reference to busy staff that has little time for cross-training of roles or sharing of knowledge is evidence that they will not have time to become in involved in other lifecycle activities.		

QUESTION	One		Scenario	One
DISTRACTER (0)	A.	Bullet 1 – Incorrect. The reference to motivated staff is evidence that this is not a risk. Bullet 2 – Incorrect. The fact there are SLAs in place, good Service Design processes and a record of good service achievement is evidence that this is not a risk. Bullet 3 – Incorrect. There is no reference in the scenario to Service Transition processes and the busy staff has little time to get involved in other lifecycle activities. This is evidence that lack of testing is a risk. Bullet 4 – Incorrect. The reference to busy staff that has little time for cross-training of roles or sharing of knowledge is evidence that they will not have time to become in involved in other lifecycle activities.		
Syllabus Unit / Module supported	ITIL SL: SO08 Challenges, Critical Success Factors and Risks			
Bloom's Taxonomy Testing Level	Level 3 Applying – Use ideas, principles and theories in new, particular and concrete situations. Behavioral tasks at this level involve both knowing and comprehension and might include choosing appropriate procedures, applying principles, using an approach or identifying the selection of options. Level 4 Analysis – The ability to use the practices and concepts in a situation or unprompted use of an abstraction. Can apply what is learned in the classroom, in workplace situations. Can separate concepts into component parts to understand structure and can distinguish between facts and inferences. Application – Candidates must apply their knowledge of organizational risks and specifically those evident in the scenario.			
Subjects covered	Categories Covered: Challenges, Critical Success Factors and Risks			
Book Section Refs	SO 9 – Challenges, Critical Success Factors and risks SO 9.2 – Challenges, Critical Success Factors and risks – Critical Success Factors SO 9.3 – Challenges, Critical Success Factors and risks – Risks			
Difficulty	Easy			

Continual Service Improvement

Scenario One

A mid-sized manufacturer specializing in educational products for children aged two to six was started seven years ago and has a great reputation. The Organization has won numerous awards. There is a growing interest in going international. The company recently showed its products at various trade shows in Europe and the Americas.

The Head Office employs about 75 people, seven of them in IT. There is currently only one manufacturing plant, employing 200 people, which has had increased difficulties keeping production in line with the demand. The Company must now expand both locally and abroad. The Company has recently announced the following business strategies:

- Streamline business operations to reduce the bottlenecks impeding the launch of new products
- Concentrate on increasing the market share of key products by eliminating the manufacturing of products that are not selling well
- Improve production capacity and capabilities by moving to new production sites in Europe and the Americas
- The Chief Information Officer (CIO) wishes to increase the awareness and acceptance of a Continual Service Improvement (CSI) approach amongst IT staff. The CIO believes that the Continual Service
- Improvement program will lead to closer integration between IT and the business. You have recently been appointed as the CSI Manager.

Previously a SWOT (Strengths, Weaknesses, Opportunities, and Threats) analysis was conducted by a selection of staff from the IT team. This SWOT was intended as input into the IT Strategy that is about to be developed. Part of this included a SWOT analysis of Continual Service Improvement within the organization.

STRENGTHS	WEAKNESSES
IT Management demonstrate their commitment to CSI A CSI manager is in place People in the organization have the right attitude, values and commitment IT processes are based on ITIL and at Level '3' of maturity	The organization is predominantly 'Reactive' in its CSI initiatives The organization has somewhat stagnant processes which have not been reviewed for improvement for some time There is a lack of monitoring and reporting tools Existing Service Management data is insufficient to provide insight into CSI opportunities
OPPORTUNITIES	THREATS
Invest in an integrated IT Service Management tool to remove IT bottlenecks Implementation of a new reporting mechanism and tools for Knowledge Management to streamline IT Operations Knowledge transfer and coaching for the personnel to make them more productive	Competition for wireless is already in existence New regulatory requirements will require additional efforts New technology as the result of the city's expansion plans is expected to be supported Lack of trained personnel creates bottlenecks in support activities Lack of use of formal Knowledge Management

Scenario analysis

Paragraph 1

1	A mid-sized manufacturer specializing in educational products for children aged two to
2	six was started seven years ago and has a great reputation. The Organization has won
3	numerous awards. There is a growing interest in going international. The company recently
4	showed its products at various trade shows in Europe and the Americas.
5	

Highlights
• Mid-sized manufacturer

What does it mean?
• A mid-sized manufacturer is about to encounter some issues

Paragraph 2

6	The Head Office employs about 75 people, seven of them in IT. There is currently only one
7	manufacturing plant, employing 200 people, which has had increased difficulties keeping
8	production in line with the demand. The Company must now expand both locally and
9	abroad. The Company has recently announced the following business strategies:
10	

Highlights
• Expand both locally and abroad

What does it mean?
• The organization needs to expand to keep up with the demand.

Paragraph 3

11	Streamline business operations to reduce the bottlenecks impeding the launch of new
12	products
13	Concentrate on increasing the market share of key products by eliminating the
14	manufacturing of products that are not selling well
15	Improve production capacity and capabilities by moving to new production sites in Europe
16	and the Americas
17	The Chief Information Officer (CIO) wishes to increase the awareness and acceptance of a
18	Continual Service Improvement (CSI) approach amongst IT staff. The CIO believes that the
19	Continual Service Improvement program will lead to closer integration between IT and the
20	business. You have recently been appointed as the CSI Manager.

Highlights
• Streamline business operations
• Increasing the market share
• Improve production capacity and capabilities
• Increase the awareness and acceptance of Continual Service Improvement (CSI)
• You have recently been appointed as the CSI Manager.

What does it mean?
• You are the CSI Manager and the organization wants to
  - Improve production capacity and capabilities to increase its the market share but also wants to streamline business operations
  - Additionally, the CIO wants to increase the awareness and acceptance of Continual Service Improvement

Paragraph 4

21	Previously a SWOT (Strengths, Weaknesses, Opportunities, and Threats) analysis was
22	conducted by a selection of staff from the IT team. This SWOT was intended as input into
23	the IT Strategy that is about to be developed. Part of this included a SWOT analysis of
24	Continual Service Improvement within the organization.
25	

Highlights
- SWOT (Strengths, Weaknesses, Opportunities, and Threats) analysis was conducted by a selection of staff from the IT team
- SWOT was intended as input into the IT Strategy that is about to be developed

What does it mean?
- An analysis of the meaning of the SWOT is important to answer the question properly
- SWOT conducted before IT strategy established, should be the other way around

Paragraph 5

	STRENGTHS	WEAKNESSES
26		
27		
28	IT Management demonstrate their	The organization is predominantly
29	commitment to CSI	'Reactive' in its CSI initiatives
30	A CSI manager is in place	The organization has somewhat stagnant
31	People in the organization have the right	processes which have not been reviewed
32	attitude, values and commitment	for improvement for some time
33	IT processes are based on ITIL and at Level	There is a lack of monitoring and reporting
34	'3' of maturity	tools
35		Existing Service Management data is
36		insufficient to provide insight into CSI
37		opportunities
38		
39	OPPORTUNITIES	THREATS
40		
41	Invest in an integrated IT Service	Competition for wireless is already in
42	Management tool to remove IT	existence
43	bottlenecks	New regulatory requirements will require
44	Implementation of a new reporting	additional efforts
45	mechanism and tools for Knowledge	New technology as the result of the city's
46	Management to streamline IT	expansion plans is expected to be
47	Operations	supported
48	Knowledge transfer and coaching for	Lack of trained personnel creates
	the personnel to make them more	bottlenecks in support activities
	productive	Lack of use of formal Knowledge
		Management

Highlights
- The whole SWOT analysis especially the weaknesses and threats
- Opportunities are actually IT objectives

What does it mean?
- Reactive organization
- Stagnant processes
- Lack of basic tools (monitoring and reporting)
- Lack of data
- SWOT does not reveal much useful information

Question One

Refer to Scenario One

Which one of the following statements about the Strength Weakness Opportunities and Threats (SWOT) analysis results BEST reveals the current gaps in the ability of IT to support the corporate objectives?

A:	The SWOT analysis indicates that IT is committed to better integration with the business by implementing Knowledge Management and better monitoring and reporting tools. They are also focused on the training and coaching of staff.
B:	The SWOT analysis does not reveal useful information in its current state as it was conducted before a desired end state for IT was defined and agreed. Additionally, IT opportunities were confused with IT strategies. The SWOT analysis should be performed again after the IT strategy is set.
C:	The SWOT analysis indicates that IT does not appear to currently have the appropriate capabilities or resources required by the Business to achieve its corporate strategies. It is far too reactive, even though the teams are generally committed.
D:	The SWOT analysis indicates that with a significant investment in both an integrated Service Management and monitoring toolset, IT could have the opportunity of addressing its weaknesses.

Question analysis

What is the question asking?
Select the BEST
- Set of current gaps in the ability of IT to support the corporate objectives?

What do you look for in the answers?
- Weaknesses section of the SWOT
- Opportunities section of the SWOT
- Not contradicting the strengths section of the SWOT
- Related to the scenario, not a theoretical answer

A:	The SWOT analysis indicates that IT is committed to better integration with the business by implementing Knowledge Management and better monitoring and reporting tools. They are also focused on the training and coaching of staff.	*Implementing knowledge management is only an opportunity and they are too reactive to be focused on training and coaching. Lack of trained personnel has been identified as a threat.* *This answer is missing the mark entirely.*
B:	The SWOT analysis does not reveal useful information in its current state as it was conducted before a desired end state for IT was defined and agreed. Additionally, IT opportunities were confused with IT strategies. The SWOT analysis should be performed again after the IT strategy is set.	*The SWOT was conducted before a desired end state for IT was defined and agreed. IT opportunities are IT objectives. The SWOT should be done after the IT strategy is set*
C:	The SWOT analysis indicates that IT does not appear to currently have the appropriate capabilities or resources required by the Business to achieve its corporate strategies. It is far too reactive, even though the teams are generally committed.	*It seems that IT does not appear to currently have the appropriate capabilities or resources required by the Business. It is true that IT is far too reactive, even if teams seem committed.* *This answer only looks at the weaknesses.*
D:	The SWOT analysis indicates that with a significant investment in both an integrated Service Management and monitoring toolset, IT could have the opportunity of addressing its weaknesses.	*Investing in technology is not the answer as an investment in personnel and processes is also required.* *This answer is marginally correct. IF the organization includes process and training as part of the tool deployment, then this answer makes more sense. However, this is not mentioned anywhere which makes it an assumption. Additionally, providing a recommendation is not what the question is asking for.*

Based on the above breakdown, the best answer is B, second best is C the third best should be D and the distracter should be A.

The rationale for this answer follows.

Answer and rationale

How to use the rationale

First   Look at the syllabus unit which in this case is Learning Unit 4.

Second   The subject covered is Analyze the measuring and reporting frameworks
             such as the Balance Scorecard and the SWOT analysis, which is bullet 1 in
             that section

Third   The book references CSI 5.4.2 – Continual Service Improvement methods
             and techniques – SWOT analysis
             For further details, please refer to the Continual Service Improvement book.

QUESTION	One		Scenario	One
Question Rationale	SWOT analysis is an important tool used in CSI. It is important for someone involved in CSI to always ensure that the Corporate goals are kept in mind at all times. This is also a key component of the seven step measuring process. See Section 5.4 'Common pitfalls of a SWOT analysis'			
MOST CORRECT (5)	B	This is the correct answer. IT's opportunities are not taking into consideration the Corporate strategies that would allow IT to improve its processes and service delivery to be better integrated with the business. The IT strategy needs to be set first.		
SECOND BEST (3)	C	This answer is partially correct. The weaknesses section supports this claim as it identifies the most significant gaps in IT capabilities. IT is not equipped to support the corporate strategies.		
THIRD BEST (1)	D	This is only marginally correct. Investing in IT technology at this time will only be a temporary solution that may address some weaknesses but will certainly not support the corporate objectives in the end.		
DISTRACTER (0)	A	This answer is obviously incorrect. With the exception of the CIO, there are no indications that IT is committed to integrate better with the business. Their opportunities are all IT wishes and reflect the fact that they have a reactive and tool focused mentality.		
Syllabus Unit / Module supported	ITIL SL: CSI04 Continual Service Improvement methods and techniques			
Bloom's Taxonomy Testing Level	Level 4 Analysis – The ability to use the practices and concepts in a situation or unprompted use of an abstraction. Can apply what is learned in the classroom, in workplace situations. Can separate concepts into component parts to understand structure and can distinguish between facts and inferences. Application – This question requires the delegate to compare the results of the SWOT against corporate objectives and come up with a gap analysis.			
Subjects covered	Analyze the Measuring and Reporting frameworks such as the Balance Scorecard and the SWOT analysis.			
Book Section Refs	CSI 5.4.2 – Continual Service Improvement methods and techniques – SWOT analysis			
Difficulty	Easy			

Managing Across The Lifecycle

Scenario One

A major IT service provider has determined that they will not be able to remain in business and maintain their current business model because of turmoil in the economy. Their financial analyst predicts that, based on current market buying trends and the cost of operations, they will only be able to remain in business for a maximum of 26 months, taking into account their current cash reserves, as well as expected expenses and projected revenues.

Several key issues are detrimental to their business survival:
• They are currently spending more money than they earn
• They are behind their competitors by about 18 months in market innovations, especially with regard to offering cloud services
• Their current credit rating does not allow them to borrow investment money
• Sales are down 30% and service demand has decreased

The Board of Directors has decided to take immediate action to cut costs and to implement the following measures:
• Reduce staff by 20%, with a focus on management positions
• Close 15% of the office locations
• Mandatory salary reduction of 10% for all employees, including management
• Mandatory one week of unpaid leave for all employees, including management

Because of the economic turmoil, and because employment is hard to find in this industry, they feel the majority of employees that remain will not leave the company. There will be morale issues, but management hopes that the remaining employees will understand this course of action is necessary for the company's survival.

Several improvement studies have been undertaken in the past by a trusted consultant to compare the organization against their competitors and to understand current service levels. The results showed:
• They were less efficient and less effective in service delivery, resulting in a significant difference in return on investment for services consumed by customers
• The services delivered are losing their competitiveness in the market because there has been very little investment in innovation
• Their customers also said that, because of innovation issues, the quality of the services are not as good as their competitors' services

Up until the current period of economic turmoil, the company had done nothing with these findings because, since the organization was quite profitable, they did not view them as urgent concerns.

Management acknowledges they need to change quickly or they will go bankrupt. It is expected that the economy will recover in the next 12 to 18 months but the recovery will not guarantee a significant increase in sales. Now, they need to not only continue to run the business, but also to transform it at the same time in order to become competitive again.

Scenario analysis

Paragraph 1

1	A major IT service provider has determined that they will not be able to remain in business
2	and maintain their current business model because of turmoil in the economy. Their
3	financial analyst predicts that, based on current market buying trends and the cost of
4	operations, they will only be able to remain in business for a maximum of 26 months,
5	taking into account their current cash reserves, as well as expected expenses and projected
6	revenues.

Highlights
- Major IT service provider
- Will only be able to remain in business for a maximum of 26 months

What does it mean?
- The organization is in serious difficulty. Something has to be done to improve revenues and either cut or control expenses better

Paragraph 2

7	Several key issues are detrimental to their business survival:
8	They are currently spending more money than they earn
9	They are behind their competitors by about 18 months in market innovations, especially
10	with regard to offering cloud services
11	Their current credit rating does not allow them to borrow investment money
12	Sales are down 30% and service demand has decreased
13	

Highlights

- Currently spending more money than they earn
- Behind their competitors by about 18 months in market innovations
- Current credit rating does not allow them to borrow investment money
- Sales are down 30% and service demand has decreased

What does it mean?

- They lag behind the competition in innovation. There are cash flow issues and they can't borrow money to ease the situation.

Paragraph 3

14	The Board of Directors has decided to take immediate action to cut costs and to implement
15	the following measures:
16	Reduce staff by 20%, with a focus on management positions
17	Close 15% of the office locations
18	Mandatory salary reduction of 10% for all employees, including management
19	Mandatory one week of unpaid leave for all employees, including management
20	

Highlights

- Reduce staff by 20%
- Close 15% of the office locations
- Mandatory salary reduction of 10% for all employees, including management
- Mandatory one week of unpaid leave for all employees, including management

What does it mean?

- Cost cutting measures affect every levels of the organization, line staff and managers
- Cost cutting measures will affect staff morale – the emotional cycle of change will happen; shock, avoidance, external blame, self-blame, acceptance, optimum performance

Paragraph 4

21	Because of the economic turmoil, and because employment is hard to find in this industry,
22	they feel the majority of employees that remain will not leave the company. There will be
23	morale issues, but management hopes that the remaining employees will understand this
24	course of action is necessary for the company's survival.
25	

Highlights
• Management hopes that the remaining employees will understand this course of action is necessary for the company's survival

What does it mean?
• Cost cutting measures will affect staff morale – the emotional cycle of change will happen; shock, avoidance, external blame, self-blame, acceptance, optimum performance

Paragraph 5

26	Several improvement studies have been undertaken in the past by a trusted consultant
27	to compare the organization against their competitors and to understand current service
28	levels. The results showed:
29	They were less efficient and less effective in service delivery, resulting in a significant
30	difference in return on investment for services consumed by customers
31	The services delivered are losing their competitiveness in the market because there has
32	been very little investment in innovation
33	Their customers also said that, because of innovation issues, the quality of the services are
34	not as good as their competitors' services

Highlights
• They were less efficient and less effective in service delivery
• Losing their competitiveness in the market because there has been very little investment in innovation
• Because of innovation issues, the quality of the services are not as good as their competitors' services

What does it mean?
• Lack of innovation, and likely complacency, led to this situation; need for a thorough assessment, analysis, possibly unpopular improvement recommendation and implementation

Paragraph 6

35	Up until the current period of economic turmoil, the company had done nothing with
36	these findings because, since the organization was quite profitable, they did not view them
37	as urgent concerns.

Highlights
- Company had done nothing [...] since the organization was quite profitable, they did not view [customer concerns] as urgent

What does it mean?
- They have no one to blame but themselves; they were complacent

Paragraph 7

38	Management acknowledges they need to change quickly or they will go bankrupt. It is
39	expected that the economy will recover in the next 12 to 18 months but the recovery will
40	not guarantee a significant increase in sales. Now, they need to not only continue to run
41	the business, but also to transform it at the same time in order to become competitive
	again.

Highlights
- Management acknowledges they need to change quickly or they will go bankrupt

What does it mean?
- Cannot shut down to implement improvements
- Need to continue trying selling products
- Implement improvements across the board (people, processes, partners and products) at the same time

Question One

Refer to Scenario One
The current Chief Information Officer (CIO) has determined that the company needs external assistance to address their issues. The CIO has a dual business objective to:
1. Survive the current period of economic turmoil; and
2. Increase competiveness

According to the study in the accompanying scenario, there are some key concerns with regard to business improvement. The Board had decided to re-hire the same consultant who carried out the initial studies.

You are that trusted consultant and you have been tasked to focus on establishing a business case to improve internal operations.

Which one of the following options is the BEST solution to help you with the business case and to assist the organization with strategic change for survival, taking into account the outcomes of the previous studies?

A:	Make the CIO aware that a re-assessment of the company needs to be carried out to confirm that the initial study results are still valid; create a business case to document the benefits of the recommended service improvements including an organizational transformation component; show how these improvements will impact the business goals for controlling spending.
B:	Inform the CIO that changes to the business will require re-training people, updating processes and maybe incorporating technology changes as well; then establish a business case for changing the current service environment to a more efficient future state, reflecting the potential benefit to the customer and payback time to the business.
C:	Advise the CIO that you need to conduct an additional process maturity assessment that will help justify how much to spend on improving the current services; establish a business case to support your recommendations; create a internal marketing and communication plan to inform employees of organizational process changes to improve market position.
D:	Recommend a major initiative to increase service efficiency, quality and innovation; build a business case for undertaking the improvement initiatives identifying changes needed in service delivery, competencies and tools, as well as additional expenses; identify expected Total Cost of Ownership (TCO), Return On Investment (ROI) and Value Of Investment (VOI); define how and when transformation success is measured relative to expected outcomes.

Question analysis

What is the question asking?
Select the BEST
- Solution to help with the business case

AND
- Assist the organization with strategic change for survival

AND
- Taking into account the outcomes of the previous studies

What do you look for in the answers?

A:	Make the CIO aware that a re-assessment of the company needs to be carried out to confirm that the initial study results are still valid; create a business case to document the benefits of the recommended service improvements including an organizational transformation component; show how these improvements will impact the business goals for controlling spending.	*Only focuses on business case benefits addressed for service improvement and innovation components*
B:	Inform the CIO that changes to the business will require re-training people, updating processes and maybe incorporating technology changes as well; then establish a business case for changing the current service environment to a more efficient future state, reflecting the potential benefit to the customer and payback time to the business.	*It is really important to address how people and processes will change: i.e. 'as is' to the 'to be' state.'* *Business values addressed current situation and future situation*
C:	Advise the CIO that you need to conduct an additional process maturity assessment that will help justify how much to spend on improving the current services; establish a business case to support your recommendations; create a internal marketing and communication plan to inform employees of organizational process changes to improve market position.	*Recommending actions and deliverables already completed is pointless and useless*
D:	Recommend a major initiative to increase service efficiency, quality and innovation; build a business case for undertaking the improvement initiatives identifying changes needed in service delivery, competencies and tools, as well as additional expenses; identify expected Total Cost of Ownership (TCO), Return On Investment (ROI) and Value Of Investment (VOI); define how and when transformation success is measured relative to expected outcomes.	*Business value measures are included such as. efficiency, quality and innovation = business value measures* *Changes needed in service delivery, competencies and tools, additional expenses; identify expected TCO, ROI, and VOI = business case* *Define how and when transformation success is measured relative to expected outcomes = expected benefits achieved*

Based on the above breakdown, the best answer is D, second best is B, the third best should be A, and the distractor should be C.

The rationale for this answer follows.

Answer and rationale

How to use the rationale

First   Look at the syllabus unit which in this case is Learning Unit 3.

Second   The subject covered is Conducting Strategic Assessments, which is bullet 1
             in that section

Third   The book references CSI 4.4.2 – Establishing a business case and CSI 4.4.3
             –Measuring benefits achieved

             For further details, please refer to the Continual Service Improvement book.

QUESTION	One	Scenario	One
Question Rationale	This question focuses on Management of Strategic Change. Data and evidence should be provided relating to the costs and expected benefits of undertaking process improvement or the Return on Investment for CSI (4.4) with specific focus on CSI (4.4.2) Establishing a Business Case, and CSI (4.4.3) Measuring Benefits Achieved. The Business Case should articulate the reason for undertaking a service or process improvement initiative. As far as possible, data and evidence should be provided relating to the costs and expected benefits of undertaking process improvement. Key focus areas: (A) – 'In developing a Business Case, the focus should not be limited to ROI but also on the business value that service improvement brings to the organization and its customers (VOI). That's because ROI alone does not capture the real value of service improvement. Should an organization choose to focus solely on ROI, much of the potential benefit achievable will not be disclosed nor reviewed after the fact. This could in turn result in worthwhile initiatives not being approved, or a review of the initiative revealing apparent failure, when it was actually successful.' (B) – 'Examples of business value measures are: Time to market Customer retention Inventory carrying cost Market share. IT's contribution can be captured as follows: Gaining agility Managing knowledge Enhancing knowledge Reducing costs Reducing risk.' (C) – 'IT should begin by defining the types of business values that each improvement will contribute to.' (D) – 'The benefits are realized from the business changes. It is really important to address how people and processes will change: i.e. 'as is' to the 'to be' state.'			

QUESTION	One		Scenario	One
	(E) – 'While the initial identification of benefits is an estimate of those likely to be realized by the proposed process improvement initiative, there is also a need to subsequently measure the benefits actually achieved.' Business Value list in scenario are Control spending Transform/Innovate the business Economy – Customer value/quality/competitiveness (efficiency and effectiveness) Current (as-is) situation to (to-be) situation.			
MOST CORRECT (5)	D.	This is the best answer because: Recommend a major initiative to increase service efficiency, quality and innovation; – Business value measures are included such as. efficiency, quality and innovation – Focus area (B) build a Business Case for undertaking the improvement initiatives identifying changes needed in service delivery, competencies and tools, as well as additional expenses; identify expected Total Cost of Ownership (TCO), Return On Investment (ROI) and Value Of Investment (VOI); – All aspects of business case – TCO, ROI, VOI – Focus area (A) Define how and when transformation success is measured relative to expected outcomes. – Collection of data related to expected benefits achieved – Focus area (D)		
SECOND BEST (3)	B.	This is the second best answer because: Inform CIO that changes to the business will require re-training people, updating processes and, maybe, incorporating technology changes as well; – Focus area (D) Then establish a business case for changing the current service environment to a more efficient future state, reflecting the potential benefit to the customer and payback time to the business. – Business values addressed current situation and future situation – Focus area (A)		
THIRD BEST (1)	A.	This is the third best answer because: Make the CIO aware that a re-assessment of the company needs to be done to validate that the initial study results are still valid; – Re-assessment is probably not necessary – No Focus area. Create a business case to document the benefits of the recommended service improvements, including an organizational transformation component; – Business case benefits addressed for service improvement and innovation components – Focus area (A) Show how these improvements will impact the business goals for controlling spending. – Missing customer value/benefits – answer B addresses both – Focus area (A)		

QUESTION	One		Scenario	One
DISTRACTER (0)	C.	This is the distracter: Advise the CIO that you need to conduct an additional process maturity assessment that will help justify how much to spend on improving the current services; – no focus area – Process Maturity assessment will not provide the data to justify how much to spend on improving process Establish a business case to support your recommendations; – recommendations not advisable, business plan supporting these recommendations will not help Create an internal marketing and communication plan to inform employees of organizational process changes to improve market position. – no focus area, Marketing and Communication plan will not help		
Syllabus Unit / Module supported	ITIL EX: MALC02 Management of Strategic change			
Bloom's Taxonomy Testing Level	Level 4 Analysis – The ability to use the practices and concepts in a situation or unprompted use of an abstraction. Can apply what is learned in the classroom, in workplace situations. Can separate concepts into component parts to understand structure, and can distinguish between facts and inferences. Level 5 Synthesis – The ability to put back together again the various parts or elements of a concept into a unified organization or whole. This putting together again and making sense of small parts is a crucial factor in intelligence and learning. Behavioral tasks at this level would include creating, writing, designing, combining, composing, organizing, revising and planning. This level of learning in order to occur must include the first four levels – knowing, comprehending, analyzing and applying. This level of learning is probably the most intense and exciting for student and teacher alike. Application – The candidate must understand the aspects of establishing a business case and relate the case to service improvements for business value needed in the scenario and ITIL guidance by determining the best approach option for addressing these.			
Subjects covered	Categories Covered: • Management of strategic change • Controlling quality			
Book Section Refs	CSI 4.4.2 – Continual Service Improvement processes – Return on Investment for CSI – Establishing a business case CSI 4.4.3 – Continual Service Improvement processes – Return on Investment for CSI – Measuring benefits achieved			
Difficulty	Moderate			

Summary

One of the most important things to remember for this type of exam and question style is to select the BEST answer according to the ones described in the literature. As mentioned numerous times, the examination is not about your personal practices or your organization's practices.

Best answers often focus on the following:
- Business outcomes
- Business requirements
- End-to-end service approach
- High level elements

During the course, instructors often lead or allow discussions about the second best, third best and distracter answers. This is actually a good thing to do.

However, during the exam, the above is pointless and a waste of time. The question ONLY asks for the BEST answer. Do not waste time on attempting to determine between the other three answers.

Of course, make notes on the exam paper if you wish (or mentally if doing the exam online). This would normally give you the elements to identify the order from Best to Distracter. Don't try to identify which is which. There is no need.

If the answer looks too IT centric or too similar to what you or your organization is currently doing, chances are that it is not the best answer. It is quite likely to be the third best or the distracter answers. Please note that the previous comment is a general statement and may not apply for a particular question.

When practicing for the examination, use some of the practice tips provided in the following chapters: Using scenarios for practice, Using exam questions for practice and Using answers and rationales for practice.

CHAPTER 8

Exploring the syllabuses

This chapter looks at the high level learning objectives of each of the syllabuses. As part of the preparation for the course as well as preparing for the exam, a candidate should not simply read the syllabus but use it to understand how to apply the concepts described in the literature.

The syllabus section called 'Syllabus at a glance' is explored for both intermediate qualifications streams. A candidate should pay close attention to this section as it provides a strong link to how to apply the practices contained in the core books to a situation. It must be pointed out that this section does not provide clues to the scenario or to the possible questions. It does, however, provide hints as to the application aspects a candidate should start preparing for.

As explained in the previous chapter, each syllabus section contains the book sections to read as well as to the core elements to be very familiar with. There is no right or wrong way in preparing for an exam, although technically 'doing nothing' is neither appropriate nor recommended. Any candidate is free to read the material in the order they feel best suits their learning style, knowledge, skills and experience.

Capabilities stream

Looking at the four syllabuses making up the capabilities stream, it can be observed that the sections are strikingly similar. The reason is simple, consistency between the qualifications. This consistency makes it easier:

- For examiners to create questions
- For examiners to support other qualifications
- For the reviewers to identify overlaps and omissions
- For training organizations to develop courses more effectively and efficiently
- For trainers to deliver the courses and prepare candidates for the exams
- For candidates to prepare for the course and for the exam

Although there are some subtle differences in the wording, the meaning is the same across the four capabilities qualifications.

Introduction section

Full understanding of < Qualification Name > terms and core concepts:

- The concept of Service Management as a practice
- How it delivers value to customers and the business
- The underpinning processes and functions that support the Service Lifecycle
- Which stages of the Service Lifecycle contribute to < Qualification Name > and how they interact

The above is straightforward. Here is a list of the key concepts.

- Utility and warranty
- Fit for purpose and fit for use
- It is always about business outcomes
- Service
- Service Management
- Knowing the processes within each stage of the lifecycle (Figure 8.1)
- Knowing the four functions (Figure 8.2)
- The relationship between each stage

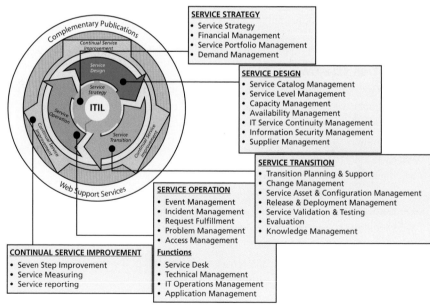

© Crown copyright 2007 Reproduced under license from OGC Figure 1.2 Service Strategy

Figure 8.1 the 26 processes

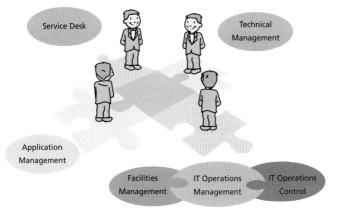

Figure 8.2 the four Service Operation functions

Each process will provide process documentation such as process controls, process activities, procedures, work instructions, process flows, authority matrix, job descriptions, roles and responsibilities, resources, capabilities, inputs, outputs and required triggers.

Of course there are more 'outputs' provided by each stage, but for the purpose of the exam the candidate should be able to extrapolate most of the required elements for any answer, based on the table below.

To → From ↓	Service Strategy	Service Design	Service Transition	Service Operation	Continual Service Improvement
Service Strategy		Service Portfolio Service Pipeline IT Strategy IT Budget Handling Demand Supplier Strategy Services Business plans Roles and responsibilities			

To → From ↓	Service Strategy	Service Design	Service Transition	Service Operation	Continual Service Improvement
Service Design			Business requirements Service catalogue Agreements – SLA, OLA, UC Availability Management Information System Capacity Management Information System Security Management Information System IT Service continuity plans Business Impact assessments Supplier Contracts database Service models Plans Roles and responsibilities		
Service Transition	Transition planning and support plan Change schedule Change models Configuration management system Service knowledge management system Release and deployment plans Validation and testing plans and results Evaluation plans and reports Roles and responsibilities				
Service Operation	Event logs Incident database Problem and known error databases Request models User profiles Access violations Roles and responsibilities for Technical Management Application Management IT Operations Management Service Desk				
Continual Service Improvement	What should be measured What can be measured Raw data Analyzed data Reports Business cases for improvements RFCs for improvements Roles and responsibilities				

Table 8.1 Relationships between lifecycle phases

Process section

- The < Process Name > inclusive of its design strategy, components, activities, roles, and operation including its organizational structure as well as any interfaces with other processes

Design strategy	High Level Only Consider people. process, partners and products as part of any design and/or implementation Look for presence or lack of other processes Look for resistance to change by personnel
Components	The elements specific to the process such as Plans Databases Management systems Policies
Activities	Consider the activities of the process to handle one transaction such as a change or an incident Consider the standard process management activities as well such as Design Implementation Control Reporting Managing personnel Improvements
Roles	Process owner Process manager Process specific In regards to role, there may be a section in the syllabus entirely dedicated to roles of the cluster. This section often includes responsibilities of the roles involved.
Operation	Relationship between the process and the four functions
Organizational structure	As part of the four functions In-sourced vs. outsourced Local, central, etc
Interfaces	Which process specific outputs are provided such as Plans Schedules Records details in databases Policies Logs

Table 8.2 Components of the process section

- Efficient < Process Name > and provide examples of how it is used to ensure Quality Service within the < Qualification Name >

Look to the purpose, goal and objectives of the process

- The benefits and business value that can be gained from < Process Name >.

Although the books mention many benefits, they can be extrapolated from the following list:
- More effective
- More efficient
- Fewer delays
- Handle more
- Integration with other processes
- Better support of the business
- Better cost control
- More consistent and repeatable across the organization
- Better reporting

Technology and implementation considerations

- The technology requirements for Service Management tools, where and how these would be used within < Qualification Name > for process implementation

The technology requirements are for implementing a specific process or set of processes. The tools usually include:
- Process flow engine
- Self help
- Integrated service management suite
- Configuration management system
- Discovery, Deployment and Licensing
- Remote Control and Diagnostics
- Monitoring tools
- Reporting tools including dashboards
- Project management

- The need and benefits of tools that support < lifecycle stage > as related to <Qualification Name >

Again, the needs and benefits of tools are high level. Look for generic needs and benefits such as:

- Need for effectiveness, efficiency, better reporting, more responsive to business needs

See the benefits list for processes above and apply them to technology.

- Implementing processes including planning and managing organizational change, operations, project management, risk management, and staff considerations

When considering the implementation of services, processes or technology, the above bullet provides most of the elements that would make up a best answer.

- Assess first then plan
- Manage or address the organizational change such as:
  - Resistance to change
  - Outsourcing
  - In-sourcing
- Manage the way process operation will now happen
- Use a project management approach
- Identify risk before, during and after the implementation. Consider risks to:
  - People
  - Process
  - Partners
  - Products
  - The business
- Staff considerations such as:
  - Too busy
  - Lack of knowledge and skills
  - Lack of personnel
- What best practices such as Deming's cycle should be used in order to alleviate challenges and risks when implementing Service Management technologies as well as designing technology architectures.

When considering other best practices for the implementation of services, processes or technology, look for some of the most common ones. There is no need to be fully versed in any of them but a generic understanding is both desirable and useful.

- Deming's cycle
- Project management
- Governance
- International standards

Challenges, critical success factors and risks

Before considering what to look for as part of an answer, there is a need to revisit the definition of these three very important terms.

A *challenge* is a potential stimulating task or problem. It is something that will need to be addressed in order to be successful. A challenge makes it more difficult or time consuming and is not necessarily insurmountable.

A *critical success factor* (CSF) is something that must happen if a Process, Project, Plan, or IT Service is to succeed. Key performance indicators (KPIs) are used to measure the achievement of each CSF.

A *risk* is a possible event that could cause harm or loss, or affect the ability to achieve Objectives. A Risk is measured by the probability of a Threat, the Vulnerability of the Asset to that Threat, and the Impact it would have if it occurred.

Examples of challenges
- Lack of something such as funding, time, knowledge, or skills
- Lack of other processes
- Lack of integration with other processes
- Personnel are too busy
- Inadequate set of tools
- Too many things going on
- Lack of data and information
- Resistance to change by personnel

Examples of critical success factors
- Ongoing management commitment
- Ongoing personnel commitment
- Proper planning
- Adequate tools
- Process integration
- Proper data for decision making
- Funding and commitment for all phases such as design, implementation, deployment and operation as well as improvements
- Having the right skills, knowledge, attitudes and aptitudes

Examples of risks
- Not completing project or task on time
- Change of mind by management or the business
- Not achieving business objectives
- Vendor going out of business
- Mergers and acquisitions
- Outsourcing and in-sourcing
- Being locked into a contract
- Obsolete technology
- Being too successful

Syllabuses at a glance

The following section provides the 'syllabus at a glance' section for the four qualifications making up the Capabilities stream.

A candidate can use the general information provided in the previous section and the practices described in the book at attempt to apply them to a specific situation.

Examples are provided in Chapters 8, 9 and 10.

Operational Support and Analysis

OSA01: Introduction to Operational Support and Analysis
Full understanding of Operational Support and Analysis (OSA) terms and core concepts:
- The concept of Service Management as a practice
- How it delivers value to customers and the business
- The underpinning processes and functions that support the Service Lifecycle
- Which stages of the Service Lifecycle contribute to Operational Support and Analysis and how they interact

OSA02: Event Management
Support problem solving by putting theory into practice, interpret principles and relationships:
- The Event Management process inclusive of its design strategy, components, activities, roles, and operation including its organizational structure as well as any interfaces with other processes
- Efficient Event Management and provide examples of how it is used to ensure Quality Service within OSA
- The benefits and business value that can be gained from Event Management

OSA03: Incident Management

Support problem solving by putting theory into practice, interpret principles and relationships

- The Incident Management process inclusive of its design strategy, components, activities, roles, and operation including its organizational structure as well as any interfaces with other processes
- The measurement model and the metrics that would be used to support Incident Management within OSA practices
- The benefits and business value that can be gained from Incident Management

OSA04: Request Fulfillment

Support problem solving by putting theory into practice, interpret principles and relationships:

- The Request Fulfillment process inclusive of its design strategy, components, activities, roles, and operation including its organizational structure as well as any interfaces with other processes
- The measurement model and the metrics that would be used to support Incident Management within OSA practices
- The benefits and business value that can be gained from Request Fulfillment as related to OSA

OSA05: Problem Management

Support problem solving by putting theory into practice, interpret principles and relationships:

- The end-to-end process flow for Problem Management inclusive of design strategy, components, activities, roles, and operation including its organizational structure as well as any interfaces with other processes
- A measurement model and the metrics that would be used to support Problem Management within OSA practices
- The benefits and business value that can be gained from Problem Management

OSA06: Access Management

Support problem solving by putting theory into practice, interpret principles and relationships:

- The end-to-end process flow for Access Management process inclusive of design strategy, components, activities, roles, and operation including its organizational structure as well as any interfaces with other processes
- A measurement model and the metrics that would be used to support Access Management within OSA practices

- The benefits and business value that can be gained from Access Management as related to OSA

OSA07: The Service Desk
Support problem solving by putting theory into practice, interpret principles and relationships:
- The complete end-to-end process flow for the Service Desk function inclusive of design strategy, components, activities, and operation as well as any interfaces with other processes or lifecycle phases
- The Service Desk validation components and activities (e.g. Service Desk role, organizational structures, challenges, issues safeguards, etc.) and how these test components are used to ensure Quality Service within OSA
- A measurement model and the metrics that would be used to support the Service Desk function within OSA practices

OSA08: Functions
Support problem solving by putting theory into practice, interpret principles and relationships:
- The end-to-end process flow for OSA Functions (i.e. Technical Management, IT Operations Management, and Applications Management) inclusive of design strategy, objectives, components, activities, roles and operation including its organizational structure as well as any interfaces with other processes
- The benefits and business value that can be gained from functions as related to OSA

Release, Control and Validation

RCV01: Introduction to Release, Control and Validation (RCV)
Full understanding of Service Strategy terms and core concepts:
- The concept of Service Management as a practice and how it delivers value to customers and the business
- The underpinning processes and functions that support the Service Lifecycle
- What makes up the Service Capability RCV cluster (i.e. which stages of the Service Lifecycle contribute to this capability and how they interact) and its specific focus on Service Transition

RCV02: Change Management
Support problem solving by putting theory into practice, interpret principles and relationships:

- The end-to-end process flow for Change Management inclusive of its design strategy, components, activities, roles and operation including its organizational structure and the interfaces with other processes
- A measurement model and the metrics that would be used to support Change Management within RCV practices
- The benefits and business value that can be gained from Change Management

RCV03: Service Asset and Configuration Management
Support problem solving by putting theory into practice, interpret principles and relationships:
- The end-to-end process flow for Asset and Configuration Management inclusive of its design strategy, components, activities, roles and operation including its organizational structure and the interfaces with other processes
- A measurement model and the metrics that would be used to support Service Asset and Configuration Management within RCV practices
- The benefits and business value that can be gained from Service Asset and Configuration Management

RCV04: Service Validation and Testing (SVT)
Support problem solving by putting theory into practice, interpret principles and relationships:
- The end-to-end process flow for SVT process inclusive of its design strategy, components, activities, roles and operation including its organizational structure and the interfaces with other processes
- SVT testing perspectives (e.g. Test requirement, conditions, environments, data, etc.) and how these test components are used to ensure service quality
- The benefits and business value that can be gained from SVT as related to RCV

RCV05: Release and Deployment Management
Support problem solving by putting theory into practice, interpret principles and relationships:
- The end-to-end process flow for Release and Deployment Management inclusive of its design strategy, components, activities, roles and operation including its organizational structure and the interfaces with other processes
- The Release and Deployment model and related activities (e.g. design, planning, build, pilots, test, transfer, deployment, retirement, etc.) and how these activities ensure service quality
- The benefits and business value that can be gained from Release and Deployment Management

RCV06: Request Fulfillment

Support problem solving by putting theory into practice, interpret principles and relationships:

- The end-to-end process flow for Request Fulfillment inclusive of its design strategy, components, activities, roles and operation including its organizational structure and the interfaces with other processes (e.g. Incident and Release)
- The Request Fulfillment model and related activities (e.g. effectiveness of designs, changes, performance, etc.) and provide examples of how these activities help to ensure Quality Service within RCV
- The benefits and business value that can be gained from Request Fulfillment Management

RCV07: Evaluation

Support problem solving by putting theory into practice, interpret principles and relationships:

- The end-to-end process flow for Evaluation inclusive of its design strategy, components, activities, roles and operation including its organizational structure and the interfaces with other processes
- The Evaluation model and related activities (e.g. effectiveness of designs, changes, performance, etc.) and how these activities help to ensure service quality

RCV08: Knowledge Management

Support problem solving by putting theory into practice, interpret principles and relationships:

- The end-to-end process flow for Knowledge Management inclusive of its design strategy, components, activities, roles and operation including its organizational structure and the interfaces with other processes (e.g. CSI processes)
- The Knowledge Management model and related activities (e.g. Data-to-Information-to-Knowledge-to- Wisdom (DIKW), stakeholder management, metrics, etc.) and how these activities help to ensure service quality
- The benefits and business value that can be gained from Knowledge Management

RCV09: Release, Control and Validation Roles and Responsibilities

Support problem solving by putting theory into practice, interpret principles and relationships:

- The roles and responsibilities related to Change Management, Service Asset and Configuration Management, Service Validation and Testing, Release and Deployment Management, Request Fulfillment, Evaluation, and Knowledge Management.

Where and how these are used, as well as how they fit within the Service Transition organization

RCV10: Technology and Implementation Considerations

Support problem solving by putting theory into practice, interpret principles and relationships:

- The technology requirements for Service Management tools, where and how these would be used within RCV for process implementation (e.g. Knowledge Management and Service Asset and Configuration Management)
- The need and benefits of tools that support Service Transition as related to RCV
- Implementing processes including planning and managing Change, Service Operation, project management, risk management, and staff considerations
- What best practices such as the Deming cycle should be used in order to alleviate challenges and risks when implementing Service Management technologies as well as designing technology architectures.

Planning, Protection and Optimization

PPO01: Introduction to Planning, Protection and Optimization (PPO)

Full understanding of PPO terms and core concepts:

- The concept of Service Management as a practice and how it delivers value to customers and the business
- The underpinning PPO processes and functions that support the Service Lifecycle
- What makes up the Service Capability cluster 'Planning, Protection and Optimization' (i.e. which phases of the Service Lifecycle contribute to this capability and how they all interact) and its specific focus on Service Design

PPO02: Capacity Management

Support problem solving by putting theory into practice, interpret principles and relationships:

- The end-to-end process flow for Capacity Management inclusive of its design strategy, components, activities, roles and operation, organizational structure and its interfaces with other processes
- A measurement model and the metrics that would be used to support Capacity Management within PPO practices
- The benefits and business value that can be gained from Capacity Management

PPO03: Availability Management

Support problem solving by putting theory into practice, interpret principles and relationships:

- The end-to-end process flow for Availability Management inclusive of its design strategy, components, activities, roles and operation, organizational structure and its interfaces with other processes
- The benefits and business value that can be gained from Availability Management
- A measurement model and the metrics that would be used to support Availability Management within PPO practices

PPO04: IT Service Continuity Management (ITSCM)

Support problem solving by putting theory into practice, interpret principles and relationships:

- The end-to-end process flow for ITSCM inclusive of its design strategy, components, activities, roles and operation, organizational structure and its interfaces with other processes
- The four stages of ITSCM (i.e. Initiation, Requirements and Strategy, Implementation and Ongoing Operation) and how each can be used to support PPO
- A measurement model and the metrics that would be used to support ITSCM within PPO practices
- The benefits and business value that can be gained from ITSCM

PPO05: Information Security Management

Support problem solving by putting theory into practice, interpret principles and relationships:

- The end-to-end process flow for Security Management inclusive of its design strategy, components, activities, roles and operation, organizational structure and its interfaces with other processes
- A measurement model and the metrics that would be used to support Security Management within PPO practices
- The benefits and business value that can be gained from Security Management

PPO06: Demand Management

Support problem solving by putting theory into practice, interpret principles and relationships:

- The end-to-end process flow for Demand Management inclusive of its design strategy, components, activities, roles and operation, organizational structure and its interfaces with other processes

- Activity-based Demand Management as it relates to business and user activity patterns and how these contribute to Core and Service Level packages
- The benefits and business value that can be gained from Demand Management in support of PPO

PPO07: Challenges, Critical Success Factors and Risks
Support problem solving by putting theory into practice, interpret principles and relationships:
- The challenges and risks (e.g. staff, funding, management, etc.) in relation to Capacity, Demand, Availability, ITSCM and Security Management and how each challenge can be addressed
- Critical success factors related to Capacity, Demand, Availability, ITSCM and Security Management and how to measure and monitor them for each process and activity
- The challenges and risks as well as related critical success factors that are associated with Service Design in its alignment with PPO

PPO08: Planning, Protection and Optimization Roles and Responsibilities
Support problem solving by putting theory into practice, interpret principles and relationships:
- The roles and responsibilities related to Capacity, Availability, ITSCM and Information Security Management, how they fit and how they are used within the Service Design organization to support PPO

PPO09: Technology and Implementation Considerations
Support problem solving by putting theory into practice, interpret principles and relationships:
- Service Management tools, where and how they can be used within PPO for process implementation
- The types of tools that support Service Design as related to PPO
- What best practices should be used in order to alleviate challenges and risks when implementing Service Management technologies and designing technology architectures

Service Offerings and Agreements

SOA01: Introduction to Service Offerings and Agreements
Full understanding of Service Offerings and Agreements (SOA) terms and core concepts:
- Service Management as a practice
- How it delivers value to customers and the business

- The underpinning processes and functions that support the Service Lifecycle
- Which stages of the Service Lifecycle contribute to Service Offerings and Agreements and how they all interact

SOA02: Service Portfolio Management

Support problem solving by putting theory into practice, interpret principles and relationships:

- Service Portfolio Management inclusive of its design strategy, components, methods, activities, roles and operation including its organizational structure and the interfaces with other processes
- Service Portfolio Management in relationship to the Service Catalogue and Service Pipeline and how these support SOA
- The benefits and business value from Service Portfolio Management

SOA03: Service Catalogue Management

Support problem solving by putting theory into practice, interpret principles and relationships:

- Service Catalogue Management inclusive of its design strategy, components, activities, roles and operation including its organizational structure and the interfaces with other processes
- Service Catalogue in relation to the Service Portfolio, the Business Catalogue, and the Technical Service Catalogue and how these components are used to ensure quality service within SOA
- Metrics and critical success factors associated with Service Catalogue Management in support of SOA

SOA04: Service Level Management

Support problem solving by putting theory into practice, interpret principles and relationships:

- Service Level Management (SLM) inclusive of design strategy, components, activities, roles and operation including its organizational structure as well as any interfaces with other processes
- SLM components and activities including Service Level Agreements (SLAs) structures, Service Level Requirements (SLRs), Operational Level Agreements (OLAs), critical success factors, Underpinning Contracts (UCs), their metrics, performance and monitoring
- How these components are used to ensure quality service within SOA
- The benefits and business value of SLM

SOA05: Demand Management

Support problem solving by putting theory into practice, interpret principles and relationships:

- Demand Management process inclusive of design strategy, components, activities, roles and operation including its organizational structure as well as any interfaces with other processes
- Demand especially as it relates to business activity patterns and how it is used within SOA
- Service Portfolio interaction with Demand Management and how demand can be managed for service in relation to providing business benefits and in support of SOA

SOA06: Supplier Management

Support problem solving by putting theory into practice, interpret principles and relationships:

- Supplier Management process inclusive of design strategy, components, activities, roles and operation including its organizational structure as well as any interfaces with other processes
- Supplier Management components and activities (e.g. Supplier Categorization, Supplier Evaluation, Supplier and Contract Database, metrics, etc.) and how these are used to ensure quality service within SOA
- The benefits and business value that can be gained from Supplier Management as related to SOA

SOA07: Financial Management

Support problem solving by putting theory into practice, interpret principles and relationships:

- Financial Management inclusive of design strategy, components, activities, roles and operation including its organizational structure as well as any interfaces with other processes
- Financial Management components and activities including funding, accounting, chargeback, Return on Investment and how these are used to ensure quality service within SOA
- The benefits and business value that can be gained from Financial Management

SOA08: Business Relationship Manager

Support problem solving by putting theory into practice, interpret principles and relationships:

- The Business Relationship Manager roles and responsibilities, and how they support SOA

- Business Relationship Manager activities and how these are used to ensure quality service within SOA

SOA09: Service Offerings and Agreement Roles and Responsibilities
Support problem solving by putting theory into practice, interpret principles and relationships:
- The roles and responsibilities related to Service Catalogue Manager, Service Level Manager and the Supplier Manager and how they fit within the Service Design organization to support SOA

SOA10: Technology and Implementation Considerations
Support problem solving by putting theory into practice, interpret principles and relationships:
- Service Management tools and where/how they would be used within SOA for process implementation
- The tools that support SOA
- Challenges and Risks when implementing SOA practices and processes

Lifecycle stream

Looking at the five syllabuses making up the lifecycle stream, it can be observed that the sections heading are quite similar, with the exception of the Service Strategy qualification which will be explored separately. It must be noted that the details vary from one qualification to the next. The reason for the similarities is simple, consistency between the qualifications. This consistency makes it easier:
- For examiners to create questions
- For examiners to support other qualifications
- For the reviewers to identify overlaps and omissions
- For training organizations to develop courses more effectively and efficiently
- For trainers to deliver the courses and prepare candidates for the exams
- For candidates to prepare for the course and for the exam

Although there are some subtle differences in the wording, the meaning is the same across the four lifecycle qualifications for Service Design, Service Transition, Service Operation and Continual Service Improvement.

The Service Strategy qualification will be discussed separately afterwards.

Introduction section

• The processes and Service Lifecycle phases that < Stage Name > interfaces with
• The fundamental aspects of < Stage Name > and be able to define them

The above is straightforward; it is about knowing and understanding each process within a particular stage of the lifecycle. The introduction covers two key elements. The first element explores the relationships between each of the processes within a particular stage and the other four stages. The second element requires the candidate be able to define the key concepts within each process.

Please refer to Figure 8.1 for the list of the processes within each stage.

Please refer to Table 8.1 on for a list of the major relationships between each stage. Look at each element provided and determine to which process they belong. After reading about each of the appropriate processes a candidate should be able to identify further elements and explain them. Another way is to list at the list of terms provided at the end of each syllabus and again identify to which process they belong and what they can be used for.

Principles

• How Service Operation is organized in relation to Functions, Groups, Teams, Department and divisions.
• How an organization can achieve balance when dealing with internal versus external organizational focus, identifying the issues related to organizations who operate at the extremes of these balances
• What 'Operational Health' means, specifically addressing examples of 'Self Healing Systems' and the processes used by them
• The creation, components and implementation of a complete communication strategy to be used with Service Operations

Processes

In preparing for this section a candidate should understand and explain each process in general. To accomplish this, concentrate on the purpose, goal and objectives of a particular process.

Tip
Here is a simple tip to remember the meaning of the purpose and goal of most processes: use Deming's cycle of Plan, Do, Check and Act.

The <Process name> is about planning for, executing, verifying and improving all aspects related to <...>.

If you remember the above you should be able to recognize the key elements in a scenario, question or answer.

The next element is to understand the relationships between the processes within a stage. Identify which process specific outputs are provided such as:
• Plans
• Schedules
• Records details in databases
• Policies
• Logs
• Outputs from methods and techniques

In preparing for the third and last element of this section, a candidate should turn to the 'value to the business' section as the ultimate purpose for any process is about supporting business outcomes.

Activities

In preparing for this section, a candidate does not need to go into the depth of understanding of the transactional activities required by the Capabilities qualification. However, it is important to know them, their use and the use of their primary outputs. In the Lifecycle stream it is important to consider the standard process management activities such as:
• Designing the process
• Implementing the process
• Controlling the process
• Reporting
• Managing the personnel involved:
  - Consider managing the process which involves managing personnel who do not directly report to your assigned role in the scenario
  - Consider managing the relationship with a third party-vendor who is involved in the execution of various process activities

- Improving the various aspects of the process, particularly reporting, business relationship and communication

Organizing

In preparing for this section a candidate should look at the stage as a whole and not to specific processes. It is important to be able to understand and appropriately apply the authority matrix (also known as the RACI model – Responsible, Accountable, Consulted and Informed). In this particular model it is important to remember the following:
- There can only be one role/person accountable for each activity
- The same role/person should be accountable for all activities
- A role may be responsible for many activities
- A role may be consulted for many activities
- A role may be kept informed for many activities
- A role may have a combination of responsible, consulted and/or informed for any activity. Possible combinations include:
  - R/C/I
  - R/C
  - R/I
  - C/I
  - A/R
  - A/C
  - A/I

When outsourcing the execution of a process or part of a process, the 'accountability' cannot be outsourced. It must remain within the organization. The third party is 'responsible' for the correct execution of the activities. It is quite likely that the third party may have an authority matrix of their own with someone accountable; however, the organization that outsourced the activities retains the accountability.

It is important to remember the four Service Operation Functions, as they are the ones who will provide the people resources for the execution of activities in each stage:
- Senior IT management are likely to be assigned various aspects and levels of authority, responsibility, consultancy and information for the Service Strategy stage
- Various IT managers are likely to be assigned the accountability or responsibility for the execution for high level activities within the other four stages while senior analysts will be responsible for the execution of specific activities within service design, transition and improvement

- The more transactional type of activities such as handling an incident, a problem, a change, testing, and deployment are quite likely to be assigned to first and second level analysts throughout the four functions

Technology considerations

- The technology that supports a particular stage and how it can be used more effectively and efficiently to support business outcomes
- The technology required to support each of the processes within a particular stage.

Keep the technology at a high level such as:
- <Process name> module in an integrated service management suite
- Monitoring tools
- Auto discovery tools
- Reporting tools
- Investigation and analysis tools
- Communication tools
- Knowledge-related tools such as the CMS and the SKMS
- The Service Portfolio, Service Pipeline and the Service Catalogue

The need and benefits of tools that support < lifecycle stage > as related to <Qualification Name >
- Again, the needs and benefits of tools are high level. Look for generic needs and benefits such as:
  - Need for effectiveness, efficiency, better reporting, more responsive to business needs
  - See the benefits list for processes in the Capabilities stream (page 221) and apply them to technology

Implementation considerations

- Strategies and models for managing a particular stage Service Operation and how to implement this activity within an organization
- Implementing the technologies related to a particular stage within an organization

When considering the implementation of a stage, services, processes or technology, the following bullets provide most of the elements that would make up a best answer:
- Assess first then plan
- Manage or address the organizational change such as:

- Resistance to change
- Outsourcing
- In-sourcing
• Manage the way process operation will now happen
• Use a project management approach
• How to assess and manage risks with in a group primarily involved with a specific stage including the interaction that needs to occur with groups primarily involved with other stages:
• Identify risk before, during and after the implementation. Consider risks to:
    - People
    - Process
    - Partners
    - Products
    - The business
• Staff considerations such as:
    - Too busy
    - Lack of knowledge and skills
    - Lack of personnel

Challenges, Critical Success Factors and Risks

Challenges, Critical Success Factors and Risks
• The challenges and risks (e.g. staff, funding, management, etc.) related to Service Operation and the details behind how each challenge can be addressed
• The Critical Success Factors (CSFs) related to Service Operation as well as a detailed model for measuring and monitoring Service Operation CSFs

Before considering what to look for as part of an answer, there is a need to revisit the definition of these three very important terms.

A *challenge* is a potential stimulating task or problem. It is something that will need to be addressed in order to be successful. A challenge makes it more difficult or time consuming and is not necessarily insurmountable.

A *critical success factor* is something that must happen if a Process, Project, Plan, or IT Service is to succeed. KPIs are used to measure the achievement of each CSF.

A *risk* is a possible event that could cause harm or loss, or affect the ability to achieve Objectives. A Risk is measured by the probability of a Threat, the Vulnerability of the Asset to that Threat, and the Impact it would have if it occurred.

Examples of challenges
- Lack of something such as funding, time, knowledge, or skills
- Lack of other processes
- Lack of integration with other processes
- Personnel are too busy
- Inadequate set of tools
- Too many things going on
- Lack of data and information
- Resistance to change by personnel

Examples of critical success factors
- Ongoing management commitment
- Ongoing personnel commitment
- Proper planning
- Adequate tools
- Process integration
- Proper data for decision making
- Funding and commitment for all phases such as design, implementation, deployment and operation as well as improvements
- Having the right skills, knowledge, attitudes and aptitudes

Examples of risks
- Not completing project or task on time
- Change of mind by management or the business
- Not achieving business objectives
- Vendor going out of business
- Mergers and acquisitions
- Outsourcing and in-sourcing
- Being locked into a contract
- Obsolete technology
- Being too successful

Syllabus at a glance

Service Strategy

SS01: Service Strategy Principles
Full understanding of Service Strategy terms and core concepts:
- Understand the strategy of differentiating value creation (attributes, perceptions and preferences) in the customer's mind
- Recognize what are assets and how to use them to create value
- Be able to define the three types of service providers and how/where they are used
- Comprehend value chain models and the vertical integration strategy they provide
- Grasp the fundamental aspects of service strategy and be able to define them

SS02: Defining Services and Market Spaces
Support problem solving by putting theory into practice, interpret principles and relationships:
- Be able to create services/strategies related to a customer's needs
- How to use assets (service and customer) to influence value creation
- How to use service archetypes to design a strategy based on asset-based and utility based positioning
- What strategies can be used to define market spaces by focusing services to support business outcome

SS03: Conducting Strategic Assessments
Support problem solving by putting theory into practice, interpret principles and relationships:
- How to mutually reinforce capabilities and resources so that Service Management will be treated as a strategic asset
- Ability to conduct a strategic assessment related to investment and financial business constraints
- Performing an analysis of a customer's needs, market spaces and alignment with business strategy to develop expansion and growth forecasts

SS04: Financial Management
Support problem solving by putting theory into practice, interpret principles and relationships:
- Be able to enhance and add value to a shared imperatives framework for business and IT

- Create, implement and measure service and financial demand modeling so that funding variations related to changes in demand can be quantified
- Provide analysis and guidance to determine how to select the appropriate IT funding models

SS05: Service Portfolio Management
Support problem solving by putting theory into practice, interpret principles and relationships:
- Be able to identify the strategic need as well as build a case for a Service Portfolio
- Design and implement a Service Portfolio management environment that includes all the methods: define, analyze, approve and charter

SS06: Managing Demand
Support problem solving by putting theory into practice, interpret principles and relationships:
- Build a case for implementing demand management related to customer and/or market space requirements
- Ability to develop a capabilities-based demand management strategy for a company
- Be able to integrate and relate all aspects of a Service Catalogue and Service Pipeline to demand and capacity
- Be able to design and implement service packages as well as to determine when/where/how service packages should be introduced and used

SS07: Driving Strategy through the Service Lifecycle
Support problem solving by putting theory into practice, interpret principles and relationships:
- Develop strategies that use all the elements of the lifecycle (e.g. Service Catalogue, Service Pipeline, contract portfolio, financial budgets, delivery schedules and improvement programs)
- Be able to construct and know where/when to use the different types of Service Models as well as where the different design 'drivers' (e.g. outcomes, constraints, pricing) affect the strategy
- How to use Service Transition for decision analysis to evaluate options, paths, risk and costs related to proposed strategies
- How to use Service Operations and Service Catalogue for deployment patterns

SS08: Critical Success Factors and Risks
Support problem solving by putting theory into practice, interpret principles and relationships:

- Be able to provide insight and guidance in the design of IT organizations through the use of five organizational structures as well as Critical Success factor
- Be able to determine the need for and selection of automated tools to support any strategic objectives you have put forward
- Use strategy to achieve operational effectiveness and to overcome organizational complexity

Service Design

SD01: Introduction to Service Design
Full understanding of Service Design terms and core concepts:

- Understand the strategy of differentiating value creation and articulate all the benefits to the business that result from efficient Service Design
- Service Acceptance Criteria and how to use them to create value
- The contents and use of Service Design Packages
- The underpinning processes, functions and assets that link business value to IT services
- The fundamental aspects of Service Design

SD02: Service Design Principles
Support problem solving by putting theory into practice, interpret principles and relationships:

- Design service solutions related to a customer's needs
- Design and use the Service Portfolio to enhance business value
- The measurement systems and metrics
- Service Design models to accommodate different service solutions

SD03: Service Design Processes
Support problem solving by putting theory into practice, interpret principles and relationships:

- The interaction of Service Design processes
- The flow of Service Design as it relates to the business and customer
- The five design aspects and how they are incorporated into the Service Design process

SD04: Service Design technology related activities
Support problem solving by putting theory into practice, interpret principles and relationships:
- Requirements engineering in the design process and using the three types of requirements as identified for any system; Functional, Management/Operations and Usability
- The design of technical architectures for Data and Information Management, and Application Management

SD05: Organizing for Service Design
Support problem solving by putting theory into practice, interpret principles and relationships:
- How to design, implement, and populate a RACI diagram for any process that is within the scope of IT Service Management
- The Service Design roles and responsibilities, where and how they are used and how a Service Design organization would be structured to use these roles

SD06: Consideration of Technology
Support problem solving by putting theory into practice, interpret principles and relationships:
- Service Design related Service Management tools, where and how they would be used
- The benefits and types of tools that support Service Design

SD07: Implementation and improvement of Service Design
Support problem solving by putting theory into practice, interpret principles and relationships:
- The creation, implementation and use of critical success factors and key performance indicators as ways to improve designed services
- The six-stage implementation/improvement cycle and how the activities in each stage of the cycle are applied
- How Business Impact Analysis, Service Level Requirements and risk assessment can affect service design solutions

Service Transition

ST01 introduction to service transition
Full understanding of Service Transition terms and core concepts:
- The flow of Service Transition and where the Service Transition evaluation points occur in the flow
- Ways that Service Transition adds value to the business
- The inputs to and outputs from Service Transition as it interfaces with the other Service Lifecycle phases
- The fundamental aspects of Service Transition and be able to define them

ST02: Service Transition Principles
Support problem solving by putting theory into practice, interpret principles and relationships:
- The utility of a service as defined in terms of the business outcomes that customers expect
- How services provide value by increasing the performance of customer assets while removing risks
- Service Transition best practices in relation to stakeholder relationships and how these best practices can be applied
- How to ensure the quality of a new or changed service

ST03: Service Transition Processes
Support problem solving by putting theory into practice, interpret principles and relationships:
- How to integrate Service Transition with the processes that interact with Service Transition
- The flow of Service Transition as it relates to the transition planning, transition support, service validation and testing as well as evaluation.

ST04: Service Transition related activities
Support problem solving by putting theory into practice, interpret principles and relationships:
- How to address and manage communication aspects/strategy of Service Transition
- How to address organizational change from planning through to communication and implementation, and the interactions with the other lifecycle stages
- How to use all the methods, practices and techniques available to manage change
- Stakeholder management and how to achieve this within an existing organization

ST05: Organizing for Service Transition
Support problem solving by putting theory into practice, interpret principles and relationships:
- Service Transition roles and responsibilities, where and how they are used as well as how a Service Transition organization would be structured to use these roles
- The interfaces that exist between Service Transition and other organizational units (including third parties) and the 'handover points'
- Why Service Transition needs Service Design and Service Operation, what it uses from them and how

ST06: Consideration of Technology
Support problem solving by putting theory into practice, interpret principles and relationships:
- Technology requirements that support Service Transition, where and how these would be used
- Types of Knowledge Management, Service Asset and Configuration Management and workflow tools that can be used to support Service Transition

ST07: Implementation and improvement of Service Transition
Support problem solving by putting theory into practice, interpret principles and relationships:
- The stages for introducing Service Transition into an organization
- The design, creation, implementation and use of critical success factors and key performance indicators as ways to measure and improve Service Transition
- Challenges, risks and prerequisites for success in Service Transition
- Qualification Learning Objectives

Service Operation

SO01: Introduction to Service Operation
Full understanding of Service Operation terms and core concepts:
- The functions contained within Service Operations including how they interact to make Service Operations work
- The processes and Service Lifecycle phases that Service Operation interfaces with
- The fundamental aspects of Service Operation and be able to define them

SO02: Service Operation Principles
Support problem solving by putting theory into practice, interpret principles and relationships:
- How Service Operation is organized in relation to Functions, Groups, Teams, Department and divisions.
- How an organization can achieve balance when dealing with internal versus external organizational focus, identifying the issues related to organizations who operate at the extremes of these balances
- What 'Operational Health' means, specifically addressing examples of 'Self Healing Systems' and the processes used by them
- The creation, components and implementation of a complete communication strategy to be used with Service Operations

SO03: Service Operation Processes
Support problem solving by putting theory into practice, interpret principles and relationships:
- The use of and interaction of each of the five key processes that make up Service Operation
- The value to the business that each of the Service Operation processes contributes
- The use of and interaction of all other lifecycle operational activities that contribute to Service Operation

SO04: Common Service Operation Activities
Support problem solving by putting theory into practice, interpret principles and relationships:
- The difference between a technology-centric and a business-centric organization, the five levels of maturity and how Service Operation can be used to move towards increasing the business-centric focus
- How the activities identified in this unit support Service Operation and provide a detailed model of how to integrate them into a Service Operation organization

SO05: Organizing Service Operation
Support problem solving by putting theory into practice, interpret principles and relationships:
- The objective, activities and roles of each of the four functions indentified in this unit and how to build a Service Operation model based on these functions
- Service Operation roles and responsibilities, where and how they are used as well as how a Service Operation organization would be structured to use these roles

SO06: Technology Considerations

Support problem solving by putting theory into practice, interpret principles and relationships:

- The technology that supports Service Operation, where and how these can be used
- The technology required to support each of the Service Operations processes and functions: Event Management, Incident Management, Request Fulfillment, Problem Management, Access Management and Service Desk

SO07: Implementation Considerations

Support problem solving by putting theory into practice, interpret principles and relationships:

- Strategies and models for managing change in Service Operation and how to implement this activity within an organization
- Implementing Service Operation technologies within a company
- How to assess and manage risk with in a Service Operation group including the interaction that needs to occur with the Service Design and Service Transition personnel

SO08: Challenges, Critical Success Factors and Risks

Support problem solving by putting theory into practice, interpret principles and relationships:

- The challenges and risks (e.g. staff, funding, management, etc.) related to Service Operation and the details behind how each challenge can be addressed
- The Critical Success Factors (CSFs) related to Service Operation as well as a detailed model for measuring and monitoring Service Operation CSFs

Continual Service Improvement

CSI01: Introduction to Continual Service Improvement

Full understanding of Continual Service Improvement terms and core concepts:

- The Service Gap Model, how Service Level Management contributes to the management of gaps and how a Service Improvement Program can be used
- The 7-Step improvement process used in Continual Service Improvement
- The processes and Service Lifecycle stages that Continual Service Improvement interfaces with
- The fundamental aspects of Continual Service Improvement and be able to define them

CSI02: Continual Service Improvement Principles

Support problem solving by putting theory into practice, interpret principles and relationships:

- How Service Level Management supports Continual Improvement, providing details and examples related to use of Service Level Agreements, Operational Level Agreements and Underpinning Contracts
- How the complete Deming cycle works and how it can be applied to a real world example
- What role benchmarking plays in Continual Service Improvement and the interaction it has with governance
- What situations require the use of frameworks and models and examples, and how each type can be used to achieve improvement

CSI03: Continual Service Improvement Process

Support problem solving by putting theory into practice, interpret principles and relationships:

- What the 7-Step improvement process is, how each step can be applied and the benefits it produces
- The use and interaction of all other lifecycle stages and activities that contribute to Continual Service Improvement
- The benefits and differences between the types of metrics (i.e. Technology, Process and Service) and how each is used to support Continual Service Improvement
- The differences between the Technology Domain and the Service Management Domain, and how each is viewed by Continual Service Improvement

CSI04: Continual Service Improvement Methods and Techniques

Support problem solving by putting theory into practice, interpret principles and relationships:

- How to use Availability Management techniques such as Component Failure Impact Analysis, Fault Tree
- How analysis is used to support Continual Service Improvement
- How Capacity, Problem, Risk and IT Service Continuity Management can all be used holistically to support Continual Service Improvement
- When and where to use benchmarking, Balanced Scorecards and SWOT (Strength, Weakness Opportunity Threat) analysis

CSI05: Organization for Continual Service Improvement

Support problem solving by putting theory into practice, interpret principles and relationships:

- How to design, implement and populate a RACI (Responsible, Accountable, Consulted, Informed) matrix as well as how to use it to support Continual Service Improvement
- The Continual Service Improvement related roles and responsibilities such as Service Manager, Continual Service Improvement Manager and Service owner and provide examples of how they can be positioned within an organization

CSI06: Technology for Continual Service Improvement
Support problem solving by putting theory into practice, interpret principles and relationships:
- The technology and tools required, as well as how these would be implemented and managed, to support Continual Service Improvement activities such as Performance, Project and Portfolio Management as well as Service Measurement and Business Intelligence reporting

CSI07: Implementing Continual Service Improvement
Support problem solving by putting theory into practice, interpret principles and relationships:
- Continual Service Improvement implementation: strategy, planning, governance, communication, project management, operation as well as how to deal with cultural and organizational change
- The day-to-day concerns, support, and operations of a large corporate Continual Service Improvement group

CSI08: Critical Success Factors and Risks
Support problem solving by putting theory into practice, interpret principles and relationships:
- The challenges and risks such as staffing, funding, management, etc., which can be related to Continual Service Improvement and the details behind how each challenge can be addressed
- The critical success factors related to Continual Service Improvement as well as how to measure and monitor them

Managing Across The Lifecycle

MALC01: Introduction to IT Service Management Business and Managerial Issues
Support problem solving by putting theory into practice and interpret principles and relationships:
- Open loop and closed-loop, when / where to apply each system

- ITSM Monitor Control loops and Complex Monitor Control loops including how/ when the control loops are used
- The benefits and business value in relation to people, process and function, supplier relationships and technological alignment

MALC02: Management of Strategic Change
The candidate can demonstrate the ability to create patterns or structure from composite elements to achieve a new meaning or outcome. The candidate can make judgment, weigh options of ideas and elements to justify and support an argument or case.
- Value creation and critical success factor components of managing strategic change
- Introduce strategic change supported by a business case that defines the business benefits and the benefits realization strategy
- Tangible/intangible business benefits and models for measuring each type of benefit
- Business Value enhancement through Variable Cost Dynamics and alignment of business policy
- IT and business alignment through Demand Management, Service Portfolios and Service Catalogues

MALC03: Risk Management
The candidate can demonstrate the ability to create patterns or structure from composite elements to achieve a new meaning or outcome. The candidate can make judgment, weigh options of ideas and elements to justify and support an argument or case.
- Risk within the IT and business relationship and models for effective evaluation, analysis and identification of risk
- Management of risk in the following areas: service providers, contracts, design, operations and markets
- Analysis of business and IT related risks as measured by specific critical success factors and the corrective actions and/or transfer of risks

MALC04: Managing the Planning and Implementation of IT Service Management
The candidate can demonstrate the ability to create patterns or structure from composite elements to achieve a new meaning or outcome. The candidate can make judgment, weigh options of ideas and elements to justify and support an argument or case.
- The Deming cycle (Plan, Do, Check, Act)
- IT Service Management implementation strategy including policy, strategy, design and transition considerations
- Directing, controlling and evaluating – achieving business goals and using feedback
- Communication, coordination, and control activities when implementing IT Service Management

MALC05: Understanding Organizational Challenges

The candidate can demonstrate the ability to create patterns or structure from composite elements to achieve a new meaning or outcome. The candidate can make judgment, weigh options of ideas and elements to justify and support an argument or case.

• Organizational maturity and organizational structure
• Governance models, achieving and maintaining balance in Service Operations
• Organizational transition

MALC06: Service Assessment

The candidate can demonstrate the ability to create patterns or structure from composite elements to achieve a new meaning or outcome. The candidate can make judgment, weigh options of ideas and elements to justify and support an argument or case.

• Service assessment measurements, metrics and monitoring
• The value of benchmarking
• Service Portfolio assessments and corrective actions

MALC07: Understanding Complementary Industry Guidance and Tool Strategies

Support problem solving by putting theory into practice, and interpret principles and relationships:

• COBIT, ISO/IEC 20000, CMMI, Balanced Scorecard, Quality Management, OSI Framework, Annuity, Service Management maturity framework, Six Sigma, Project Management, TQM, Management Governance framework, and tool strategies, Qualification Learning Objectives

Summary

A syllabus is a very useful tool for exam preparation. The 'at a glance' section provides useful insight into the applicability of the concepts in many situations. The way to use this section is to refer to the appropriate section in the core books and to think of ways to apply these concepts into a scenario picked at random or to a candidate's own organization.

The high-level applicability of the concepts is quite similar from one organization to the next. This is not to say that the details will be the same.

For an organization to be successful it requires financial capital, a product to sell, a price point, placement for the product and promoting the product. The successful execution of business activities requires a strategy, a business plan, executing the plan and verifying the plan has been achieved.

And so on.

The concepts described in the core books are just that, simple common business practices however directed at IT Service Management.

The more a candidate can relate and recognize the concepts out of their IT context and apply them to a regular business situation, the easier it becomes to understand them and their applicability.

CHAPTER 9

Using scenarios for practice

There are only so many available sample papers (practice exams) available through the examining institutes. Trainers are often, if not always, asked if they can provide additional practice questions. The answer is more often than not negative.

There are ways around this lack of available sample papers. Create your own.

Don't worry – it is not too difficult, and with a little practice and the guidance provided in this chapter, a candidate can easily create multiple additional questions.

This chapter will explore how one scenario can be used for all questions within the same sample paper. This means that it is possible to create seven additional questions. But it does not have to stop there. A candidate could use a scenario for all questions in all the sample papers. It is not implied here that a candidate should go to this extreme or that every scenario will work with every question.

All the above is saying is that with a little imagination and a little bit of effort, you can use the existing sample papers in many permutations to help you better prepare for an examination.

Note from the author
As a trainer for the now defunct Service Manager course, I looked at some of the sample questions and, by simply changing the topic, was able to create the same question for all the topics. This examination was based on an 8 to 10 page case study. There were two papers, three hours per paper, five questions per paper and two to four parts per question. The answers were hand written on paper (Ok, there were available the last few years in electronic form – typing). The questions were worth 20 marks each.

Here is an example of how to proceed.

The organization wants to implement the Availability Management process. Identify three challenges the organization currently faces that need to be addressed during the implementation phase. Explain how best to address these challenges.

By simply changing the name of the process to any other one, I was able to create eleven additional practice questions. Of course as the nice person that I am, I also provided the marking guidelines for my fellow instructors and for our students. It goes without saying that I always mentioned these questions were not official sample questions, but they were nonetheless an excellent exam preparation tool for the students.

Using one of the sample scenarios already used in this book, here is how to apply this scenario for various situations within the same paper.

The scenario selected is from the Service Strategy Sample Paper 1. This scenario can be used for many of the questions in Sample Paper 1.

Service Strategy

Scenario One

A large IT training provider has a training center containing twenty classrooms fully equipped with PCs and servers for delivering technical training courses. The building also contains the organization's administrative offices. A wireless network serving the administrative areas was installed about two years ago.

The wireless network can be accessed from the training area. Management decided to allow students who bring their own laptops, to access the internet via the wireless network as a free 'value-added' service. Students appreciate this additional service.

Over time, usage of the wireless network by both the administrative staff and students has increased. This is affecting the availability and performance of the administrative systems, therefore it is occasionally necessary to restrict and prevent student access.

The availability and performance issues continue to increase in frequency, and the training center staff is overwhelmed with complaints from students when the network is not available to them. The management team is very concerned as the course evaluation forms show increasing student dissatisfaction.

The decision has been taken to withdraw the wireless network access service from students immediately and notices have been posted in the training areas informing students of the decision.

Management must now consider what further action should be taken.

Question Two

Refer to Scenario One
As an ITSM Consultant, you have been asked by the CIO to advise what the next step should be for improvement of IT Service Management.

Which of the following approaches is the BEST one in this situation?

A:	Move forward with design, documentation and implementation of new processes as planned. Service Portfolio Management should be considered first as it is the basis for Service Catalogue Management and Service Level Management. As measurements are an important element in Service Level Management, the measurements for the existing processes and services should not be established before Service Level Management has been implemented.
B:	Measurements are the basis of both Service improvement and Process improvement. To ensure the operational processes are effective in serving the needs of the business and the IT Unit, effective measurements should be established. To ensure that the IT staff understand the measurements and take them seriously, the measurements should be operationally oriented; therefore the IT unit should start by setting up monitoring and measurement of components relevant to Event Management, Incident Management, Request Fulfillment and Access Management, the processes which are directly related to customer satisfaction.
C:	All measurements should be useful and relevant to the context in which value is created. The IT unit should have thorough discussions with the business unit leaders on how services affect business performance and outcomes. Measurements can then be defined that provide IT decision support across the Service Lifecycle, with strong underpinnings related to the concerns and needs of customers and users. Finally, it is important to relate IT assets with services and the business processes to ensure end-to-end visibility and control for IT managers.
D:	End-to-end measurements should be established to ensure that services and processes are measured in their full extent and not as discrete components or activities. Even though they are more demanding to aggregate, the IT unit should strive to achieve end-to-end measurements. These would provide a top-level picture of the services and processes, and would prevent the situation where some areas are measured and others are poorly measured or not measured at all. They would also prevent inconsistency in methods, presentation and calculation of the measurements.

Relating the scenario to the question
The important thing to remember about the scenario is that Management wants to address the issue of providing internet access to the students in the training center. The last two paragraphs of the scenario are:

The decision has been taken to withdraw the wireless network access service from students immediately and notices have been posted in the training areas informing students of the decision.

Management must now consider what further action should be taken.

Question rationale
This question focuses on value creation. Value is defined not only strictly in terms of the customers' economic business outcome but also highly on the customers' perceptions. Perceptions of added value are influenced by expectations.

The answers are provided at the end of the chapter.

Question Three

Refer to Scenario One
The IT Director wants advice on sourcing the services currently provided by the IT group. The director wants to know whether the IT group should continue with its current services in future, or whether it should focus on its unique services by supporting and maintaining the business application and outsource the generic services.

What would be the BEST next stage so that an informed decision may be made?

A:	The Strategic Review should continue in order to better understand and quantify the value and cost of IT service provision to the business created by the IT services in the Service Catalogue. The viability of continuing to provide these services can then be evaluated together with the potential to improve the management of the services. Once the costs and value are better understood, a clear sourcing strategy can be formulated and published.
B:	The Strategic Review should continue in order to better understand the costs of providing each of the IT services in the Service Catalogue. If the cost of providing desktop PC support and server hosting services internally is greater than the price proposed by the external provider, then these services should be outsourced. The IT group will then be able to focus on providing those services in which they have most expertise.

C:	The Strategic Review should continue in order to fully identify and understand the actual costs of providing the services in the Service Portfolio. Once this greater understanding of the business value has been achieved, the focus should be to consider outsourcing those services that are most costly to provide.
D:	The Service Catalogue should be enhanced to become a Service Portfolio in order to provide a better understanding of the existing services' positions within the full Service Lifecycle. The costs of providing services can then be fully identified and understood. The strategy should then focus on ways of reducing costs in order to make the services more attractive to the business.

Relating the scenario to the question
The important thing to remember about the scenario is that Management wants to address the issue of providing internet access to the students in the training center. The last two paragraphs of the scenario are:

The decision has been taken to withdraw the wireless network access service from students immediately and notices have been posted in the training areas informing students of the decision.

Management must now consider what further action should be taken.

Question rationale
This question focuses on the development of service potential and service management as a strategic asset by understanding market spaces and value creation principles.

The answers are provided at the end of the chapter.

Question Four

Refer to Scenario One
As a Financial Management specialist you have been asked for advice on the proposed approach. Based on the situation and ITIL Financial Management practices, is the Finance Director's proposal the BEST way to inform the outsourcing decision?

A:	Yes. However it requires thorough planning and may take longer than five months. If approached carefully, the business will be able to quantify the value of IT services because they will be paying for what they need. This will help to inform the decision on outsourcing.

B:	Yes, because the price the customers are required to pay will help them quantify the value of the IT services. However, it is important that Notional Charging is introduced. This is because the proposal is to evaluate the relative costs of outsourcing versus the current situation rather than recovering costs. The proposal can be introduced within the timescales proposed by the Finance Director because current costs are well understood.
C:	No, because the timescales are too short. Introducing an internal charging mechanism needs longer timescales, including a period of Notional Charging so that any anomalies in charging mechanisms and budget allocations can be resolved amicably before charging is introduced. Introducing charging too quickly may make it difficult to evaluate the factors determining the strategic decision.
D:	No. Introducing an internal charging mechanism may eventually enable the IT unit to recover operational costs fairly, but this will not provide sufficient information for the outsourcing decision. The decision would be better informed by quantifying the value that the services create for business customers and comparing this with the costs of providing those services. Introducing a charge-back scheme may also be an unnecessary and costly overhead.

Relating the scenario to the question

The important thing to remember about the scenario is that Management wants to address the issue of providing internet access to the students in the training center. The last two paragraphs of the scenario are:

The decision has been taken to withdraw the wireless network access service from students immediately and notices have been posted in the training areas informing students of the decision.

Management must now consider what further action should be taken.

Question rationale

This question focuses on the use of Financial Management to provide an effective basis for service valuation.

The answers are provided at the end of the chapter.

Question Five

Refer to Scenario One

You are a consultant engaged by the CIO to provide advice on this strategy. Which of the following options is the BEST advice?

A:	The IT services that support contracts with car manufacturers are a good candidate for consolidation and centralization and would be likely to provide significant cost savings through sharing resources and infrastructure. Since the business services that they support are low value and high volume, it would make good business sense to consolidate them and to provide them centrally.
B:	The IT services that support the ad hoc customer requirement provide important business differentiation, and so it is important that these services are well served locally. These IT services should not be consolidated or centralized. Instead, the services that are similar across multiple different situations should be considered for centralization. This will ensure that ad hoc services can be easily geared to each customer as required.
C:	It is possible that there are aspects of all the IT services supporting all end-customer types that would be capable of consolidation, and it would be appropriate to investigate further a service model for each of the IT service types which at least match existing levels of utility and warranty at a lower cost.
D:	At this stage it is difficult to determine where consolidation would be most effective. It is likely that some consolidation would be cost effective through sharing resources and infrastructure. However, first it would be appropriate to consider dependencies between services, then determine how the IT services are deployed and used locally and finally to evaluate both relevant user costs and IT costs. It will then be possible to determine whether consolidation of any aspects of service would be cost effective.

Relating the scenario to the question

The important thing to remember about the scenario is that Management wants to address the issue about providing internet access to the students in the training center. The last two paragraphs of the scenario are:

> The decision has been taken to withdraw the wireless network access service from students immediately and notices have been posted in the training areas informing students of the decision.

> Management must now consider what further action should be taken.

Question rationale

The question looks at service strategies linked to end-customer requirements and their strategic importance and considers aspects of IT service costs through the service delivery chain including hidden costs.

The answers are provided at the end of the chapter.

Question Six

Refer to Scenario One

As the CIO, which one of the following approaches is the BEST to determine the investment strategy that creates the most value to the organization?

A:	The best way to calculate value is to focus on the economic return of each of the initiatives. To ensure consistency, all initiatives should be evaluated in the same way, using financial calculations that are meaningful to both IT and the business. In this way the infrastructure resilience and business initiatives can be compared and the highest return on investment chosen.
B:	It is true that improving the resilience of the IT infrastructure does not add value in itself. The Business Relationship Managers (BRMs) will not be able to demonstrate any real value of the innovative ideas until the infrastructure has been stabilized. The CIO should re-prioritize the internal projects and only then encourage implementation of the innovative projects if the business is willing to fund them, and in the order in which the business prioritizes them.
C:	What the customer values is frequently different from what the IT department believes it provides. Therefore, in addition to quantifying the financial return of the initiatives, the BRMs should also focus on evaluating the expectations and perceptions of the customers. The best initiative is the one with the optimal combination of financial outcome and the value added (in terms of how each service meets the expectations of the customers). This means that there must be a balance between projects focusing on internal IT dependencies and the ability to deliver innovative new services.
D:	Value is highly dependent on the customers' perceptions. The financial outcome of the initiatives should be calculated to quantify the returns, but in addition to that, the perceptions of the customer should be identified by the BRMs to get the full picture of which of the initiatives creates most value to the organization. If the customers do not perceive any value from improving the resilience of the IT infrastructure then this project should be dealt with as a lower priority.

Relating the scenario to the question

The important thing to remember about the scenario is that Management wants to address the issue of providing internet access to the students in the training center. The last two paragraphs of the scenario are:

The decision has been taken to withdraw the wireless network access service from students immediately and notices have been posted in the training areas informing students of the decision.

Management must now consider what further action should be taken.

Question rationale
This question focuses on value creation. Value is defined not only strictly in terms of the customers' economic business outcome but also highly on the customers' perceptions. Perceptions of added value are influenced by expectations.

The answers are provided at the end of the chapter.

Question Seven

Refer to Scenario One
You have been asked to analyze the responses from the questionnaire and help decide the relative importance of the two attributes with respect to fulfilling customer needs.

Which one of the following is the BEST analysis of the customer responses?

A:	The data is quite conclusive about the need to provide both Stock Enquiry AND Mobile Update attributes. Customers across all three business functions perceive value in having BOTH attributes in the new service. The 'Must NOT have' and 'Questionable' responses should be considered statistically insignificant relative to the overall number of responses.
B:	The data is ambiguous or inconclusive about the need to provide a Stock Enquiry OR Mobile Update option. There are customers who do not care about the service attributes and customers who do. Some responses are questionable. There are differences in perceptions between the Sell, Buy and Store functions. It would be difficult and expensive to design and deliver a service that will satisfy all three types of customers. Further analysis and research are necessary.
C:	Customers across all three business functions perceive value in BOTH proposed attributes, although NOT providing the Mobile Update is likely to cause more dissatisfaction than NOT providing a Stock Enquiry feature. The 'Must NOT have' and 'Questionable' responses possibly reflect anxiety or uncertainty over how the service attributes will be compatible with their respective work environments.
D:	Customers in the Sales or 'Sell' function and those in Purchasing or 'Buy' are much more eager to know about current stock levels than those in the Warehouse or 'Store' function. However, the 'Buy' side customers are suspicious of how Interactive Voice Response (IVR) technology works, possibly because they are less accustomed to the latest devices and technology, compared with the Sales staff. Customers in the 'Store' function are probably not very keen on the need to provide alerts and updates until they know how it affects their roles and responsibilities.

Relating the scenario to the question
The important thing to remember about the scenario is that Management wants to address the issue of providing internet access to the students in the training center. The last two paragraphs of the scenario are:

The decision has been taken to withdraw the wireless network access service from students immediately and notices have been posted in the training areas informing students of the decision.

Management must now consider what further action should be taken.

Question rationale
The question looks at requirements, constraints and limiting factors for IT services linked to developing appropriate service models. It covers some of the links between service strategy and service design. It specifically considers decisions on the importance of service attributes in the style of a Kano model, and how this needs to be considered alongside other constraints and factors.

The answers are provided at the end of the chapter.

Question Eight

Refer to Scenario One
Which one of the following options BEST defines the market spaces and the CORRECT steps to take in this situation?

A:	Market spaces define opportunities for services to deliver value.
	• Define the outcomes that each business division needs to achieve
	• Identify the customer assets used to achieve these outcomes
	• Identify Technology Department service archetypes
	• Map customer assets and service archetypes to create market spaces. These show how each service enables outcomes for each division
	• Update the Service Catalogue and differentiate between services which are used similarly by all divisions and those which are used differently
B:	Each business division represents a distinct market space.
	• Define the activities, outcomes and customer assets of each market space
	• Identify the service archetypes in the Technology Department
	• Link each service archetype to each market space
	• Determine how each market space uses each service archetype
	• Service archetypes which are used similarly by different market spaces should be catalogued as core service packages. Service archetypes dedicated to a single market space should be listed as a Service Level Package

C:	Market spaces represent points of opportunity between a service provider and its customers. • Since services are already well defined, first document service archetypes • Identify the customer assets • Map service archetypes and customer assets to create a baseline for how value can be delivered • Document business outcomes for each division and validate that the market spaces can support these • Catalogue the services for each market space so the Technology Department clearly understands what is delivered to each division
D:	Market spaces are defined by mapping service archetypes to customer assets. • The best starting point is to identify the service archetypes and customer assets • Determine the desired business outcomes for each division • Map the Service archetypes, customer assets and business outcomes. This identifies the market spaces • Document these in the Service Portfolio. This becomes the basis for defining services, ensuring that the Technology Department is able to deliver exactly what each division requires

Relating the scenario to the question

The important thing to remember about the scenario is that Management wants to address the issue of providing internet access to the students in the training center. The last two paragraphs of the scenario are:

The decision has been taken to withdraw the wireless network access service from students immediately and notices have been posted in the training areas informing students of the decision.

Management must now consider what further action should be taken.

Question rationale

This question focuses on the role that market spaces play in defining services and articulating value the value of those services. Candidates should be able to demonstrate an understanding of the relationship of business outcomes, service archetypes, market spaces and customer assets. Specifically, candidates should be able to understand:

• That market spaces are sets of opportunities for delivering value, and not simply customers or groups of customers

• Market spaces are created by understanding the outcomes desired by customers, and then identifying the combination of customer assets and service archetypes that will enable the customer to achieve those outcomes

- When market spaces are mapped, it becomes possible to define the structure of services that will be documented in the Service Catalogue (which is the appropriate reference for staff in this situation)

The answers are provided at the end of the chapter

How to approach each question in relation to Scenario One

The important thing to remember about the scenario is that Management wants to address the issue of providing internet access to the students in the training center. The last two paragraphs of the scenario are:

> The decision has been taken to withdraw the wireless network access service from students immediately and notices have been posted in the training areas informing students of the decision.

> Management must now consider what further action should be taken.

Question 2

As an ITSM consultant, you have been asked by the CIO to advise what the next step should be for improvement of IT Service Management.

Overall, improving Service Management is a good idea. This should help the organization to avoid making similar planning mistakes in the future. Therefore it is possible to answer the question using this scenario.

Question 3

The IT Director wants advice on sourcing the services currently provided by the IT group. The director wants to know whether the IT group should continue with its current services in future, or whether it should focus on its unique services by supporting and maintaining the business application and outsource the generic services.

Outsourcing wireless internet access could provide the organization with more bandwidth and the ability to negotiate a discount for the students. The connectivity could be provided using a 'WI-FI hot spot' approach or by renting wireless internet modems.

Question 4
As a Financial Management specialist you have been asked for advice on the proposed approach. Based on the situation and ITIL Financial Management practices, is the Finance Director's proposal the BEST way to inform the outsourcing decision?

Assume the decision has been made to outsource internet access for students. This question makes a lot of sense for this particular scenario.

Question 5
You are a consultant engaged by the CIO to provide advice on this strategy. Which of the following options is the BEST advice?

Although the original scenario is about an organization manufacturing car parts in multiple locations with for three different types of customers, this question can still be used with a little imagination. Assume the training organization is present in multiple cities. Assume the three types of customers are the business, corporate customers (sending many people for training) and individual customers. The question is still relevant to Scenario One.

Question 6
As the CIO, which one of the following approaches is the BEST to determine the investment strategy that creates the most value to the organization?

An investment strategy is an investment strategy. This situation applies to Scenario One, as the organization must decide whether to resume providing the wireless service to the students or not, as well as how to go about it.

Question 7
You have been asked to analyze the responses from the questionnaire and help decide the relative importance of the two attributes with respect to fulfilling customer needs.

This question seems a bit more difficult to relate to Scenario One because of the survey responses provided in the original Scenario Seven for this question. However, assume a survey is conducted with the students and the business regarding the wireless access service. There would be differences of opinions as to the importance, the usefulness, and other factors. The question is not so much about the results but about perceptions and making sure the survey is well constructed. The other important element to remember is to keep looking at the answers that provide a business outcome point of view.

Question 8
Which one of the following options BEST defines the market spaces and the CORRECT steps to take in this situation?

It is possible to use a similar approach for this question as suggested for question five. The students and the business represent two distinct market spaces. This type of exercise needs to be conducted for all services in all organizations.

Answers to Service Strategy Sample Paper 1

Question	Best	2nd Best	3rd Best	Distractor
Two	C	D	B	A
Three	A	B	C	D
Four	D	C	A	B
Five	D	C	B	A
Six	C	D	A	B
Seven	C	D	A	B
Eight	A	D	C	B

Summary

The point of this type of practice is primarily to recognize that the practices described in the core books are relevant to any organization. Of course, coming up with the best answer is nice but a candidate should focus instead on approaching a question as if it were a real assignment with the parameters provided. The parameters are along the following lines:

- You are a/the < insert role here >...
- The CIO wants you to <action verb here >...
- The business wants to < accomplish something >...

The major learning point here is that all activities need to be performed within an organization. All organizations have issues that need to be addressed, things that need to be changed, things that need to be improved, and things that are outsourced. The differences lie in the scale, magnitude and type of industry and organization.

Replace the name of the product being sold with the one your organization is selling. Replace the service/system/application name with one in your organization with similar issues. Imagine yourself in that situation. What should be done according to the practices describes in the core books?

CHAPTER 10

Using exam questions for practice

Using a technique similar to the one described and used in Chapter 8, this chapter will illustrate how to use various questions and build other similar questions for the same paper or for different ones as well.

For the purpose of this chapter, the scenarios and the question come from Service Strategy Sample Paper 1 has been selected. The question selected is number three.

The IT Director wants advice on sourcing the services currently provided by the IT group. The director wants to know whether the IT group should continue with its current services in future, or whether it should focus on its unique services by supporting and maintaining the business application and outsource the generic services.

What would be the BEST next stage so that an informed decision may be made?

A:	The Strategic Review should continue in order to better understand and quantify the value and cost of IT service provision to the business created by the IT services in the Service Catalogue. The viability of continuing to provide these services can then be evaluated together with the potential to improve the management of the services. Once the costs and value are better understood, a clear sourcing strategy can be formulated and published.
B:	The Strategic Review should continue in order to better understand the costs of providing each of the IT services in the Service Catalogue. If the cost of providing desktop PC support and server hosting services internally is greater than the price proposed by the external provider, then these services should be outsourced. The IT group will then be able to focus on providing those services in which they have most expertise.
C:	The Strategic Review should continue in order to fully identify and understand the actual costs of providing the services in the Service Portfolio. Once this greater understanding of the business value has been achieved, the focus should be to consider outsourcing those services that are most costly to provide.
D:	The Service Catalogue should be enhanced to become a Service Portfolio in order to provide a better understanding of the existing services' positions within the full Service Lifecycle. The costs of providing services can then be fully identified and understood. The strategy should then focus on ways of reducing costs in order to make the services more attractive to the business.

Answers to Question 3 Service Strategy Sample Paper 1

Question	Best	2nd Best	3rd Best	Distractor
Three	A	B	C	D

From the rationale we have

This question focuses on the development of service potential and service management as a strategic asset by understanding market spaces and value creation principles.

Best answer	A.	Answer A is the best option as it has no pre-conceptions about which services are most worthy of retaining in-house. In order to make a sourcing decision it is correct to understand the value created by services for the business using the Service Catalogue, and then balance this against the true costs of providing the service. It recognizes ITSM as being potentially a valuable asset.
Second best	B.	Answer B adopts a sensible approach to an extent, but it would be wrong to automatically assume that if the cost of providing desktop PC support and server hosting services internally is greater than the proposed price from the external provider, then the services should be outsourced. This does not take into account the value created for the business by those services, particularly as the infrastructure supports a strategic application and confidential data. The strategy needs to take into account cost and value.
Third best	C.	This is the third best answer. The suggested answer focuses on the Service Portfolio without offering any plausible explanation why analysis should be done at that level. Also it only focuses on cost of service provision, without balancing this against the potential value created. Just focusing on the least costly services ignores the needs and perception of the business customers.
Distractor	D.	This is the least viable of the answers. Just producing a Service Portfolio will not necessarily provide the information alluded to in the answer. Implementing cost reductions will not necessarily make services more attractive to customers – it could in fact squeeze service potential so much that service level performance and value to customers would also reduce.

Scenario One

A large IT training provider has a training center containing twenty classrooms fully equipped with PCs and servers for delivering technical training courses. The building also contains the organization's administrative offices. A wireless network serving the administrative areas was installed about two years ago.

The wireless network can be accessed from the training area. Management decided to allow students who bring their own laptops to access the internet via the wireless network as a free 'value-added' service. Students appreciate this additional service.

Over time, usage of the wireless network by both the administrative staff and students has increased. This is affecting the availability and performance of the administrative systems, therefore it is occasionally necessary to restrict and prevent student access.

The availability and performance issues continue to increase in frequency, and the training center staff is overwhelmed with complaints from students when the network is not available to them. The management team is very concerned as the course evaluation forms show increasing student dissatisfaction.

The decision has been taken to withdraw the wireless network access service from students immediately and notices have been posted in the training areas informing students of the decision.

Management must now consider what further action should be taken.

Relating the question to the scenario
Looking at the scenario, is a question such as 'What would be the BEST next stage so that an informed decision may be made?' a valid one to ask?

The wording in the answers is generic enough to apply to the scenario. At the end of the scenario we have:
- The decision has been taken to withdraw the wireless network access service from students immediately and notices have been posted in the training areas informing students of the decision.
- Management must now consider what further action should be taken.

The additional information in the question can be broken down as follows:
- The IT Director wants advice on sourcing the services currently provided by the IT group.
- The director wants to know if the IT group should...
  - Continue with its current services in future
  - Focus on its unique services by supporting and maintaining the business application and outsource the generic services

The question and the scenario are both looking at 'next steps'. Of course, something about the wireless network will have to be done but overall, the answer does provide insight into what an organization will have to do eventually as part of improving the delivery of its services.

Scenario Two

The IT unit of a medium sized transportation company has been implementing Service Management processes for a few years. The IT unit has focused on more operational processes such as Event Management, Incident Management, Request Fulfillment and Access Management. These processes are now documented and implemented to some degree, but the IT unit still struggles with managing and improving these processes. It is felt that one main reason for this is that performance measurements are lacking.

The implementation of the first Service Management processes was undertaken as a result of numerous operational quality issues, but no strategic considerations were taken into account to support the implementation. The Chief Information Officer (CIO) feels the implementation of the operational processes to a certain extent has not been consistent with the business environment's support needs, but so far the CIO has not been able to make the case with specific evidence and arguments.

Based on business requirements, the IT unit now sees the need to formalize and improve other Service Management processes such as Service Portfolio Management, Service Catalogue Management and Service Level Management, but the CIO is unsure if it is a good idea to start this before basic performance measurements are in place.

Relating the question to the scenario
Looking at the scenario, is a question such as 'What would be the BEST next stage so that an informed decision may be made?' a valid one to ask?

The wording in the answers is generic enough to apply to the scenario. At the end of the scenario we have:
• Based on business requirements, the IT unit now sees the need to formalize and improve other Service Management processes such as Service Portfolio Management, Service Catalogue Management and Service Level Management, but the CIO is unsure if it is a good idea to start this before basic performance measurements are in place.

The additional information in the question can be broken down as follows:
• The IT Director wants advice on sourcing the services currently provided by the IT group.
• The director wants to know if the IT group should...
    - Continue with its current services in future
    - Focus on its unique services by supporting and maintaining the business application and outsource the generic services

The question and the scenario are both looking at 'next steps'. Is this scenario significantly different from Scenario Three? The answer is no.

Scenario Three

A law firm provides specialist legal services to large companies. It has a head office and lawyers' offices in six locations.

The IT group, based at the head office, supports and maintains the main business application which was developed in-house several years ago. This application supports business processes including case logging and tracking, customer relationship management and production of customer accounts and invoices. It is considered to be a strategic service, providing a source of differentiation for the business and the data is considered to be highly confidential. The application runs on servers at head office linked to servers at the other offices.

The IT group provides desktop PC and server support using technicians located at each site who deal with incidents as they arise using their local site knowledge and their close relationship with the business users to provide effective and timely incident resolutions. The IT group also offers training courses ranging from basic word-processing to more specialized training in the business application. There are no structured Service Management processes in place and most of the support activity is reactive.

The IT Director has instigated a Strategic Review and, acting on the advice from an external ITSM consultant, arranged for the development of a Service Catalogue.

The Review revealed that the services provided by the IT group are mostly very basic and generic, apart from the specialized support and training for the business application. In fact, an external company has made an informal approach offering desktop PC support and server hosting at a competitive price. The Strategic Review also revealed that many of the services offered by the IT group fall into a market space already well served by other IT providers.

Relating the question to the scenario
This is the original scenario for this question. As already mentioned, the additional information in the question can be broken down as follows:
- The IT Director wants advice on sourcing the services currently provided by the IT group.

- The director wants to know if the IT group should…
  - Continue with its current services in future
  - Focus on its unique services by supporting and maintaining the business application and outsource the generic services

Scenario Four

An organization provides consultancy services to large companies. There is an IT unit which supports and maintains some specialized business applications which were developed in-house, and provides IT infrastructure support to business users.

The IT unit develops a budget plan on an annual basis. Operational funds are allocated according to the budget plan by the corporate Finance Department. The overall actual expenditure is usually within 5% of the budget.

Business changes are managed via projects. Project managers are responsible for identifying the required funding for the one-time initial cost of new IT infrastructure required by their projects. Project managers are also responsible for estimating ongoing annual costs of any new IT infrastructure, which is then taken into account in the next round of operational budget planning.

The Finance Director has suggested that some of the IT unit's services might be outsourced in future, thus allowing more of the internal IT resources to focus on business change projects which will bring value to the business. The Finance Director also believes that outsourcing may reduce the costs of IT services in the longer term.

In order to help inform a strategic decision on the business value created, as well as whether and what to outsource, the Finance Director has proposed that initially the IT unit shall introduce internal charging and recover its operational costs from the business units. Under this proposal, the IT unit's annual operational budget will be allocated between business units using a method of apportionment which will be decided by the Finance Director in consultation with other directors. The IT unit will propose the charge-back method based on their understanding of the operational costs. The objective will be for the IT unit to 'break even' each year.

The Finance Director believes that the IT unit already has a good understanding of its operational costs and has therefore proposed that operational cost-recovery should be introduced at the start of the next financial year in five months' time.

Relating the question to the scenario

Looking at the scenario, is a question such as 'What would be the BEST next stage so that an informed decision may be made?' a valid one to ask?

The wording in the answers is generic enough to apply to the scenario. At the end of the scenario we have:

- The IT unit will propose the charge-back method based on their understanding of the operational costs. The objective will be for the IT unit to 'break even' each year.
- The Finance Director believes that the IT unit already has a good understanding of its operational costs and has therefore proposed that operational cost-recovery should be introduced at the start of the next financial year in five months' time.

The additional information in the question can be broken down as follows:

- The IT Director wants advice on sourcing the services currently provided by the IT group.
- The director wants to know if the IT group should...
  - Continue with its current services in future
  - Focus on its unique services by supporting and maintaining the business application and outsource the generic services

Scenario Five

An organization makes car parts in four factories in Europe. The Head Office is based in a large city close to one of the factories. All four factories have small administrative offices supporting local purchasing, sales and distribution. Shared Services such as Finance and Human Resources are based at the Head Office.

The customers are mainly comprised of the following three types:

- Large car manufacturers who have an ongoing requirement for standard parts, which are planned a long time in advance. This business is fairly secure, based upon relatively long term contracts, and brings in steady, low margin income.
- Car repairers who have a mixture of steady requirements and ad-hoc requirements, and require parts at relatively short notice. This type of business is based upon a mix of medium and short term contracts. There is strong competition for this business, and the level of service and responsiveness is seen as a differentiator.
- Development units of car manufacturers and car specialists who have specific one-off requirements for which they are willing to pay a high premium and to wait for delivery. Sometimes these arrangements lead to lucrative long term manufacturing

contracts. Customers are supplied by their local factory and the larger customers may be served by more than one factory.

Most of the organization's IT services are managed from the Head Office by a central IT unit. However, smaller local IT units serve each of the factories with infrastructure management and support. The IT services for the factories and sales run on distributed IT infrastructure and are supported locally.

The Chief Information Officer (CIO) has been asked by the Chief Executive Officer (CEO) to reduce the cost of IT across the whole organization, as part of an overall cost-cutting initiative. The CIO has decided to investigate a strategy of consolidation and centralization of the local IT infrastructure and IT services into the central IT unit to provide savings through economies of scale.

Relating the question to the scenario
Looking at the scenario, is a question such as 'What would be the BEST next stage so that an informed decision may be made?' a valid one to ask?

The wording in the answers is generic enough to apply to the scenario. At the end of the scenario we have:
• Based on business requirements, the IT unit now sees the need to formalize and improve other Service Management processes such as Service Portfolio Management, Service Catalogue Management and Service Level Management, but the CIO is unsure if it is a good idea to start this before basic performance measurements are in place.

The additional information in the question can be broken down as follows:
• The IT Director wants advice on sourcing the services currently provided by the IT group.
• The director wants to know if the IT group should...
  - Continue with its current services in future
  - Focus on its unique services by supporting and maintaining the business application and outsource the generic services

Although this scenario mentions that the IT unit has a good understanding of costs, it may be a good exercise to review the costs and compare against outsourcing options to demonstrate the competitiveness of IT.

This is an exercise which is often done in many organizations. Organizations are always looking at core competencies and non-core competencies and looking at better ways to reduce or control costs.

Scenario Six
A financial company's IT department has recently spent time and effort in improving the quality of IT services delivered to its customers and business users. The department is now considering the opportunities for significant investment to improve the resilience of the IT infrastructure, particularly to deliver and support critical business services. This investment is driven primarily by the need to prevent recurrence of several recent major outages affecting critical business services.

Business Relationship Managers (BRMs) within the IT department are responsible for interacting with customers within business units. The BRMs do not agree that improving resilience is the highest priority need at present. Based on feedback from customers they have identified other needs which should be fulfilled by a number of initiatives, some of them innovative. One such example is a Smartphone application that enables the prospective borrowers to compare different loan options and choose the one that best fits their needs. Another need is an automated service that retrieves credit reports from multiple credit rating agencies (credit bureaus) and automatically generates alerts based on rules or triggers set by account holders.

The Chief Information Officer (CIO) is uncertain which initiative creates the most value to the organization: the improvement of the infrastructure resilience or the innovative initiatives from the business units. The CIO's preference is to avoid major outages; however the CIO also realizes that the BRMs provide an important function to proactively identify the business needs and direction. The IT department also has limited resources and funding.

Relating the question to the scenario
Looking at the scenario, is a question such as 'What would be the BEST next stage so that an informed decision may be made?' a valid one to ask?

The wording in the answers is generic enough to apply to the scenario. At the end of the scenario we have:
• The Chief Information Officer (CIO) is uncertain which initiative creates the most value to the organization: the improvement of the infrastructure resilience or the innovative initiatives from the business units. The CIO's preference is to avoid major outages; however the CIO also realizes that the BRMs provide an important function

to proactively identify the business needs and direction. The IT department also has limited resources and funding.

The additional information in the question can be broken down as follows:

- The IT Director wants advice on sourcing the services currently provided by the IT group.
- The director wants to know if the IT group should...
  - Continue with its current services in future
  - Focus on its unique services by supporting and maintaining the business application and outsource the generic services

Improving the resilience of the infrastructure may involve outsourcing some or all of it. This question and scenario do go well together.

Scenario Seven

A manufacturer has decided to upgrade some of its legacy IT applications and become more service-oriented in its approach to fulfilling customer needs. The Inventory Control application was developed in-house many years ago along with its supporting infrastructure, systems and processes. It is used to maintain proper stocks, flows of raw materials and finished products through the manufacturing system. New business needs have emerged and the Chief Information Officer (CIO) would like to offer a new and improved solution in the form of an Inventory Management Service.

An internal design team will study the new business needs and translate them into specific attributes of the new service to be offered using the Software-as-a-Service (SaaS) delivery model. It is very important to determine what attributes provide the most value for customers in terms of utility and warranty, since availability and accessibility typically dominate perceptions in SaaS-based environments. Sales teams have become increasingly mobile in their work patterns. They are expected to pursue opportunities aggressively, generate and close new sales while on visits to their customers. Knowledge of production and shipping lead times is therefore valuable to have on mobile devices such as Smart-phones.

A design questionnaire has been developed to understand the value customers perceive from a set of six service attributes. Sixty key customers from Sales, Purchasing and Warehouse functions were asked to respond by characterizing each attribute with labels such as 'Must have', 'Should have' and Does not matter', organized into each of three business contexts: Sell, Buy and Store. The table below shows the responses to the questionnaire for two of the six service attributes. The numbers in the boxes indicate the number of customers who chose each label. Instances where a customer's response was ambiguous, ambivalent or contradictory were categorized as 'Questionable'.

Each attribute has certain cost implications over the lifecycle of the service, therefore an efficient trade-off must be made between them to have a service design that best meets customer needs while minimizing lifecycle costs.

ATTRIBUTE DESCRIPTION:	ATTRIBUTE #1: Stock Enquiry				ATTRIBUTE #2: Mobile Update			
	Inquire on Stock Levels using Interactive Voice Response (IVR) System				Push Alerts and Updates on Stock Levels to Mobile Devices and Laptops			
LABELS	Sell	Buy	Store	Total	Sell	Buy	Store	Total
Must have	4	1	5	10	7	4	2	13
Should have	5	2	8	15	10	10	4	24
Does not matter	4	6	3	13	2	6	9	17
Should NOT have	3	6	2	11	1	0	2	3
Must NOT have	2	5	0	7	0	0	1	1
Questionable	2	0	2	4	0	0	2	2
TOTAL	20	20	20	60	20	20	20	60

Relating the question to the scenario
Looking at the scenario, is a question such as 'What would be the BEST next stage so that an informed decision may be made?' a valid one to ask?

The wording in the answers is generic enough to apply to the scenario. At the end of the scenario we have:
• Each attribute has certain cost implications over the lifecycle of the service, therefore an efficient trade-off must be made between them to have a service design that best meets customer needs while minimizing lifecycle costs.

The additional information in the question can be broken down as follows:
• The IT Director wants advice on sourcing the services currently provided by the IT group.
• The director wants to know if the IT group should…
  - Continue with its current services in future
  - Focus on its unique services by supporting and maintaining the business application and outsource the generic services

This scenario is about new business requirements and the question is about doing internal or outsourcing some services. This organization should look at all possibilities regarding this new SaaS delivery model. Should it be done internally or by an external party? The question and the scenario do go well together.

Scenario Eight

A transport company operates within a major city. It comprises three divisions:
- Passenger Shuttles: This division has 35 vehicles used to shuttle passengers to and from the airport. During sporting and cultural events, these vehicles also provide transport from hotels and for residents in outlying areas.
- Freight Transport: This division has a fleet of 75 small cargo vans. They provide clearing and forwarding services from the airport; and are also contracted by a global courier company to provide local deliveries. They also distribute newspapers to hotels and newsstands.
- Taxis: This division maintains and leases 200 vehicles to licensed taxi drivers.

Every vehicle is equipped with:
- Global Positioning System (GPS) to enable drivers to navigate the city streets
- Satellite tracking systems to enable dispatchers to track their location. This helps the dispatchers schedule deliveries and passenger pick-ups, and provides protection against the theft of vehicles.
- Two-way radio communication to enable drivers to communicate with dispatchers
- A device to accept credit card payments

The Technology Department supports this technology and IT services including:
- Driver Dispatch software
- Financial Systems
- Driver Compensation
- Supplier Contract Management
- Vehicle Lease and Maintenance Tracking

Drivers and division managers have been complaining about the quality of service from the Technology Department. It appears that Technology Department staff believes that all services are used in the same way by all divisions. This has resulted in incorrect guidance on how to use services and significant business disruptions because incidents are often prioritized incorrectly. The Technology Director has initiated a project to clearly define each service and how each supports the business.

Relating the question to the scenario
Looking at the scenario, is a question such as 'What would be the BEST next stage so that an informed decision may be made?' a valid one to ask?

The wording in the answers is generic enough to apply to the scenario. At the end of the scenario we have:
- The Technology Director has initiated a project to clearly define each service and how each supports the business.

The additional information in the question can be broken down as follows:
- The IT Director wants advice on sourcing the services currently provided by the IT group.
- He wants to know if the IT group should…
  - Continue with its current services in future
  - Focus on its unique services by supporting and maintaining the business application and outsource the generic services

Similarly to Scenario Seven, this one is about business requirements. It wants to properly define the services and how each supports the business. Looking at providing the services internally versus an external provider may not be the first thing to do but it has to be done eventually. Assume you are at that stage. Can you still answer the question based on this scenario? Of course you can. The question and the scenario do go well together.

Summary
The point of this type of practice is primarily to recognize that the practices described in the core books are relevant to any organization. Of course, coming up with the best answer is nice but a candidate should focus instead on approaching a scenario as if it were a real assignment with the parameters provided. The parameters are along the following lines:
- You are a/the < insert role here >…
- The CIO wants you to <action verb here >…
- The business wants to < accomplish something >…

The major learning point here is that all activities need to be performed within an organization. All organizations have issues that need to be addressed, things that need to be changed, things that need to be improved, and things that are outsourced. The differences lie in the scale, magnitude and type of industry and organization.

Replace the name of the product being sold with the one your organization is selling. Replace the service/system/application name with one in your organization with similar issues. Imagine yourself in that situation. What should be done according to the practices describes in the core books? Although the question used for all scenarios may not be a perfect fit, such as not really be the first thing that should be done, eventually the topic of the question needs to be answered regardless of the scenario.

The work we all do in IT is not that different. The scale and the scope do vary of course. The point of this exercise is to demonstrate that these questions will have to be considered at some point and that the answers are portable from one organization to the next.

CHAPTER 11

Using answers and rationales for practice

The sample papers provide a third and final section, the answers and rationale. This section may be useful to understand the application of the concepts in a simulated situation. In this chapter we will look at how to use the question rationale to identify the concepts, how they are applied and how to extract the rationale from the core books.

There is no need to repeat this exercise too often so only one rationale (No. 1) from the Service Strategy Sample Paper 1 will be covered.

How to use the rationale

You will need:
- The sample paper
- The syllabus
- The appropriate core books

Do the following:
- Identify the subjects covered
- Identify the syllabus unit
- Look at the syllabus and identify the appropriate bullet within that unit
- Identify the book references section
- Identify which book sections to read
- Read the 'Application' section within the Bloom's section
- Read the appropriate book section
- Read the best answer and identify which part of the book was used for inspiration for the question
- Understand the best answer based on the Bloom's application, the syllabus, the book, and the question rationale sections
- Repeat for the second best, third best and distracter answers.

Yes there is work to do and yes, there is a need to consult all the appropriate documents. Is this so different than the work you do? No, it is not.

QUESTION	One		SCENARIO	One
Question rationale	This question focuses on the development of service potential and service management as a strategic asset by understanding market spaces and value creation principles.			
Most correct	D.	This answer is the most comprehensive as it recognizes the value that the internet access creates for students and also considers the cost justification of providing it. By treating internet access as a service in its own right, proper decisions can be made regarding costs and value creation. This answer also correctly identifies the relationship between market spaces, customers and services.		
Second best	C.	This is a reasonable answer as it recognizes the value potential of internet access for students. Providing an 'internet café' approach would enable better control over demand for the resources devoted to student internet access. It doesn't address the potential for developing the internet access facility as a service in its own right. Also the utility of wireless connectivity is taken away in the case of internet access from the café. Students may be able to do quick references and download lecture slides while they are in class. Answer C therefore does not fully explore the nature of demand for wireless access.		
Third best	B.	This is a solution that lacks any consideration of the possibilities of developing internet access for students. It has merit in the sense that it would result in a clearer setting of student expectations, but fails to consider the value creation possibilities.		
Distracter	A.	This is an incorrect answer as it incorrectly identifies the market spaces and fails to address any considerations of costs and risks. It also makes untested assumptions regarding the level of cost compared with customer satisfaction. Also the assumption that only the needs of external customers need to be taken into account is incorrect. Poorly performing administrative services can be just as damaging to the business (e.g. late billing)		
Syllabus unit / module supported	ITIL SL: SS03 Conducting Strategic Assessments			
Bloom's taxonomy testing level	Level 3 Applying – Use ideas, principles and theories in new, particular and concrete situations. Behavioral tasks at this level involve both knowing and comprehension and might include choosing appropriate procedures, applying principles, using an approach or identifying the selection of options. Application – The candidate must apply their knowledge of Demand Management and place this into the context of the scenario in order to determine the service potential and best choice for the organization depicted.			
Subjects covered:	Categories covered: Strategic analysis Service potential Demand Management			
Book section refs	SS 4.3 – Service strategy – Develop strategic assets SS 4.4 – Service strategy – Prepare for Execution			
Difficulty	Moderate			

<table>
<tr><td colspan="2">1. Identify the subject covered</td><td colspan="2">Categories covered:
Strategic analysis
Service potential
Demand Management</td></tr>
<tr><td colspan="2">2. Identify the syllabus unit</td><td colspan="2">SS03 Conducting Strategic Assessments</td></tr>
<tr><td colspan="2">3. Look at the syllabus and identify the appropriate bullet within that unit</td><td colspan="2">Strategic assets of an organization and their performance potential for serving particular customers or market spaces (internal or external)</td></tr>
<tr><td colspan="2">4. Identify the book references section</td><td colspan="2">SS 4.3 – Service strategy – Develop strategic assets
SS 4.4 – Service strategy – Prepare for Execution</td></tr>
<tr><td>5. Identify which book sections to read</td><td colspan="2">SS 4.3
4.3.1
4.3.2
4.3.2.1
4.3.2.2
4.3.2.3</td><td>SS 4.4
4.4.1
4.4.2
4.4.3
4.4.4
4.4.5
4.4.6
4.4.7
4.4.8
4.4.9
4.4.10</td></tr>
<tr><td colspan="2">6. Read the 'Application' section within the Bloom's section</td><td colspan="2">Application – The candidate must apply their knowledge of Demand Management and place this into the context of the scenario in order to determine the service potential and best choice for the organization depicted.</td></tr>
<tr><td colspan="2">7. Read the appropriate book section</td><td colspan="2">See '5' above</td></tr>
<tr><td colspan="2">8. Read the best answer and identify which part of the book was used for inspiration for the question</td><td colspan="2">This answer is the most comprehensive as it recognizes the value that the internet access creates for students and also considers the cost justification of providing it. By treating internet access as a service in its own right, proper decisions can be made about costs and value creation. This answer also correctly identifies the relationship between market spaces, customers and services.</td></tr>
<tr><td colspan="2">9. Understand the best answer based on the Bloom's application, the syllabus, the book, and the question rationale sections</td><td colspan="2"></td></tr>
<tr><td colspan="2">10. Repeat for the second best, third best and distracter answers.</td><td colspan="2"></td></tr>
</table>

Summary

Although a candidate may not agree totally with the explanations provided in the rationale document, the learning point is the BEST answer in this particular situation, based on the information provided in the scenario and the four choices available.

That's the key point. AMONG the four available choices, which one is the BEST? Since the applicability of the concepts is actually based on too many variables and the fact that no two organizations are the same, there can be no one CORRECT answer for ALL situations.

In our day-to-day activities within our organizations we are faced with the same dilemmas all the time. Given the particular situation, the resources available, the capabilities our organization possesses and the finite timeframe allocated, what is the BEST solution we can come up with?

In many situations, we know what SHOULD be done. However, given the limited resources and the fact we have often been in similar situations before, certain steps are either omitted or cut short. The more we skip those steps the more the rest becomes our common practices and eventually, they become the best we can do.

The framework brings us out of our comfort levels. It brings us back to the 'what should be done' in order to be successful. Typically, the most successful organizations are the ones who adhere to all the steps all the time. OK, let's agree to almost all the steps, almost all the time. You get the point.

Successful candidates are those capable of accepting that the BEST answer is based on the information provided. Successful candidates accept that other steps that may or should have been done before or as part of a more complete solution are simply not mentioned. Successful candidates accept the best answer may actually be incomplete. Successful candidates play the game and do not disparage the conditions imposed by the scenario and the question; they accept them.

Stop looking for what is not there. Stop asking 'but if the question had been about or if this information had been provided'. The question is not about what you want it to be and the information provided is the one you need to use. Play within the parameters imposed by the situation. That's all the examinations are doing. They put you in a particular situation with limited information and ask you to come up with the best choice given theses circumstances.

A few final words from the author

I would like to remind the reader as a potential examination candidate that it is ultimately up to them to put in the effort and get good results in their exams.

I (and a few other people) call this 'sweat equity'. Here is an example.

You do not get in better physical condition by purchasing a membership to a gym.
You do not get in better physical condition by purchasing trendy exercise wear.
You do not get in better physical condition by going to the gym.

You do get in better physical condition by properly utilizing the equipment in the gym.
You do get in better physical condition through multiple repetitions of an exercise.
You do get in better physical condition through multiple repetitions of multiple exercises.
You do get in better physical condition by practicing on a regular basis, at leas 3 times a week, for about an hour each visit.

The same logic applies for anyone wishing to become an expert in any field.
* *Purchase the books*
* *Read the books*
* *Re-read the books*
* *Consult the books*
* *Purchase education and training*
* *Attend the education and training courses and workshops*
* *Pay attention in class*
* *Avoid distractions such as emails, phone calls, and text messaging*
* *Ask questions – the only 'stupid question' is the one not asked*
* *Provide examples*
* *Do the homework*
* *In the evening, prepare for the following day*
* *Ensure you keep a good work/life balance*
* *Oh, and don't forget to have fun*

About the Accredited Training Organizations (ATO)

The syllabus is only a guide providing a list of the material to cover. Each ATO is free to present the material in the format and order they wish as long at they cover the entire syllabus. By the way, it is also up to the ATO to decide which diagrams to use or not.

The ATO must meet their EI's strict requirements regarding the organizational processes, the course material, the instructors, and the instructor notes. For intermediate level courses, instructors must have a minimum number of years of experience and hold both the ITIL Expert certification and the certification for the course they are teaching.

Of course, there are organizations offering online (computer-based) courses. The EIs do have specific evaluation criteria for theses types of courses as well.

Becoming an (ITIL) Expert

In order to be an expert in any field or discipline, one must put in effort and time; what people refer to at «sweat equity» or the «heavy lifting». One does not become an expert by attending an introductory class on a particular topic.

In the case of ITIL, read the books! Read the books! Read the books! Discuss the topics with others, make them you own, identify where they are in your organization, read blogs and whitepapers. You should attend a set of courses covering the entire spectrum of the framework. Look to the syllabuses/syllabi for details of what is covered in each course.

About the exams

Finally, the examiners do not go out of their way to «trick» people with a «nasty» examination scheme. There are no «trick» questions. There are no «trick» answers. There are no situations where the difference between the best answer and the second best answer is only one word or a misplaced comma.

If you firmly believe there are tricked questions and answers and that you can do a better job at writing exam scenarios, questions, answers and relevant rationales, please contact APMG and apply to become an examiner. Creating exam questions is not as easy as it seems.

About statistics

If you are looking for the number of people that have achieved a particular qualification, for example, the number of people who followed the Manager Bridge route versus the ITIL V3 route to become and ITIL Expert please contact your Examining Institute and/or APMG. They publish statistics on a regular basis.

Appendices

Owner, Publisher, and Accreditor

ORGANIZATION	ROLE	WEBSITE
OGC	Owner of ITIL	www.ogc.gov.uk
TSO	Official Publisher	www.tso.co.uk
APM Group Ltd	Accreditor	www.apmgroup.co.uk

The ITIL Accreditation Scheme
The APM Group Limited as the Official Accreditor is authorized to assess and license Examination Institutes (EIs) to administer ITIL qualification and accreditation activities.

Examination Institute Accreditation
All organizations approved by APM Group as EIs will be audited by independent auditors appointed by APM Group in accordance with the principles of international best practice standards. If the systems used by the applicant organizations are found to be in line with these guidelines, they will be granted permission to operate under the ITIL scheme and will also be offered a place on the qualifications board.

Under the contracts signed with APM Group, EIs are allowed to undertake the following activities:
* Approve training organizations through the standards and mechanisms audited and agreed by APM Group
* Administer examinations via those organizations they have approved using the standards and mechanisms agreed by APM Group.

Under the contracts signed with APM Group, EIs are not permitted to undertake any of the following activities –
* Amend approved ITIL syllabuses
* Develop their own ITIL examinations
* Develop products which may be perceived as competition to those within the ITIL scheme

- Offer training or consulting in ITIL in competition with those organizations they approve to do this
- Make any amendments to the pass mark agreed by the qualification board
- Issue trademark licenses to their approved organizations directly
- Outsource the running of their ITIL activities to any third party other than authorized examination agents, as agreed with the Accreditor.

Any Examination Institute can operate internationally.

Information about the Examining Institutes

Professional qualifications based on ITIL are offered by Examination Institutes (EIs). An EI is an organization accredited by the APM Group. EIs are permitted to operate an ITIL examination scheme through a network of Accredited Training Organizations (ATOs), and Accredited Trainers with Accredited materials. All EIs also have representation on the ITIL qualifications board, the governance and standards setting body for the ITIL scheme.

The Examination Institutes are listed below.

APMG-International http://www.apmg-uk.com/	

APMG-International specializes in the accreditation and certification of organizations, processes and people. APMG-International is an ITIL Examination Institute, which offers global accreditation and examination services for training providers.
Email: servicedesk@apmg-internantional.com

BCS-ISEB http://www.bcs.org/	iseb

The Information Systems Examination Board (BCS-ISEB) is a wholly owned subsidiary of the British Computer Society. BCS-ISEB provides industry recognized qualifications that measure competence, ability and performance in many areas of IT, including ITIL.
Email: isebenq@hq.bcs.org.uk

CSME http://www.csme.us/	

CSME has been working to promote IT professionalism in the US and the Americas for over half a decade. While it has been focused on ITIL to date, CSME is positioned to support all IT certification schemes that promote IT professionalism. CSME is committed to maintaining and advancing the integrity of the examination processes for all IT professional certifications. CSME does this while always putting customer service first.
Email: info@csme.us

DANSK IT http://www.dansk-it.dk/	

With more than 6,000 members DANSK IT is a leading interest organization for IT professionals in Denmark. The core activities evolve around member networks, conferences, courses, certification programs and IT political advice to the Danish government and its agencies. Founded in 1958, DANSK IT is among the first IT societies in the world.
Email: dansk-it@dansk-it.dk

DF Certifiering AB http://www.dfs.se/dfcertifiering/	DF CERTIFIERING AB

DF Certifiering AB (DFC), is a wholly owned subsidiary of Dataföreningen i Sverige, the Swedish Computer Society with 26 000 IT professionals as members in Sweden. DFC's role is to give accreditation to training providers and certify IT. DFC also provides products in the field of Information Security and self-assessing tests for e-Citizens.
Email: certifiering@dfs.se

EXIN http://www.exin-exams.com/	EXIN

The Examination Institute for Information Science in the Netherlands (EXIN) is a global, independent IT examination provider. EXIN establishes educational requirements and develops and organizes examinations and learning tracks in the field of IT.
Email: service@exin-exams.com

LCS http://www.loyalistexams.com/	

Loyalist Certification Services (LCS) delivers ITIL exams to training organizations around the world. Since 2001, LCS has delivered over 200,000 ITIL exams in many languages and locations. As an independent ITIL examination institute, LCS provides neutral information and is dedicated to maintaining the integrity of the exam process. Responsive...Reliable...Trusted.
Email: exams@loyalistexams.com

PEOPLECERT Group http://www.peoplecert.org/	PEOPLECERT GROUP

PEOPLECERT Group is a prominent personnel certification body that has issued to date more than 2.2 million certificates globally in a variety of certification schemes. Its schemes range from IT to Language assessment, including schemes from prestigious organizations such as ECDL Foundation, City & Guilds and many others. The integrity and reliability of the certification process is ensured by being accredited according to ISO17024 and certified according to ISO27001, ISO14001, ISO10002 and ISO9001.
Email: info@peoplecert.org

TÜV SÜD Akademie http://www.tuev-sued.de/	

The TÜV SÜD Group is well known for consulting, testing, certification and training on behalf of industry, trade and commerce, public institutions and private individuals. TÜV SÜD creates increased safety and added economic value by supporting the competitive strength of its customers through the world. TÜV SÜD Mission: Choose certainty. Add value.
Email: akd.it@tuev-sued.de

References

ITIL BOOKS

From TSO

TITLE	ISBN
Service Strategy	ISBN–10:0113310455
Service Design	ISBN–10:0113310471
Service Transition	ISBN–10:011331048X
Service Operation	ISBN–10:0113310463
Continual Service Improvement	ISBN–10:0113310498
Introduction to ITIL v3 Service Lifecycle	ISBN–13:9780113310616
ITIL Lifecycle Approach Based on ITIL V3 Suite 5 Management Guides	ISBN–13:9789087531089
Passing Your ITIL Foundation Exam	ISBN–13:9780113312061

From Van Haren Publishing

TITLE	ISBN
ITIL® V3 – A Pocket Guide	ISBN–13:9789087531027
Foundations of ITIL® V3	ISBN–13:9789087530570
ITIL® V3 Foundation Exam: The Study Guide	ISBN–13:9789087530693

Other titles suggested by the author

TITLE	AUTHOR(s)	ISBN
A Sense of Urgency	John P. Kotter	ISBN–10:1422179710 ISBN–13:9781422179710
Big Bucks	Ken Blanchard Sydney Sheldon	ISBN–10:0688170358 ISBN–13:9780688170356
Gung HO	Ken Blanchard Sydney Sheldon	ISBN–10:068815428X ISBN–13:9780688154288
Heart of change	John P. Kotter	ISBN–10:1578512549 ISBN-13:9781578512546

TITLE	AUTHOR(s)	ISBN
Helping People Win at Work: A Business Philosophy called "Don't Mark My Paper, Help Me Get an A"	Ken Blanchard Garry Ridge	ISBN–10:0137011717 ISBN–13:9780137011711
High Five	Ken Blanchard Sydney Sheldon	ISBN–10:0688170366 ISBN–13:9780688170363
Leadership & One Min Man: Increasing Effectiveness Through Situational Leadership	Ken Blanchard Drea Zigarmi Patricia Zigarmi	ISBN–10:0688039693 ISBN–13:9780688039691
Leading change	John P. Kotter	ISBN–10:0875847471 ISBN–13:9780875847474
Our Iceberg Is Melting: Changing and Succeeding Under Any Conditions	Holger Rathgeber John Kotter	ISBN–10:031236198X ISBN–13:9780312361983
Raving Fans	Ken Blanchard Sydney Sheldon	ISBN–10:0688123163 ISBN–13:9780688123161
The cookie thief	Kirk Weisler	www.morebetterbooks.com
The dog poop initiative	Kirk Weisler	www.morebetterbooks.com
The one minute manager	Ken Blanchard Spencer Johnson	ISBN–10:0688014291 ISBN–13:9780688014292
Whale Done! The Power of Positive Relationships	Ken Blanchard Thad Lacinak Chuck Tompkins	ISBN–10:074323538x ISBN–13:9780743235389
When Fish Fly: Lessons for Creating a Vital and Energized Workplace from the World Famous Pike Place Fish Market	John Yokoyama Joseph Michelli	ISBN–10:0739311565 ISBN–13:9780739311561
Who Killed Change?	Ken Blanchard	ISBN–10:0061778931 ISBN–13:9780061778933
Who moved my cheese?	Spencer Johnson	ISBN–10:0399144463 ISBN–13:9780399144462
Seven Habits Of Highly Effective People: Powerful Lessons in Personal Change	Stephen R. Covey	ISBN–10:0671708635 ISBN–13:9780671708634
The 12 Bad Habits That Hold Good People Back: Overcoming the Behavior Patterns That Keep You From Getting Ahead	James Waldroop Timothy Butler	ISBN–10:0385498500 ISBN–13:9780385498500
101 Things to do before you die	Richard Horne	ISBN–10:1582344930 ISBN–13:9781582344935
101 Things NOT to do before you die	Richard Horne	ISBN–10:0312357583 ISBN–13:9780312357580
How full is your bucket? Expanded anniversary edition	Tom Rath Donald O. Clifton	ISBN–10:1595620036 ISBN–13:9781595620033
ABC of ICT	Paul Wilkinson Jan Schilt	ISBN–13:9789087531409
Andragogy in Action: Applying Modern Principles of Adult Learning (Jossey-Bass Management Series)	Malcolm S. Knowles	ISBN-10: 0875896219 ISBN-13: 9780875896212

Some complementary frameworks, methodologies and standards

Public frameworks, methodologies, and standards are all relevant to Service Management. Some of the better-known ones are listed below, in alphabetical order of their organization

Carnegie Mellon University – Software Engineering Institute Carnegie Mellon
Capability Maturity Model Integration (CMMI®)
   http://www.sei.cmu.edu/cmmi/general/eSourcing

Capability Model for Service Providers (eSCM-SP™)
   http://itsqc.cmu.edu/models/escm-sp/index.asp

International Organization for Standardization (ISO)
IO/IEC 20000
ISO/IEC 27001
   www.iso.org

ISACA
Control Objectives for Information and related Technology (COBIT®)
Val IT
Risk IT
   www.isaca.org

Motorola
Six Sigma™
   www.motorola.com

Office of Government Commerce (OGC)
Managing Successful Programs®
Portfolio, Programme and Project Offices®
Portfolio, Programme, and Project Management Maturity Model®
Projects in Controlled Environments (PRINCE2®)

Management of Risk (M_o_R®)
ITIL®
www.best-management-practice.com

Project Management Institute (PMI)
Project Management Body of Knowledge (PMBOK®)
www.pmi.org

TeleManagement Forum (TM Forum)
Telecom Operations Map (eTOM®)
www.tmforum.org

Frameworks and methodologies for ITSM

The following list is taken from the book Framework for IT Management published by Van Haren Publishing (www.vanharen.net) in collaboration with itSMF International (www.itsmfi.org).

ISBN-13: 9789077212905

Quality Management & Business Process Management
TAM
EFQM
ISO9000
ISO/IEC 20000
TOGAF™
TickIT

ISO/IEC 19770
ISO/IEC 15504
ISO/IEC 27001

Quality Improvement
CMMI
Six Sigma
e-SCM-SP
IT Balanced Scorecard

IT Governance
As 8015
COBIT
M_o_R

Information Management
Generic framework for information management
ITIL
BiSL
ISPL
eTOM®
ASL

Project Management
MSP
PRINCE2™
PMBOK
IPMA Competence baseline

List of tables

List of figures

Glossary

The following glossary is a consolidation of the glossary found at the end of each of the five core books. This approach ensured that all terms are present. Of course, duplicate terms have been removed

TERM	DEFINITION
Acceptance	Formal agreement that an IT Service, Process, Plan, or other Deliverable is complete, accurate, Reliable and meets its specified Requirements. Acceptance is usually preceded by Evaluation or Testing and is often required before proceeding to the next stage of a Project or Process. See also Service Acceptance Criteria
Access Management	(Service Operation) The Process responsible for allowing Users to make use of IT Services, data, or other Assets. Access Management helps to protect the Confidentiality, Integrity and Availability of Assets by ensuring that only authorized Users are able to access or modify the Assets. Access Management is sometimes referred to as Rights Management or Identity Management.
Account Manager	(Service Strategy) A Role that is very similar to Business Relationship Manager, but includes more commercial aspects. Most commonly used when dealing with External Customers.
Accounting	(Service Strategy) The Process responsible for identifying actual costs of delivering IT Services, comparing these with budgeted costs, and managing variance from the Budget.
Accredited	Officially authorized to carry out a Role. For example, an Accredited body may be authorized to provide training or to conduct Audits.
Active Monitoring	(Service Operation) Monitoring of a Configuration Item or an IT Service that uses automated regular checks to discover the current status. See also Passive Monitoring.
Activity	A set of actions designed to achieve a particular result. Activities are usually defined as part of Processes or Plans, and are documented in Procedures.
Agreed Service Time	(Service Design) A synonym for Service Hours, commonly used in formal calculations of Availability. See also Downtime
Agreement	A Document that describes a formal understanding between two or more parties. An Agreement is not legally binding, unless it forms part of a Contract. See also Service Level Agreement, Operational Level Agreement

TERM	DEFINITION
Alert	(Service Operation) A warning that a threshold has been reached, something has changed, or a Failure has occurred. Alerts are often created and managed by System Management tools and are managed by the Event Management Process.
Analytical modeling	(Service Strategy) (Service Design) (Continual Service Improvement) A technique that uses mathematical Models to predict the behavior of a Configuration Item or IT Service. Analytical Models are commonly used in Capacity Management and Availability Management. See also Modeling.
Application	Software that provides Functions that are required by an IT Service. Each Application may be part of more than one IT Service. An Application runs on one or more Servers or Clients. See also Application Management, Application Portfolio
Application Management	(Service Design) (Service Operation) The Function responsible for managing Applications throughout their Lifecycle
Application Portfolio	(Service Design) A database or structured Document used to manage Applications throughout their Lifecycle. The Application Portfolio contains key Attributes of all Applications. The Application Portfolio is sometimes implemented as part of the Service Portfolio, or as part of the Configuration Management System
Application Sizing	(Service Design) The Activity responsible for understanding the Resource Requirements needed to support a new Application, or a major Change to an existing Application. Application Sizing helps to ensure that the IT Service can meet its agreed Service Level Targets for Capacity and Performance.
Architecture	(Service Design) The structure of a System or IT Service, including the Relationships of Components to each other and to the environment they are in. Architecture also includes the Standards and Guidelines that guide the design and evolution of the System.
Assembly	(Service Transition) A Configuration Item (CI) that is made up of a number of other CIs. For example a Server CI may contain CIs for CPUs, Disks, Memory, etc.; an IT Service CI may contain much Hardware, Software and other CIs. See also Build.
Assessment	Inspection and analysis to check whether a Standard or set of Guidelines is being followed, that Records are accurate, or that Efficiency and Effectiveness targets are being met. See also Audit.
Assessment	Inspection and analysis to check whether a Standard or set of Guidelines is being followed, that Records are accurate, or that Efficiency and Effectiveness targets are being met. See also Audit

TERM	DEFINITION
Asset	(Service Strategy) Any Resource or Capability. Assets of a Service Provider including anything that could contribute to the delivery of a Service. Assets can be one of the following types: Management, Organization, Process, Knowledge, People, Information, Applications, Infrastructure, and Financial Capital.
Asset Management	(Service Transition) Asset Management is the Process responsible for tracking and reporting the value and ownership of financial assets throughout their Lifecycle. Asset Management is part of an overall Service Asset and Configuration Management Process.
Asset Register	(Service Transition) A list of Assets that includes their ownership and value. Asset Management maintains the Asset Register.
Attribute	(Service Transition) A piece of information about a Configuration Item. Examples are: name, location, Version number, and cost. Attributes of CIs are recorded in the Configuration Management Database (CMDB). See also Relationship.
Audit	Formal inspection and verification to check whether a Standard or set of Guidelines is being followed, that Records are accurate, or that Efficiency and Effectiveness targets are being met. An Audit may be carried out by internal or external groups. See also Certification, Assessment.
Authority Matrix	See RACI.
Automatic Call Distribution (ACD)	(Service Operation) Use of Information Technology to direct an incoming telephone call to the most appropriate person in the shortest possible time. ACD is sometimes called Automated Call Distribution
Availability	(Service Design) Ability of a Configuration Item or IT Service to perform its agreed Function when required. Availability is determined by Reliability, Maintainability, Serviceability, Performance, and Security. Availability is usually calculated as a percentage. This calculation is often based on Agreed Service Time and Downtime. It is best practice to calculate Availability using measurements of the business output of the IT Service.
Availability Management	(Service Design) The Process responsible for defining, analyzing, Planning, measuring and improving all aspects of the Availability of IT Services. Availability Management is responsible for ensuring that all IT Infrastructure, Processes, Tools, Roles, etc. are appropriate for the agreed Service Level Targets for Availability.
Availability Management Information System (AMIS)	(Service Design) A virtual repository of all Availability Management data, usually stored in multiple physical locations. See also Service Knowledge Management System

TERM	DEFINITION
Availability Plan	(Service Design) A Plan to ensure that existing and future Availability Requirements for IT Services can be provided Cost Effectively
Back-out	See Remediation.
Backup	(Service Design) (Service Operation) Copying data to protect against loss of Integrity or Availability of the original.
Balanced scorecard	(Continual Service Improvement) A management tool developed by Drs. Robert Kaplan (Harvard Business School) and David Norton. A balanced scorecard enables a Strategy to be broken down into Key Performance Indicators. Performance against the KPIs is used to demonstrate how well the Strategy is being achieved. A balanced scorecard has four major areas, each of which has a small number of KPIs. The same four areas are considered at different levels of detail throughout the Organization.
Baseline	(Continual Service Improvement) A Benchmark used as a reference point. For example; An ITSM Baseline can be used as a starting point to measure the effect of a Service Improvement Plan; A Performance Baseline can be used to measure changes in Performance over the lifetime of an IT Service; A Configuration Management Baseline can be used to enable the IT infrastructure to be restored to a known Configuration if a Change or Release fails.
Benchmark	(Continual Service Improvement) The recorded state of something at a specific point in time. A Benchmark can be created for a Configuration, a Process, or any other set of data. For example, a benchmark can be used in Continual Service Improvement, to establish the current state for managing improvements; Capacity Management, to document performance characteristics during normal operations. See also Benchmarking, Baseline.
Benchmarking	(Continual Service Improvement) Comparing a Benchmark with a Baseline or with best practice. The term Benchmarking is also used to mean creating a series of Benchmarks over time, and comparing the results to measure progress or improvement.
Best practice	Proven Activities or Processes that have been successfully used by multiple Organizations. ITIL is an example of best practice.
Brainstorming	(Service Operation) A technique that helps a team to generate ideas. Ideas are not reviewed during the Brainstorming session, but at a later stage. Brainstorming is often used by Problem Management to identify possible causes
British Standards Institution (BSI)	The UK National Standards body, responsible for creating and maintaining British Standards. See www.bsiglobal.com for more information. See also ISO.

TERM	DEFINITION
Budget	A list of all the money an Organization or business unit plans to receive, and plans to pay out, over a specified period of time. See also Budgeting, Planning.
Budgeting	The Activity of predicting and controlling the spending of money. Consists of a periodic negotiation cycle to set future Budgets (usually annual) and the day-to-day monitoring and adjusting of current Budgets.
Build	(Service Transition) The Activity of assembling a number of Configuration Items to create part of an IT Service. The term Build is also used to refer to a Release that is authorized for distribution. For example Server Build or laptop Build. See also Configuration Baseline
Build Environment	(Service Transition) A controlled Environment where Applications, IT Services and other Builds are assembled prior to being moved into a Test or Live Environment.
Business	(Service Strategy) An overall corporate entity or Organization formed of a number of Business Units. In the context of ITSM, the term Business includes public sector and not-for-profit organizations, as well as companies. An IT Service Provider provides IT Services to a Customer within a Business. The IT Service Provider may be part of the same Business as its Customer (Internal Service Provider), or part of another Business (External Service Provider)
Business Capacity Management (BCM)	(Service Design) In the context of ITSM, Business Capacity Management is the Activity responsible for understanding future Business Requirements for use in the Capacity Plan. See also Service Capacity Management
Business Case	(Service Strategy) Justification for a significant item of expenditure. Includes information about costs, benefits, options, issues, Risks, and possible problems.
Business Continuity Management (BCM)	(Service Design) The business process responsible for managing Risks that could seriously affect the business. BCM safeguards the interests of key stakeholders, reputation, brand and value-creating activities. The BCM Process involves reducing Risks to an acceptable level and planning for the recovery of business processes should a disruption to the business occur. BCM sets the Objectives, Scope and Requirements for IT Service Continuity Management.
Business Continuity Plan (BCP)	(Service Design) A Plan defining the steps required to Restore Business Processes following a disruption. The Plan will also identify the triggers for Invocation, people to be involved, communications, etc. IT Service Continuity Plans form a significant part of Business Continuity Plans

TERM	DEFINITION
Business customer	(Service Strategy) A recipient of a product or a Service from the business. For example, if the business is a car manufacturer then the business customer is someone who buys a car.
Business Impact Analysis (BIA)	(Service Strategy) BIA is the Activity in Business Continuity Management that identifies Vital Business Functions and their dependencies. These dependencies may include Suppliers, people, other business processes, IT Services, etc. BIA defines the recovery requirements for IT Services. These requirements include Recovery Time Objectives, Recovery Point Objectives and minimum Service Level Targets for each IT Service.
Business objective	(Service Strategy) The Objective of a Business Process, or of the business as a whole. Business objectives support the Business Vision, provide guidance for the IT Strategy, and are often supported by IT Services.
Business operations	(Service Strategy) The day-to-day execution, monitoring and management of business processes.
Business perspective	(Continual Service Improvement) An understanding of the Service Provider and IT Services from the point of view of the business, and an understanding of the business from the point of view of the Service Provider.
Business process	A Process that is owned and carried out by the business. A business process contributes to the delivery of a product or Service to a business customer. For example, a retailer may have a purchasing Process that helps to deliver Services to its business customers. Many business processes rely on IT Services.
Business Relationship Management	(Service Strategy) The Process or Function responsible for maintaining a Relationship with the Business. Business Relationship Management usually includes: Managing personal Relationships with Business managers. Providing input to Service Portfolio Management. Ensuring that the IT Service Provider is satisfying the Business needs of the Customers This Process has strong links with Service Level Management
Business Relationship Manager (BRM)	(Service Strategy) A Role responsible for maintaining the Relationship with one or more Customers. This Role is often combined with the Service Level Manager Role. See also Account Manager.
Business service	An IT Service that directly supports a Business Process, as opposed to an infrastructure service, which is used internally by the IT Service Provider and is not usually visible to the business. The term business service is also used to mean a Service that is delivered to business customers by business units. For example, delivery of financial services to Customers of a bank, or goods to the Customers of a retail store. Successful delivery of business services often depends on one or more IT Services.

TERM	DEFINITION
Business Service Management (BSM)	(Service Strategy) (Service Design) An approach to the management of IT Services that considers the business processes supported and the business value provided. This term also means the management of business services delivered to business customers.
Business unit	(Service Strategy) A segment of the business that has its own Plans, Metrics, income and costs. Each business unit owns Assets and uses these to create value for Customers in the form of goods and Services.
Call	(Service Operation) A telephone call to the Service Desk from a User. A Call could result in an Incident or a Service Request being logged.
Call centre	(Service Operation) An Organization or business unit that handles large numbers of incoming and outgoing telephone calls. See also Service Desk.
Call Type	(Service Operation) A Category that is used to distinguish incoming requests to a Service Desk. Common call types are Incident, Service Request and Complaint.
Capability	(Service Strategy) The ability of an Organization, person, Process, Application, Configuration Item or IT Service to carry out an Activity. Capabilities are intangible Assets of an Organization. See also Resource.
Capability Maturity Model Integration (CMMI)	(Continual Service Improvement) Capability Maturity Model(r) Integration (CMMI) is a process improvement approach developed by the Software Engineering Institute (SEI) of Carnegie Melon University, US. CMMI provides organizations with the essential elements of effective processes. It can be used to guide process improvement across a project, a division, or an entire organization CMMI helps integrate traditionally separate organizational functions, set process improvement goals and priorities, provide guidance for quality processes, and provide a point of reference for appraising current processes. See www.sei.cmu.edu/cmmi for more information. See also Maturity.
Capacity	(Service Design) The maximum Throughput that a Configuration Item or IT Service can deliver whilst meeting agreed Service Level Targets. For some types of CI, Capacity may be the size or volume, for example a disk drive.
Capacity Management	(Service Design) The Process responsible for ensuring that the Capacity of IT Services and the IT infrastructure is able to deliver agreed Service Level Targets in a cost-effective and timely manner. Capacity Management considers all Resources required delivering the IT Service, and plans for short-, medium- and long-term business requirements.
Capacity Management Information System (CMIS)	(Service Design) A virtual repository of all Capacity Management data, usually stored in multiple physical locations. See also Service Knowledge Management System

TERM	DEFINITION
Capacity Plan	(Service Design) A Capacity Plan is used to manage the Resources required to deliver IT Services. The Plan contains scenarios for different predictions of Business demand, and costed options to deliver the agreed Service Level Targets
Capacity Planning	(Service Design) The Activity within Capacity Management responsible for creating a Capacity Plan.
Capital Expenditure (CAPEX)	(Service Strategy) The cost of purchasing something that will become a financial asset, for example computer equipment and buildings. The value of the Asset is Depreciated over multiple accounting periods.
Capital item	(Service Strategy) An Asset that is of interest to Financial Management because it is above an agreed financial value.
Capitalization	(Service Strategy) Identifying major cost as Capital, even though no Asset is purchased. This is done to spread the impact of the cost over multiple accounting periods. The most common example of this is software development, or purchase of a software license.
Category	A named group of things that have something in common. Categories are used to group similar things together. For example, Cost Types are used to group similar types of cost. Incident Categories are used to group similar types of Incident, CI Types are used to group similar types of Configuration Item.
Certification	Issuing a certificate to confirm Compliance to a Standard. Certification includes a formal Audit by an independent and Accredited body. The term Certification is also used to mean awarding a certificate to verify that a person has achieved a qualification.
Change	(Service Transition) The addition, modification or removal of anything that could have an effect on IT Services. The Scope should include all IT Services, Configuration Items, Processes, Documentation, etc.
Change Advisory Board (CAB)	(Service Transition) A group of people that advises the Change Manager in the Assessment, prioritization and scheduling of Changes. This board is usually made up of representatives from all areas within the IT Service Provider, representatives from the Business and Third Parties such as Suppliers
Change Case	(Service Operation) A technique used to predict the impact of proposed Changes. Change Cases use specific scenarios to clarify the scope of proposed Changes and to help with Cost Benefit Analysis. See also Use Case.
Change History	(Service Transition) Information about all changes made to a Configuration Item during its life. Change History consists of all those Change Records that apply to the CI

TERM	DEFINITION
Change Management	(Service Transition) The Process responsible for controlling the Lifecycle of all Changes. The primary objective of Change Management is to enable beneficial Changes to be made, with minimum disruption to IT Services.
Change Model	(Service Transition) A repeatable way of dealing with a particular Category of Change. A Change Model defines specific pre-defined steps that will be followed for a change of this Category. Change Models may be very simple, with no requirement for approval (e.g. Password Reset) or may be very complex with many steps that require approval (e.g. major software release). See also Standard Change, Change Advisory Board.
Change Record	(Service Transition) A Record containing the details of a Change. Each Change Record documents the Lifecycle of a single Change. A Change Record is created for every Request for Change that is received, even those that are subsequently rejected. Change Records should reference the Configuration Items that are affected by the Change. Change Records are stored in the Configuration Management System.
Change Request	See Request for Change.
Change Schedule	(Service Transition) A Document that lists all approved Changes and their planned implementation dates. A Change Schedule is sometimes called a Forward Schedule of Change, even though it also contains information about Changes that have already been implemented
Change Window	(Service Transition) A regular, agreed time when Changes or Releases may be implemented with minimal impact on Services. Change Windows are usually documented in SLAs
Charging	(Service Strategy) Requiring payment for IT Services. Charging for IT Services is optional, and many Organizations choose to treat their IT Service Provider as a Cost Centre.
Chronological Analysis	(Service Operation) A technique used to help identify possible causes of Problems. All available data about the Problem is collected and sorted by date and time to provide a detailed timeline. This can make it possible to identify which Events may have been triggered by others.
CI Type	(Service Transition) A Category that is used to Classify CIs. The CI Type identifies the required Attributes and Relationships for a Configuration Record. Common CI Types include: Hardware, Document, User, etc.
Classification	The act of assigning a Category to something. Classification is used to ensure consistent management and reporting. CIs, Incidents, Problems, Changes, etc. are usually classified.

TERM	DEFINITION
Client	A generic term that means a Customer, the business or a business customer. For example, Client Manager may be used as a synonym for Account Manager. The term client is also used to mean; A computer that is used directly by a User, for example a PC, Handheld Computer, or Workstation; The part of a Client-Server Application that the User directly interfaces with. For example an e-mail Client.
Closed	(Service Operation) The final Status in the Lifecycle of an Incident, Problem, Change, etc. When the Status is Closed, no further action is taken
Closure	(Service Operation) The act of changing the Status of an Incident, Problem, Change, etc. to Closed
COBIT	(Continual Service Improvement) Control Objectives for Information and related Technology (COBIT) provides guidance and best practice for the management of IT Processes. COBIT is published by the IT Governance Institute. See www.isaca.org for more information.
Code of Practice	A Guideline published by a public body or a Standards Organization, such as ISO or BSI. Many Standards consist of a Code of Practice and a Specification. The Code of Practice describes recommended best practice.
Cold Standby	See Gradual Recovery
Commercial Off-The-Shelf (COTS)	(Service Design) Application software or Middleware that can be purchased from a Third Party.
Compliance	Ensuring that a Standard or set of Guidelines is followed, or that proper, consistent accounting or other practices are being employed.
Component	A general term that is used to mean one part of something more complex. For example, a computer System may be a component of an IT Service; an Application may be a Component of a Release Unit. Components that need to be managed should be Configuration Items.
Component Capacity Management (CCM)	(Service Design) (Continual Service Improvement) The Process responsible for understanding the Capacity, Utilization, and Performance of Configuration Items. Data is collected, recorded and analyzed for use in the Capacity Plan. See also Service Capacity Management.
Component CI	(Service Transition) A Configuration Item that is part of an Assembly. For example, a CPU or Memory CI may be part of a Server CI
Component Failure Impact Analysis (CFIA)	(Service Design) A technique that helps to identify the impact of CI failure on IT Services. A matrix is created with IT Services on one edge and CIs on the other. This enables the identification of critical CIs (that could cause the failure of multiple IT Services) and of fragile IT Services (that have multiple Single Points of Failure)

TERM	DEFINITION
Computer Telephony Integration (CTI)	(Service Operation) Computer Telephony Integration (CTI) is a general term covering any kind of integration between computers and telephone Systems. It is most commonly used to refer to Systems where an Application displays detailed screens relating to incoming or outgoing telephone calls. See also Automatic Call Distribution, Interactive Voice Response.
Concurrency	A measure of the number of Users engaged in the same Operation at the same time
Confidentiality	(Service Design) A security principle that requires that data should only be accessed by authorized people.
Configuration	(Service Transition) A generic term, used to describe a group of Configuration Items that work together to deliver an IT Service, or a recognizable part of an IT Service. Configuration is also used to describe the parameter settings for one or more CIs.
Configuration Baseline	(Service Transition) A Baseline of a Configuration that has been formally agreed and is managed through the Change Management process. A Configuration Baseline is used as a basis for future Builds, Releases and Changes
Configuration Control	(Service Transition) The Activity responsible for ensuring that adding, modifying or removing a CI is properly managed, for example by submitting a Request for Change or Service Request
Configuration Identification	(Service Transition) The Activity responsible for collecting information about Configuration Items and their Relationships, and loading this information into the CMDB. Configuration Identification is also responsible for labeling the CIs themselves, so that the corresponding Configuration Records can be found
Configuration Item (CI)	(Service Transition) Any Component that needs to be managed in order to deliver an IT Service. Information about each CI is recorded in a Configuration Record within the Configuration Management System and is maintained throughout its Lifecycle by Configuration Management. CIs are under the control of Change Management. CIs typically include IT Services, hardware, software, buildings, people, and formal documentation such as Process documentation and SLAs
Configuration Management	(Service Transition) The Process responsible for maintaining information about Configuration Items required delivering an IT Service, including their Relationships. This information is managed throughout the Lifecycle of the CI. Configuration Management is part of an overall Service Asset and Configuration Management Process.

TERM	DEFINITION
Configuration Management Database (CMDB)	(Service Transition) A database used to store Configuration Records throughout their Lifecycle. The Configuration Management System maintains one or more CMDBs, and each CMDB stores attributes of CIs, and Relationships with other CIs.
Configuration Management System (CMS)	(Service Transition) A set of tools and databases that are used to manage an IT Service Provider's Configuration data. The CMS also includes information about Incidents, Problems, Known Errors, Changes and Releases; and may contain data about employees, Suppliers, locations, business units, Customers and Users. The CMS includes tools for collecting, storing, managing, updating, and presenting data about all Configuration Items and their Relationships. The CMS is maintained by Configuration Management and is used by all IT Service Management Processes. See also Configuration Management Database.
Configuration Record	(Service Transition) A Record containing the details of a Configuration Item. Each Configuration Record documents the Lifecycle of a single CI. Configuration Records are stored in a Configuration Management Database.
Configuration Structure	(Service Transition) The hierarchy and other Relationships between all the Configuration Items that comprise a Configuration.
Continual Service Improvement (CSI)	(Continual Service Improvement) A stage in the Lifecycle of an IT Service and the title of one of the Core ITIL publications. Continual Service Improvement is responsible for managing improvements to IT Service Management Processes and IT Services. The Performance of the IT Service Provider is continually measured and improvements are made to Processes, IT Services and IT Infrastructure in order to increase Efficiency, Effectiveness, and Cost Effectiveness. See also Plan-Do-Check-Act.
Continuous Availability	(Service Design) An approach or design to achieve 100% Availability. A Continuously Available IT Service has no planned or unplanned Downtime
Continuous Operation	(Service Design) An approach or design to eliminate planned Downtime of an IT Service. Note that individual Configuration Items may be down even though the IT Service is Available
Contract	A legally binding Agreement between two or more parties.
Contract Portfolio	(Service Strategy) A database or structured Document used to manage Service Contracts or Agreements between an IT Service Provider and their Customers. Each IT Service delivered to a Customer should have a Contract or other Agreement that is listed in the Contract Portfolio. See also Service Portfolio, Service Catalogue.

TERM	DEFINITION
Control	A means of managing a Risk, ensuring that a business objective is achieved, or ensuring that a Process is followed. Example Controls include Policies, Procedures, Roles, RAID, door locks, etc. A control is sometimes called a Countermeasure or safeguard. Control also means to manage the utilization or behavior of a Configuration Item, System or IT Service.
Control Objectives for Information and related Technology (COBIT)	See COBIT.
Control perspective	(Service Strategy) An approach to the management of IT Services, Processes, Functions, Assets, etc. There can be several different Control Perspectives on the same IT Service, Process, etc., allowing different individuals or teams to focus on what is important and relevant to their specific Role. Example Control Perspectives include Reactive and Proactive management within IT Operations, or a Lifecycle view for an Application Project team.
Core service	(Service Strategy) An IT Service that delivers basic Outcomes desired by one or more Customers. See also Supporting Service, Core service package.
Core service package (CSP)	(Service Strategy) A detailed description of a core service that may be shared by two or more Service Level Packages. See also Service Package.
Cost	The amount of money spent on a specific Activity, IT Service, or business unit. Costs consist of real cost (money), notional cost such as people's time, and Depreciation.
Cost Benefit Analysis	An Activity that analyses and compares the costs and the benefits involved in one or more alternative courses of action. See also Business Case, Return on Investment
Cost Centre	(Service Strategy) A business unit or Project to which costs are assigned. A Cost Centre does not charge for Services provided. An IT Service Provider can be run as a Cost Centre or a Profit Centre.
Cost Effectiveness	A measure of the balance between the Effectiveness and Cost of a Service, Process or activity. A Cost Effective Process is one that achieves its Objectives at minimum Cost. See also KPI, Return on Investment, Value for Money
Cost Element	(Service Strategy) The middle level of category to which costs are assigned in Budgeting and Accounting. The highest-level category is Cost Type. For example a Cost Type of 'people' could have cost elements of payroll, staff benefits, expenses, training, overtime, etc. cost elements can be further broken down to give Cost Units. For example the cost element 'expenses' could include Cost Units of Hotels, Transport, Meals, etc.
Cost Management	(Service Strategy) A general term that is used to refer to Budgeting and Accounting, sometimes used as a synonym for Financial Management.

TERM	DEFINITION
Cost Type	(Service Strategy) The highest level of category to which costs are assigned in Budgeting and Accounting. For example hardware, software, people, accommodation, external and Transfer. See also Cost element, Cost Unit.
Cost Unit	(Financial Management) The lowest level of category to which costs are assigned, Cost Units are usually things that can be easily counted (e.g. staff numbers, software licenses) or things easily measured (e.g. CPU usage, Electricity consumed). Cost Units are included within cost elements. For example a cost element of 'expenses' could include Cost Units of Hotels, Transport, Meals, etc. See also Cost Type.
Countermeasure	Can be used to refer to any type of Control. The term Countermeasure is most often used when referring to measures that increase Resilience, Fault Tolerance or Reliability of an IT Service
Course Corrections	Changes made to a Plan or Activity that has already started to ensure that it will meet its Objectives. Course corrections are made as a result of Monitoring progress.
Crisis Management	(IT Service Continuity Management) Crisis Management is the Process responsible for managing the wider implications of Business Continuity. A Crisis Management team is responsible for Strategic issues such as managing media relations and shareholder confidence, and decides when to invoke Business Continuity Plans
Critical success factor (CSF)	Something that must happen if a Process, Project, Plan, or IT Service is to succeed. KPIs are used to measure the achievement of each CSF. For example a CSF of 'protect IT Services when making Changes' could be measured by KPIs such as 'percentage reduction of unsuccessful Changes', 'percentage reduction in Changes causing Incidents', etc.
Culture	A set of values that is shared by a group of people, including expectations about how people should behave, their ideas, beliefs, and practices. See also Vision.
Customer	Someone who buys goods or Services. The Customer of an IT Service Provider is the person or group that defines and agrees the Service Level Targets. The term Customers is also sometimes informally used to mean Users, for example 'this is a Customer-focused Organization'.
Customer Portfolio	(Service Strategy) A database or structured Document used to record all Customers of the IT Service Provider. The Customer Portfolio is the Business Relationship Manager's view of the Customers who receive Services from the IT Service Provider. See also Contract Portfolio, Service Portfolio.

TERM	DEFINITION
Dashboard	(Service Operation) A graphical representation of overall IT Service Performance and Availability. Dashboard images may be updated in real-time, and can also be included in management reports and web pages. Dashboards can be used to support Service Level Management, Event Management or Incident Diagnosis
Data-to-Information-to-Knowledge-to- Wisdom (DIKW)	A way of understanding the relationships between data, information, knowledge, and wisdom. DIKW shows how each of these builds on the others.
Definitive Media Library (DML)	(Service Transition) One or more locations in which the definitive and approved versions of all software Configuration Items are securely stored. The DML may also contain associated CIs such as licenses and documentation. The DML is a single logical storage area even if there are multiple locations. All software in the DML is under the control of Change and Release Management and is recorded in the Configuration Management System. Only software from the DML is acceptable for use in a Release.
Deliverable	Something that must be provided to meet a commitment in a Service Level Agreement or a Contract. Deliverable is also used in a more informal way to mean a planned output of any Process.
Demand Management	Activities that understand and influence Customer demand for Services and the provision of Capacity to meet these demands. At a Strategic level Demand Management can involve analysis of patterns of business activity and User Profiles. At a tactical level it can involve use of Differential Charging to encourage Customers to use IT Services at less busy times. See also Capacity Management.
Deming Cycle	See Plan-Do-Check-Act.
Dependency	The direct or indirect reliance of one Process or Activity on another.
Deployment	(Service Transition) The Activity responsible for movement of new or changed hardware, software, documentation, Process, etc. to the Live Environment. Deployment is part of the Release and Deployment Management Process.
Depreciation	(Service Strategy) A measure of the reduction in value of an Asset over its life. This is based on wearing out, consumption or other reduction in the useful economic value.
Design	(Service Design) An Activity or Process that identifies Requirements and then defines a solution that is able to meet these Requirements. See also Service Design.

TERM	DEFINITION
Detection	(Service Operation) A stage in the Incident Lifecycle. Detection results in the Incident becoming known to the Service Provider. Detection can be automatic, or can be the result of a user logging an Incident.
Development	(Service Design) The Process responsible for creating or modifying an IT Service or Application. Also used to mean the Role or group that carries out Development work.
Development Environment	(Service Design) An Environment used to create or modify IT Services or Applications. Development Environments are not typically subjected to the same degree of control as Test Environments or Live Environments. See also Development
Diagnosis	(Service Operation) A stage in the Incident and Problem Lifecycles. The purpose of Diagnosis is to identify a Workaround for an Incident or the Root Cause of a Problem.
Diagnostic Script	(Service Operation) A structured set of questions used by Service Desk staff to ensure they ask the correct questions, and to help them Classify, Resolve and assign Incidents. Diagnostic Scripts may also be made available to Users to help them diagnose and resolve their own Incidents.
Differential Charging	A technique used to support Demand Management by charging different amounts for the same IT Service Function at different times
Direct cost	(Service Strategy) A cost of providing an IT Service which can be allocated in full to a specific Customer, Cost Centre, Project, etc. For example, the cost of providing non-shared servers or software licenses. See also Indirect Cost.
Directory service	(Service Operation) An Application that manages information about IT infrastructure available on a network, and corresponding User access Rights.
Document	Information in readable form. A Document may be paper or electronic. For example, a Policy statement, Service Level Agreement, Incident Record, diagram of computer room layout. See also Record.
Document	Information in readable form. A Document may be paper or electronic. For example, a Policy statement, Service Level Agreement, Incident Record, diagram of computer room layout. See also Record.
Downtime	(Service Design) (Service Operation) The time when a Configuration Item or IT Service is not Available during its Agreed Service Time. The Availability of an IT Service is often calculated from Agreed Service Time and Downtime.
Driver	Something that influences Strategy, Objectives or Requirements. For example, new legislation or the actions of competitors.

TERM	DEFINITION
Early Life Support	(Service Transition) Support provided for a new or Changed IT Service for a period of time after it is Released. During Early Life Support the IT Service Provider may review the KPIs, Service Levels and Monitoring Thresholds, and provide additional Resources for Incident and Problem Management.
Economies of scale	(Service Strategy) The reduction in average cost that is possible from increasing the usage of an IT Service or Asset. See also Economies of scope.
Economies of scope	(Service Strategy) The reduction in cost that is allocated to an IT Service by using an existing Asset for an additional purpose. For example, delivering a new IT Service from existing IT infrastructure. See also Economies of scale.
Effectiveness	(Continual Service Improvement) A measure of whether the Objectives of a Process, Service or Activity have been achieved. An Effective Process or activity is one that achieves its agreed Objectives.
Efficiency	(Continual Service Improvement) A measure of whether the right amount of resources have been used to deliver a Process, Service or Activity. An Efficient Process achieves its Objectives with the minimum amount of time, money, people or other resources.
Emergency Change	(Service Transition) A Change that must be introduced as soon as possible. For example, to resolve a Major Incident or implement a Security patch. The Change Management Process will normally have a specific Procedure for handling Emergency Changes. See also Emergency Change Advisory Board (ECAB).
Emergency Change Advisory Board (ECAB)	(Service Transition) A sub-set of the Change Advisory Board that makes decisions about high-impact Emergency Changes. Membership of the ECAB may be decided at the time a meeting is called, and depends on the nature of the Emergency Change.
Environment	(Service Transition) A subset of the IT infrastructure that is used for a particular purpose. For example: Live Environment, Test Environment, and Build Environment. It is possible for multiple Environments to share a Configuration Item, for example Test and Live Environments may use different partitions on a single mainframe computer. Also used in the term Physical Environment to mean the accommodation, air conditioning, power system, etc. Environment is also used as a generic term to mean the external conditions that influence or affect something.
Error	(Service Operation) A design flaw or malfunction that causes a Failure of one or more Configuration Items or IT Services. A mistake made by a person or a faulty Process that affects a CI or IT Service is also an Error.

TERM	DEFINITION
Escalation	(Service Operation) An Activity that obtains additional Resources when these are needed to meet Service Level Targets or Customer expectations. Escalation may be needed within any IT Service Management Process, but is most commonly associated with Incident Management, Problem Management and the management of Customer complaints. There are two types of Escalation: Functional Escalation and Hierarchic Escalation.
eSourcing Capability Model for Service Providers (eSCM-SP)	(Service Strategy) A framework to help IT Service Providers develop their IT Service Management Capabilities from a Service Sourcing perspective. eSCM-SP was developed by Carnegie Mellon University, US.
Estimation	The use of experience to provide an approximate value for a Metric or cost. Estimation is also used in Capacity and Availability Management as the cheapest and least accurate Modeling method.
Evaluation	(Service Transition) The Process responsible for assessing a new or Changed IT Service to ensure that Risks have been managed and to help determine whether to proceed with the Change. Evaluation is also used to mean comparing an actual Outcome with the intended Outcome, or comparing one alternative with another.
Event	(Service Operation) A change of state that has significance for the management of a Configuration Item or IT Service. The term Event is also used to mean an Alert or notification created by any IT Service, Configuration Item or Monitoring tool. Events typically require IT Operations personnel to take actions, and often lead to Incidents being logged.
Event Management	(Service Operation) The Process responsible for managing Events throughout their Lifecycle. Event Management is one of the main Activities of IT Operations.
Exception Report	A Document containing details of one or more KPIs or other important targets that have exceeded defined Thresholds. Examples include SLA targets being missed or about to be missed, and a Performance Metric indicating a potential Capacity problem
Expanded Incident Lifecycle	(Availability Management) Detailed stages in the Lifecycle of an Incident. The stages are Detection, Diagnosis, Repair, Recovery, and Restoration. The Expanded Incident Lifecycle is used to help understand all contributions to the Impact of Incidents and to Plan how these could be controlled or reduced
External Customer	A Customer who works for a different Business to the IT Service Provider. See also External Service Provider.
External Metric	A Metric that is used to measure the delivery of IT Service to a Customer. External Metrics are usually defined in SLAs and reported to Customers. See also Internal Metric.

TERM	DEFINITION
External Service Provider	(Service Strategy) An IT Service Provider that is part of a different Organization from its Customer. An IT Service Provider may have both Internal Customers and External Customers.
External Sourcing	See Outsourcing
Facilities Management	(Service Operation) The Function responsible for managing the physical Environment where the IT Infrastructure is located. Facilities Management includes all aspects of managing the physical Environment, for example power and cooling, building Access Management, and environmental Monitoring
Failure	(Service Operation) Loss of ability to Operate to Specification, or to deliver the required output. The term Failure may be used when referring to IT Services, Processes, Activities, Configuration Items, etc. A Failure often causes an Incident.
Failure Modes and Effects Analysis (FMEA)	An approach to assessing the potential Impact of Failures. FMEA involves analyzing what would happen after Failure of each Configuration Item, all the way up to the effect on the business. FMEA is often used in Information Security Management and in IT Service Continuity Planning.
Fast Recovery	(Service Design) A Recovery Option that is also known as Hot Standby. Provision is made to Recover the IT Service in a short period of time: typically less than 24 hours. Fast Recovery typically uses a dedicated Fixed Facility with computer Systems, and software configured ready to run the IT Services. Immediate Recovery may take up to 24 hours if there is a need to Restore data from Backups.
Fault	See Error.
Fault tolerance	(Service Design) The ability of an IT Service or Configuration Item to continue to Operate correctly after Failure of a Component part.
Fault Tree Analysis (FTA)	(Service Design) (Continual Service Improvement) A technique that can be used to determine the chain of events that leads to a Problem. Fault Tree Analysis represents a chain of events using Boolean notation in a diagram
Financial Management	(Service Strategy) The Function and Processes responsible for managing an IT Service Provider's Budgeting, Accounting and Charging Requirements.
First-line Support	(Service Operation) The first level in a hierarchy of Support Groups involved in the resolution of Incidents. Each level contains more specialist skills, or has more time or other resources. See also Escalation.
Fishbone Diagram	See Ishikawa Diagram.

TERM	DEFINITION
Fit for purpose	An informal term used to describe a Process, Configuration Item, IT Service, etc. that is capable of meeting its objectives or Service Levels. Being fit for purpose requires suitable design, implementation, control and maintenance.
Fixed cost	(Service Strategy) A cost that does not vary with IT Service usage. For example the cost of Server hardware. See also Variable Cost.
Follow the Sun	(Service Operation) A methodology for using Service Desks and Support Groups around the world to provide seamless 24 * 7 Service. Calls, Incidents, Problems and Service Requests are passed between groups in different time zones.
Follow the Sun	(Service Operation) A methodology for using Service Desks and Support Groups around the world to provide seamless 24/7 Service. Calls, Incidents, Problems and Service Requests are passed between groups in different time zones.
Fulfillment	Performing Activities to meet a need or Requirement. For example, by providing a new IT Service, or meeting a Service Request.
Function	A team or group of people and the tools they use to carry out one or more Processes or Activities. For example the Service Desk. The term Function also has two other meanings; An intended purpose of a Configuration Item, Person, Team, Process, or IT Service. For example one Function of an e-mail Service may be to store and forward outgoing mails, one Function of a business process may be to dispatch goods to Customers.; To perform the intended purpose correctly, 'The computer is Functioning'.
Functional Escalation	(Service Operation) Transferring an Incident, Problem or Change to a technical team with a higher level of expertise to assist in an Escalation.
Gap Analysis	(Continual Service Improvement) An Activity that compares two sets of data and identifies the differences. Gap Analysis is commonly used to compare a set of Requirements with actual delivery.
Governance	Ensuring that Policies and Strategy are actually implemented, and that required Processes are correctly followed. Governance includes defining Roles and responsibilities, measuring and reporting, and taking actions to resolve any issues identified.
Gradual Recovery	(Service Design) A Recovery Option that is also known as Cold Standby. Provision is made to Recover the IT Service in a period of time greater than 72 hours. Gradual Recovery typically uses a Portable or Fixed Facility that has environmental support and network cabling, but no computer Systems. The hardware and software are installed as part of the IT Service Continuity Plan

TERM	DEFINITION
Guideline	A Document describing best practice, which recommends that which should be done. Compliance with a guideline is not normally enforced. See also Standard.
Help desk	(Service Operation) A point of contact for Users to log Incidents. A help desk is usually more technically focused than a Service Desk and does not provide a Single Point of Contact for all interaction. The term help desk is often used as a synonym for Service Desk.
Hierarchic Escalation	(Service Operation) Informing or involving more senior levels of management to assist in an Escalation.
High Availability	(Service Design) An approach or design that minimizes or hides the effects of Configuration Item Failure on the users of an IT Service. High Availability solutions are designed to achieve an agreed level of Availability and make use of techniques such as fault tolerance, Resilience and Fast Recovery to reduce the number of Incidents, and the Impact of Incidents.
Hot Standby	See Fast Recovery or Immediate Recovery.
Identity	(Service Operation) A unique name that is used to identify a User, person or Role. The Identity is used to grant Rights to that User, person, or Roles. Example identities might be the username SmithJ or the Role 'Change manager'.
Immediate Recovery	(Service Design) A Recovery Option that is also known as Hot Standby. Provision is made to Recover the IT Service with no loss of Service. Immediate Recovery typically uses Mirroring, Load Balancing and Split Site technologies.
Impact	(Service Operation) (Service Transition) A measure of the effect of an Incident, Problem or Change on business processes. Impact is often based on how Service Levels will be affected. Impact and Urgency are used to assign Priority.
Incident	(Service Operation) An unplanned interruption to an IT Service or reduction in the Quality of an IT Service. Failure of a Configuration Item that has not yet affected Service is also an Incident. For example Failure of one disk from a mirror set.
Incident Management	(Service Operation) The Process responsible for managing the Lifecycle of all Incidents. The primary Objective of Incident Management is to return the IT Service to Customers as quickly as possible.
Incident Record	(Service Operation) A Record containing the details of an Incident. Each Incident record documents the Lifecycle of a single Incident

TERM	DEFINITION
Indirect cost	(Service Strategy) A cost of providing an IT Service, which cannot be allocated in full to a specific customer. For example, the Cost of providing shared Servers or software licenses. Also known as Overhead. See also Direct cost.
Information Security Management (ISM)	(Service Design) The Process that ensures the Confidentiality, Integrity and Availability of an Organization's Assets, information, data and IT Services. Information Security Management usually forms part of an Organizational approach to Security Management that has a wider scope than the IT Service Provider, and includes handling of paper, building access, phone calls, etc., for the entire Organization.
Information Security Management System (ISMS)	(Service Design) The framework of Policy, Processes, Standards, Guidelines and tools that ensures an Organization can achieve its Information Security Management Objectives
Information Security Policy	(Service Design) The Policy that governs the Organization's approach to Information Security Management
Information Technology (IT)	The use of technology for the storage, communication or processing of information. The technology typically includes computers, telecommunications, Applications and other software. The information may include business data, voice, images, video, etc. Information Technology is often used to support business processes through IT Services.
Infrastructure service	An IT Service that is not directly used by the business, but is required by the IT Service Provider so they can provide other IT Services. For example directory services, naming services, or communication services.
Infrastructure Service	An IT Service that is not directly used by the Business, but is required by the IT Service Provider so they can provide other IT Services. For example directory services, naming services, or communication services.
Insourcing	See Internal Sourcing
Integrity	(Service Design) A security principle that ensures data and Configuration Items are modified only by authorized personnel and Activities. Integrity considers all possible causes of modification, including software and hardware Failure, environmental Events, and human intervention.
Interactive Voice Response (IVR)	(Service Operation) A form of Automatic Call Distribution that accepts User input, such as key presses and spoken commands, to identify the correct destination for incoming Calls.

TERM	DEFINITION
Intermediate Recovery	(Service Design) A Recovery Option that is also known as Warm Standby. Provision is made to Recover the IT Service in a period of time between 24 and 72 hours. Intermediate Recovery typically uses a shared Portable or Fixed Facility that has Computer Systems and Network Components. The hardware and software will need to be configured, and data will need to be restored, as part of the IT Service Continuity Plan
Internal Customer	A Customer who works for the same Business as the IT Service Provider. See also Internal Service Provider, External Customer.
Internal Metric	A Metric that is used within the IT Service Provider to Monitor the Efficiency, Effectiveness or Cost Effectiveness of the IT Service Provider's internal Processes. Internal Metrics are not normally reported to the Customer of the IT Service. See also External Metric.
Internal Rate of Return (IRR)	(Service Strategy) A technique used to help make decisions about capital expenditure. IRR calculates a figure that allows two or more alternative investments to be compared. A larger IRR indicates a better investment. See also Net Present Value, Return on Investment.
Internal service provider	(Service Strategy) An IT Service Provider that is part of the same Organization as its Customer. An IT Service Provider may have both Internal Customers and External Customers. See also Type I Service Provider, Type II Service Provider.
Internal Sourcing	(Service Strategy) Using an Internal Service Provider to manage IT Services. See also Service Sourcing, Type I Service Provider, and Type II Service Provider.
International Organization for Standardization (ISO)	The International Organization for Standardization (ISO) is the world's largest developer of Standards. ISO is a nongovernmental organization that is a network of the national standards institutes of 156 countries. See www.iso.org for further information about ISO.
International Standards Organization	See International Organization for Standardization (ISO).
Internet Service Provider (ISP)	An External Service Provider that provides access to the Internet. Most ISPs also provide other IT Services such as web hosting.
Invocation	(Service Design) Initiation of the steps defined in a plan. For example initiating the IT Service Continuity Plan for one or more IT Services.
Ishikawa Diagram	(Service Operation) (Continual Service Improvement) A technique that helps a team to identify all the possible causes of a Problem. Originally devised by Kaoru Ishikawa, the output of this technique is a diagram that looks like a fishbone.

TERM	DEFINITION
ISO 9000	A generic term that refers to a number of international Standards and Guidelines for Quality Management Systems. See www.iso.org for more information. See also ISO.
ISO 9001	An international Standard for Quality Management Systems. See also ISO 9000, Standard
ISO/IEC 17799	(Continual Service Improvement) ISO Code of Practice for Information Security Management. See also Standard.
ISO/IEC 20000	ISO Specification and Code of Practice for IT Service Management. ISO/IEC 20000 is aligned with ITIL best practice.
ISO/IEC 27001	(Service Design) (Continual Service Improvement) ISO Specification for Information Security Management. The corresponding Code of Practice is ISO/IEC 17799. See also Standard.
IT infrastructure	All of the hardware, software, networks, facilities, etc. that are required to develop, Test, deliver, Monitor, Control or support IT Services. The term IT infrastructure includes all of the Information Technology but not the associated people, Processes and documentation.
IT Operations	(Service Operation) Activities carried out by IT Operations Control, including Console Management, Job Scheduling, Backup and Restore, and Print and Output Management. IT Operations is also used as a synonym for Service Operation.
IT Operations Control	(Service Operation) The Function responsible for Monitoring and Control of the IT Services and IT Infrastructure. See also Operations Bridge.
IT Operations Management	(Service Operation) The Function within an IT Service Provider that performs the daily Activities needed to manage IT Services and the supporting IT infrastructure. IT Operations Management includes IT Operations Control and Facilities Management.
IT Service	A Service provided to one or more Customers by an IT Service Provider. An IT Service is based on the use of Information Technology and supports the Customer's business processes. An IT Service is made up from a combination of people, Processes and technology and should be defined in a Service Level Agreement.
IT Service Continuity Management (ITSCM)	(Service Design) The Process responsible for managing Risks that could seriously affect IT Services. ITSCM ensures that the IT Service Provider can always provide minimum agreed Service Levels, by reducing the Risk to an acceptable level and Planning for the Recovery of IT Services. ITSCM should be designed to support Business Continuity Management

TERM	DEFINITION
IT Service Continuity Plan	(Service Design) A Plan defining the steps required Recovering one or more IT Services. The Plan will also identify the triggers for Invocation, people to be involved, communications, etc. The IT Service Continuity Plan should be part of a Business Continuity Plan
IT Service Management (ITSM)	The implementation and management of Quality IT Services that meet the needs of the business. IT Service Management is performed by IT Service Providers through an appropriate mix of people, Process and Information Technology. See also Service Management.
IT Service Management Forum (itSMF)	The IT Service Management Forum is an independent Organization dedicated to promoting a professional approach to IT Service Management. The itSMF is a not-for-profit membership Organization with representation in many countries around the world (itSMF Chapters). The itSMF and its membership contribute to the development of ITIL and associated IT Service Management Standards.
IT Service Provider	(Service Strategy) A Service Provider that provides IT Services to Internal Customers or External Customers.
IT Steering Group (ISG)	A formal group that is responsible for ensuring that Business and IT Service Provider Strategies and Plans are closely aligned. An IT Steering Group includes senior representatives from the Business and the IT Service Provider
ITIL	A set of best practice guidance for IT Service Management. ITIL is owned by the OGC and consists of a series of publications giving guidance on the provision of Quality IT Services, and on the Processes and facilities needed to support them. See www.itil.co.uk for more information.
Job Description	A Document that defines the Roles, responsibilities, skills and knowledge required by a particular person. One Job Description can include multiple Roles, for example the Roles of Configuration Manager and Change Manager may be carried out by one person
Job Scheduling	(Service Operation) Planning and managing the execution of software tasks that are required as part of an IT Service. Job Scheduling is carried out by IT Operations Management, and is often automated using software tools that run batch or online tasks at specific times of the day, week, month or year.
Kano Model	Service Strategy) A Model developed by Noriaki Kano that is used to help understand Customer preferences. The Kano Model considers attributes of an IT Service grouped into areas such as basic factors, excitement factors, performance factors, etc.
Kepner & Tregoe Analysis	(Service Operation) (Continual Service Improvement) A structured approach to Problem solving. The Problem is analyzed in terms of what, where, when and extent. Possible causes are identified. The most probable cause is tested. The true cause is verified.

TERM	DEFINITION
Key Performance Indicator (KPI)	(Service Design) (Continual Service Improvement) A Metric that is used to help manage a Process, IT Service or Activity. Many Metrics may be measured, but only the most important of these are defined as KPIs and used to actively manage and report on the Process, IT Service or Activity. KPIs should be selected to ensure that Efficiency, Effectiveness, and Cost Effectiveness are all managed. See also Critical Success Factor
Knowledge Base	(Service Transition) A logical database containing the data used by the Service Knowledge Management System
Knowledge Management	(Service Transition) The Process responsible for gathering, analyzing, storing and sharing knowledge and information within an Organization. The primary purpose of Knowledge Management is to improve Efficiency by reducing the need to rediscover knowledge. See also Data-to-Information-to-Knowledge-to-Wisdom, Service Knowledge Management System.
Known Error	(Service Operation) A Problem that has a documented Root Cause and a Workaround. Known Errors are created and managed throughout their Lifecycle by Problem Management. Known Errors may also be identified by Development or Suppliers
Known Error Database (KEDB)	(Service Operation) A database containing all Known Error Records. This database is created by Problem Management and used by Incident and Problem Management. The Known Error Database is part of the Service Knowledge Management System.
Known Error Record	(Service Operation) A Record containing the details of a Known Error. Each Known Error Record documents the Lifecycle of a Known Error, including the Status, Root Cause and Workaround. In some implementations a Known Error is documented using additional fields in a Problem Record.
Lifecycle	The various stages in the life of an IT Service, Configuration Item, Incident, Problem, Change, etc. The Lifecycle defines the Categories for Status and the Status transitions that are permitted. For example; The Lifecycle of an Application includes Requirements, Design, Build, Deploy, Operate, Optimize; The Expanded Incident Lifecycle includes Detect, Respond, Diagnose, Repair, Recover, Restore; The Lifecycle of a Server may include: Ordered, Received, In Test, Live, Disposed, etc.
Line of Service (LOS)	(Service Strategy) A core service or Supporting Service that has multiple Service Level Packages. A Line of Service is managed by a Product Manager and each Service Level Package is designed to support a particular market segment.
Live	(Service Transition) Refers to an IT Service or Configuration Item that is being used to deliver Service to a Customer

TERM	DEFINITION
Live Environment	(Service Transition) A controlled Environment containing Live Configuration Items used to deliver IT Services to Customers
Maintainability	(Service Design) A measure of how quickly and Effectively a Configuration Item or IT Service can be restored to normal working after a Failure. Maintainability is often measured and reported as MTRS. Maintainability is also used in the context of Software or IT Service Development to mean ability to be Changed or Repaired easily.
Major Incident	(Service Operation) The highest Category of Impact for an Incident. A Major Incident results in significant disruption to the Business
Managed Services	(Service Strategy) A perspective on IT Services which emphasizes the fact that they are managed. The term Managed Services is also used as a synonym for Outsourced IT Services.
Management Information	Information that is used to support decision making by managers. Management Information is often generated automatically by tools supporting the various IT Service Management Processes. Management Information often includes the values of KPIs such as 'Percentage of Changes leading to Incidents', or 'first-time fix rate'
Management of Risk (M_o_R)	The OGC methodology for managing Risks. M_o_R includes all the Activities required to identify and Control the exposure to Risk, which may have an impact on the achievement of an Organization's Business Objectives.
Management System	The framework of Policy, Processes and Functions that ensures an Organization can achieve its Objectives.
Manual Workaround	A Workaround that requires manual intervention. Manual Workaround is also used as the name of a Recovery Option in which the Business Process Operates without the use of IT Services. This is a temporary measure and is usually combined with another Recovery Option
Marginal Cost	(Service Strategy) The cost of continuing to provide the IT Service. Marginal Cost does not include investment already made, for example the cost of developing new software and delivering training.
Market Space	(Service Strategy) All opportunities that an IT Service Provider could exploit to meet business needs of Customers. The Market Space identifies the possible IT Services that an IT Service Provider may wish to consider delivering.
Maturity	(Continual Service Improvement) A measure of the Reliability, Efficiency and Effectiveness of a Process, Function, Organization, etc. The most mature Processes and Functions are formally aligned to Business Objectives and Strategy, and are supported by a framework for continual improvement

TERM	DEFINITION
Maturity Level	A named level in a Maturity model such as the Carnegie Mellon Capability Maturity Model Integration.
Mean Time Between Failures (MTBF)	(Service Design) A Metric for measuring and reporting Reliability. MTBF is the average time that a Configuration Item or IT Service can perform its agreed Function without interruption. This is measured from when the CI or IT Service starts working, until it next fails.
Mean Time Between Service Incidents (MTBSI)	(Service Design) A Metric used for measuring and reporting Reliability. MTBSI is the mean time from when a System or IT Service fails, until it next fails. MTBSI is equal to MTBF + MTRS
Mean Time To Repair (MTTR)	The average time taken to repair a Configuration Item or IT Service after a Failure. MTTR is measured from when the CI or IT Service fails until it is repaired. MTTR does not include the time required to Recover or Restore. MTTR is sometimes incorrectly used to indicate Mean Time to Restore Service.
Mean Time to Restore Service (MTRS)	The average time taken to restore a Configuration Item or IT Service after a Failure. MTRS is measured from when the CI or IT Service fails until it is fully restored and delivering its normal functionality. See also Maintainability, Mean Time to Repair.
Metric	(Continual Service Improvement) Something that is measured and reported to help manage a Process, IT Service or Activity.
Middleware	(Service Design) Software that connects two or more software Components or Applications. Middleware is usually purchased from a Supplier, rather than developed within the IT Service Provider. See also Off the Shelf
Mission Statement	The Mission Statement of an Organization is a short but complete description of the overall purpose and intentions of that Organization. It states what is to be achieved, but not how this should be done.
Model	A representation of a System, Process, IT Service, Configuration Item, etc. that is used to help understand or predict future behavior.
Modeling	A technique that is used to predict the future behavior of a System, Process, IT Service, Configuration Item, etc. Modeling is commonly used in Financial Management, Capacity Management and Availability Management.
Monitor Control Loop	(Service Operation) Monitoring the output of a Task, Process, IT Service or Configuration Item; comparing this output to a predefined Norm; and taking appropriate action based on this comparison.
Monitoring	(Service Operation) Repeated observation of a Configuration Item, IT Service or Process to detect Events and to ensure that the current status is known.

TERM	DEFINITION
Near-shore	(Service Strategy) Provision of Services from a country near the country where the Customer is based. This can be the provision of an IT Service, or of supporting Functions such as Service Desk. See also On-shore, Off-shore.
Net Present Value (NPV)	(Service Strategy) A technique used to help make decisions about capital expenditure. NPV compares cash inflows with cash outflows. Positive NPV indicates that an investment is worthwhile. See also Internal Rate of Return, Return on Investment.
Notional Charging	(Service Strategy) An approach to Charging for IT Services. Charges to Customers are calculated and Customers are informed of these charges, but no money is actually transferred. Notional Charging is sometimes introduced to ensure that Customers are aware of the costs they incur or as a stage during the introduction of real Charging.
Objective	The defined purpose or aim of a Process, an Activity or an Organization as a whole. Objectives are usually expressed as measurable targets. The term Objective is also informally used to mean a Requirement. See also Outcome.
Off the Shelf	See Commercial Off the Shelf.
Office of Government Commerce (OGC)	OGC owns the ITIL brand (copyright and trademark). OGC is a UK Government department that supports the delivery of the government's procurement agenda through its work in collaborative procurement and in raising levels of procurement skills and capability with departments. It also provides support for complex public sector projects.
Off-shore	(Service Strategy) Provision of Services from a location outside the country where the Customer is based, often in a different continent. This can be the provision of an IT Service, or of supporting Functions such as Service Desk. See also On-shore, Near-shore.
Off-The-Shelf	See Commercial Off-The-Shelf
On-shore	(Service Strategy) Provision of Services from a location within the country where the Customer is based. See also Off-shore, Near-shore.
Operate	To perform as expected. A Process or Configuration Item is said to Operate if it is delivering the Required outputs. Operate also means to perform one or more Operations. For example, to Operate a computer is to do the day-today Operations needed for it to perform as expected.
Operation	(Service Operation) Day-to-day management of an IT Service, System, or other Configuration Item. Operation is also used to mean any pre-defined Activity or Transaction. For example loading a magnetic tape, accepting money at a point of sale, or reading data from a disk drive.

TERM	DEFINITION
Operation	(Service Operation) Day-to-day management of an IT Service, System, or other Configuration Item. Operation is also used to mean any pre-defined Activity or Transaction. For example loading a magnetic tape, accepting money at a point of sale, or reading data from a disk drive
Operational	The lowest of three levels of Planning and delivery (Strategic, Tactical, Operational). Operational Activities include the day-to-day or short-term Planning or delivery of a business process or IT Service Management Process. The term Operational is also a synonym for Live.
Operational Cost	Cost resulting from running the IT Services. Often repeating payments. For example staff costs, hardware maintenance and electricity (also known as 'current expenditure' or 'revenue expenditure')
Operational Expenditure (OPEX)	See Operational Cost.
Operational Level Agreement (OLA)	(Service Design) (Continual Service Improvement) An Agreement between an IT Service Provider and another part of the same Organization. An OLA supports the IT Service Provider's delivery of IT Services to Customers. The OLA defines the goods or Services to be provided and the responsibilities of both parties. For example there could be an OLA: Between the IT Service Provider and a procurement department to obtain hardware in agreed times. Between the Service Desk and a Support Group to provide Incident Resolution in agreed times. See also Service Level Agreement
Operations Bridge	(Service Operation) A physical location where IT Services and IT Infrastructure are monitored and managed.
Operations Control	See IT Operations Control.
Operations Management	See IT Operations Management.
Opportunity Cost	(Service Strategy) A Cost that is used in deciding between investment choices. Opportunity Cost represents the revenue that would have been generated by using the Resources in a different way. For example, the Opportunity Cost of purchasing a new Server may include not carrying out a Service Improvement activity that the money could have been spent on. Opportunity cost analysis is used as part of a decision making processes, but is not treated as an actual Cost in any financial statement.
Optimize	Review, Plan and request Changes, in order to obtain the maximum Efficiency and Effectiveness from a Process, Configuration Item, Application, etc.

TERM	DEFINITION
Organization	A company, legal entity or other institution. Examples of Organizations that are not companies include International Standards Organization or itSMF. The term Organization is sometimes used to refer to any entity that has People, Resources and Budgets. For example a Project or Business Unit.
Outcome	The result of carrying out an Activity; following a Process; delivering an IT Service, etc. The term Outcome is used to refer to intended results, as well as to actual results. See also Objective.
Outsourcing	(Service Strategy) Using an external service provider to manage IT Services. See also Service Sourcing.
Overhead	See Indirect cost.
Pain Value Analysis	(Service Operation) A technique used to help identify the Business Impact of one or more Problems. A formula is used to calculate Pain Value based on the number of Users affected, the duration of the Downtime, the Impact on each User, and the cost to the Business (if known).
Pareto Principle	(Service Operation) A technique used to prioritize Activities. The Pareto Principle says that 80% of the value of any activity is created with 20% of the effort. Pareto Analysis is also used in Problem Management to prioritize possible Problem causes for investigation.
Partnership	A relationship between two Organizations that involves working closely together for common goals or mutual benefit. The IT Service Provider should have a Partnership with the business, and with Third Parties who are critical to the delivery of IT Services. See also Value Network.
Passive Monitoring	(Service Operation) Monitoring of a Configuration Item, an IT Service or a Process that relies on an Alert or notification to discover the current status
Pattern of business activity (PBA)	(Service Strategy) A Workload profile of one or more business activities. Patterns of business activity are used to help the IT Service Provider understand and plan for different levels of business activity. See also User Profile.
Performance	A measure of what is achieved or delivered by a System, person, team, Process, or IT Service.
Performance Anatomy	(Service Strategy) An approach to Organizational Culture that integrates, and actively manages, leadership and strategy, people development, technology enablement, performance management and innovation.
Performance Management	(Continual Service Improvement) The Process responsible for day-to-day Capacity Management Activities. These include monitoring, threshold detection, Performance analysis and Tuning, and implementing changes related to Performance and Capacity.

TERM	DEFINITION
Pilot	(Service Transition) A limited Deployment of an IT Service, a Release or a Process to the Live Environment. A pilot is used to reduce Risk and to gain User feedback and Acceptance. See also Test, Evaluation.
Plan	A detailed proposal that describes the Activities and Resources needed to achieve an Objective. For example a Plan to implement a new IT Service or Process. ISO/IEC 20000 requires a Plan for the management of each IT Service Management Process.
Plan-Do-Check-Act	(Continual Service Improvement) A four-stage cycle for Process management, attributed to Edward Deming. Plan-Do-Check-Act is also called the Deming Cycle; PLAN: Design or revise Processes that support the IT Services; DO: Implement the Plan and manage the Processes; CHECK: Measure the Processes and IT Services, compare with Objectives and produce reports. ACT: Plan and implement Changes to improve the Processes.
Planned Downtime	(Service Design) Agreed time when an IT Service will not be available. Planned Downtime is often used for maintenance, upgrades and testing. See also Change Window, Downtime
Planning	An Activity responsible for creating one or more Plans. For example, Capacity Planning.
PMBOK	A Project management Standard maintained and published by the Project Management Institute. PMBOK stands for Project Management Body of Knowledge. See www.pmi.org for more information. See also PRINCE2.
Policy	Formally documented management expectations and intentions. Policies are used to direct decisions, and to ensure consistent and appropriate development and implementation of Processes, Standards, Roles, Activities, IT infrastructure, etc.
Portable Facility	(Service Design) A prefabricated building, or a large vehicle, provided by a Third Party and moved to a site when needed by an IT Service Continuity Plan. See also Recovery Option
Post-Implementation Review (PIR)	A Review that takes place after a Change or a Project has been implemented. A PIR determines if the Change or Project was successful, and identifies opportunities for improvement
Practice	A way of working or a way in which work must be done. Practices can include Activities, Processes, Functions, Standards and Guidelines. See also Best practice.
Prerequisite for Success (PFS)	An Activity that needs to be completed, or a condition that needs to be met, to enable successful implementation of a Plan or Process. A PFS is often an output from one Process that is a required input to another Process

TERM	DEFINITION
Pricing	(Service Strategy) The Activity for establishing how much Customers will be Charged.
PRINCE2	The standard UK government methodology for Project management. See www.ogc.gov.uk/prince2 for more information. See also PMBOK.
Priority	(Service Transition) (Service Operation) A Category used to identify the relative importance of an Incident, Problem or Change. Priority is based on Impact and Urgency, and is used to identify required times for actions to be taken. For example the SLA may state that Priority 2 Incidents must be resolved within 12 hours.
Proactive Monitoring	(Service Operation) Monitoring that looks for patterns of Events to predict possible future Failures. See also Reactive Monitoring.
Proactive Problem Management	(Service Operation) Part of the Problem Management Process. The Objective of Proactive Problem Management is to identify Problems that might otherwise be missed. Proactive Problem Management analyses Incident Records, and uses data collected by other IT Service Management Processes to identify trends or significant problems.
Problem	(Service Operation) A cause of one or more Incidents. The cause is not usually known at the time a Problem Record is created, and the Problem Management Process is responsible for further investigation.
Problem Management	(Service Operation) The Process responsible for managing the Lifecycle of all Problems. The primary objectives of Problem Management are to prevent Incidents from happening, and to minimize the Impact of Incidents that cannot be prevented.
Problem Record	(Service Operation) A Record containing the details of a Problem. Each Problem Record documents the Lifecycle of a single Problem.
Procedure	A Document containing steps that specify how to achieve an Activity. Procedures are defined as part of Processes.
Process	A structured set of Activities designed to accomplish a specific Objective. A Process takes one or more defined inputs and turns them into defined outputs. A Process may include any of the Roles, responsibilities, tools and management Controls required to reliably deliver the outputs. A Process may define Policies, Standards, Guidelines, Activities, and Work Instructions if they are needed.
Process Control	The Activity of planning and regulating a Process, with the Objective of performing the Process in an Effective, Efficient, and consistent manner.

TERM	DEFINITION
Process Manager	A Role responsible for Operational management of a Process. The Process Manager's responsibilities include Planning and coordination of all Activities required to carry out, monitor and report on the Process. There may be several Process Managers for one Process, for example regional Change Managers or IT Service Continuity Managers for each data centre. The Process Manager Role is often assigned to the person who carries out the Process Owner Role, but the two Roles may be separate in larger Organizations.
Process Owner	A Role responsible for ensuring that a Process is fit for purpose. The Process Owner's responsibilities include sponsorship, Design, Change Management and continual improvement of the Process and its Metrics. This Role is often assigned to the same person who carries out the Process Manager Role, but the two Roles may be separate in larger Organizations.
Production Environment	See Live Environment.
Profit Centre	(Service Strategy) A business unit that charges for Services provided. A Profit Centre can be created with the objective of making a profit, recovering costs, or running at a loss. An IT Service Provider can be run as a Cost Centre or a Profit Centre.
Pro-forma	A template, or example Document containing example data that will be replaced with the real values when these are available
Programme	A number of Projects and Activities that are planned and managed together to achieve an overall set of related Objectives and other Outcomes.
Project	A temporary Organization, with people and other Assets required achieving an Objective or other Outcome. Each Project has a Lifecycle that typically includes initiation, Planning, execution, Closure, etc. Projects are usually managed using a formal methodology such as PRINCE2.
Projected Service Outage (PSO)	(Service Transition) A Document that identifies the effect of planned Changes, maintenance Activities and Test Plans on agreed Service Levels.
PRojects IN Controlled Environments (PRINCE2)	See PRINCE2.
Qualification	(Service Transition) An Activity that ensures that IT infrastructure is appropriate, and correctly configured, to support an Application or IT Service.
Quality	The ability of a product, Service, or Process to provide the intended value. For example, a hardware Component can be considered to be of high Quality if it performs as expected and delivers the required Reliability. Process Quality also requires an ability to monitor Effectiveness and Efficiency, and to improve them if necessary.

TERM	DEFINITION
Quality Assurance (QA)	(Service Transition) The Process responsible for ensuring that the Quality of a product, Service or Process will provide its intended Value.
Quality Management System (QMS)	(Continual Service Improvement) The set of Processes responsible for ensuring that all work carried out by an Organization is of a suitable Quality to reliably meet Business Objectives or Service Levels. See also ISO 9000
Quick Win	(Continual Service Improvement) An improvement Activity that is expected to provide a Return on Investment in a short period of time with relatively small Cost and effort.
RACI	(Service Design) (Continual Service Improvement) A Model used to help define Roles and Responsibilities. RACI stands for Responsible, Accountable, Consulted and Informed. See also Stakeholder.
Reactive Monitoring	(Service Operation) Monitoring that takes action in response to an Event. For example submitting a batch job when the previous job completes, or logging an Incident when an Error occurs. See also Proactive Monitoring.
Reciprocal Arrangement	(Service Design) A Recovery Option. An agreement between two Organizations to share resources in an emergency. For example, Computer Room space or use of a mainframe
Record	A Document containing the results or other output from a Process or Activity. Records are evidence of the fact that an activity took place and may be paper or electronic. For example, an Audit report, an Incident Record, or the minutes of a meeting.
Recovery	(Service Design) (Service Operation) Returning a Configuration Item or an IT Service to a working state. Recovery of an IT Service often includes recovering data to a known consistent state. After Recovery, further steps may be needed before the IT Service can be made available to the Users (Restoration).
Recovery Option	(Service Design) A Strategy for responding to an interruption to Service. Commonly used Strategies are Do Nothing, Manual Workaround, Reciprocal Arrangement, Gradual Recovery, Intermediate Recovery, Fast Recovery, and Immediate Recovery. Recovery Options may make use of dedicated facilities, or Third Party facilities shared by multiple Businesses
Recovery Point Objective (RPO)	(Service Operation) The maximum amount of data that may be lost when Service is Restored after an interruption. Recovery Point Objective is expressed as a length of time before the Failure. For example a Recovery Point Objective of one day may be supported by daily Backups, and up to 24 hours of data may be lost. Recovery Point Objectives for each IT Service should be negotiated, agreed and documented, and used as requirements for Service Design and IT Service Continuity Plans.

TERM	DEFINITION
Redundancy	See Fault tolerance. The term Redundant also has a generic meaning of obsolete, or no longer needed.
Relationship	A connection or interaction between two people or things. In Business Relationship Management it is the interaction between the IT Service Provider and the business. In Configuration Management it is a link between two Configuration Items that identifies a dependency or connection between them. For example Applications may be linked to the Servers they run on, IT Services have many links to all the CIs that contribute to them.
Relationship Processes	The ISO/IEC 20000 Process group that includes Business Relationship Management and Supplier Management
Release	(Service Transition) A collection of hardware, software, documentation, Processes or other Components required to implement one or more approved Changes to IT Services. The contents of each Release are managed, tested, and deployed as a single entity.
Release and Deployment Management	(Service Transition) The Process responsible for both Release Management and Deployment
Release Identification	(Service Transition) A naming convention used to uniquely identify a Release. The Release Identification typically includes a reference to the Configuration Item and a version number. For example, Microsoft Office 2003 SR2.
Release Management	(Service Transition) The Process responsible for Planning, scheduling and controlling the movement of Releases to Test and Live Environments. The primary Objective of Release Management is to ensure that the integrity of the Live Environment is protected and that the correct Components are released. Release Management is part of the Release and Deployment Management Process.
Release Process	The name used by ISO/IEC 20000 for the Process group that includes Release Management. This group does not include any other Processes. Release Process is also used as a synonym for Release Management Process.
Release Record	(Service Transition) A Record in the CMDB that defines the content of a Release. A Release Record has Relationships with all Configuration Items that are affected by the Release
Release Unit	(Service Transition) Components of an IT Service that are normally Released together. A Release Unit typically includes sufficient components to perform a useful Function. For example, one Release Unit could be a Desktop PC, including Hardware, Software, Licenses, Documentation, etc. A different Release Unit may be the complete Payroll Application, including IT Operations Procedures and user training.
Release Window	See Change Window.

TERM	DEFINITION
Reliability	(Service Design) (Continual Service Improvement) A measure of how long a Configuration Item or IT Service can perform its agreed Function without interruption. Usually measured as MTBF or MTBSI. The term Reliability can also be used to state how likely it is that a Process, Function, etc. will deliver its required outputs. See also Availability.
Remediation	(Service Transition) Recovery to a known state after a failed Change or Release.
Repair	(Service Operation) The replacement or correction of a failed Configuration Item.
Request for Change (RFC)	(Service Transition) A formal proposal for a Change to be made. An RFC includes details of the proposed Change, and may be recorded on paper or electronically. The term RFC is often misused to mean a Change Record, or the Change itself.
Request Fulfillment	(Service Operation) The Process responsible for managing the Lifecycle of all Service Requests.
Requirement	(Service Design) A formal statement of what is needed. For example, a Service Level Requirement, a Project Requirement or the required Deliverables for a Process. See also Statement of Requirements.
Resilience	(Service Design) The ability of a Configuration Item or IT Service to resist Failure or to Recover quickly following a Failure. For example an armored cable will resist failure when put under stress. See also Fault Tolerance
Resolution	(Service Operation) Action taken to repair the Root Cause of an Incident or Problem, or to implement a Workaround. In ISO/IEC 20000, Resolution Processes is the Process group that includes Incident and Problem Management.
Resource	(Service Strategy) A generic term that includes IT Infrastructure, people, money or anything else that might help to deliver an IT Service. Resources are considered to be Assets of an Organization. See also Capability, Service Asset.
Response Time	A measure of the time taken to complete an Operation or Transaction. Used in Capacity Management as a measure of IT infrastructure Performance, and in Incident Management as a measure of the time taken to answer the phone, or to start Diagnosis.
Responsiveness	A measurement of the time taken to respond to something. This could be Response Time of a Transaction, or the speed with which an IT Service Provider responds to an Incident or Request for Change, etc.
Restoration of Service	See Restore

TERM	DEFINITION
Restore	(Service Operation) Taking action to return an IT Service to the Users after Repair and Recovery from an Incident. This is the primary Objective of Incident Management.
Retire	(Service Transition) Permanent removal of an IT Service, or other Configuration Item, from the Live Environment. Retired is a stage in the Lifecycle of many Configuration Items.
Return on Investment (ROI)	(Service Strategy) (Continual Service Improvement) A measurement of the expected benefit of an investment. In the simplest sense it is the net profit of an investment divided by the net worth of the assets invested. See also Net Present Value. See also Value on Investment.
Return to Normal	(Service Design) The phase of an IT Service Continuity Plan during which full normal operations are resumed. For example, if an alternate data centre has been in use, then this phase will bring the primary data centre back into operation, and restore the ability to invoke IT Service Continuity Plans again
Review	An evaluation of a Change, Problem, Process, Project, etc Reviews are typically carried out at predefined points in the Lifecycle, and especially after Closure. The purpose of a Review is to ensure that all Deliverables have been provided, and to identify opportunities for improvement See also Post-Implementation Review.
Rights	(Service Operation) Entitlements, or permissions, granted to a User or Role. For example the Right to modify particular data, or to authorize a Change.
Risk	A possible event that could cause harm or loss, or affect the ability to achieve Objectives. A Risk is measured by the probability of a Threat, the Vulnerability of the Asset to that Threat, and the Impact it would have if it occurred.
Risk Assessment	The initial steps of Risk Management. Analyzing the value of Assets to the business, identifying Threats to those Assets, and evaluating how Vulnerable each Asset is to those Threats. Risk Assessment can be quantitative (based on numerical data) or qualitative
Risk Management	The Process responsible for identifying, assessing and controlling Risks. See also Risk Assessment
Role	A set of responsibilities, Activities and authorities granted to a person or team. A Role is defined in a Process. One person or team may have multiple Roles, for example the Roles of Configuration Manager and Change Manager may be carried out by a single person.
Rollout	(Service Transition) See Deployment. Most often used to refer to complex or phased Deployments or Deployments to multiple locations.

TERM	DEFINITION
Root Cause	(Service Operation) The underlying or original cause of an Incident or Problem
Root Cause Analysis (RCA)	(Service Operation) An Activity that identifies the Root Cause of an Incident or Problem. RCA typically concentrates on IT Infrastructure failures. See also Service Failure Analysis.
Running Costs	See Operational Cost
Scalability	The ability of an IT Service, Process, Configuration Item, etc. to perform its agreed Function when the Workload or Scope changes.
Scope	The boundary, or extent, to which a Process, Procedure, Certification, Contract, etc. applies. For example the Scope of Change Management may include all Live IT Services and related Configuration Items; the Scope of an ISO/IEC 20000 Certificate may include all IT Services delivered out of a named data centre.
Second-line Support	(Service Operation) The second level in a hierarchy of Support Groups involved in the resolution of Incidents and investigation of Problems. Each level contains more specialist skills, or has more time or other resources.
Security	See Information Security Management.
Security Management	See Information Security Management
Security Policy	See Information Security Policy
Separation of Concerns (SoC)	(Service Strategy) An approach to Designing a solution or IT Service that divides the problem into pieces that can be solved independently. This approach separates 'what' is to be done from 'how' it is to be done.
Server	(Service Operation) A computer that is connected to a network and provides software Functions that are used by other Computers.
Service	A means of delivering value to customers by facilitating outcomes customers want to achieve without the ownership of specific costs and risks.
Service Acceptance Criteria (SAC)	(Service Transition) A set of criteria used to ensure that an IT Service meets its functionality and Quality Requirements and that the IT Service Provider is ready to Operate the new IT Service when it has been Deployed. See also Acceptance
Service Analytics	(Service Strategy) A technique used in the assessment of the business impact of Incidents. Service Analytics models the dependencies between Configuration Items and the dependencies of IT Services on Configuration Items.
Service Asset	Any Capability or Resource of a Service Provider. See also Asset.

TERM	DEFINITION
Service Asset and Configuration Management (SACM)	(Service Transition) The Process responsible for both Configuration Management and Asset Management.
Service Capacity Management (SCM)	(Service Design) (Continual Service Improvement) The Activity responsible for understanding the Performance and Capacity of IT Services. The Resources used by each IT Service and the pattern of usage over time are collected, recorded, and analyzed for use in the Capacity Plan. See also Business Capacity Management, Component Capacity Management
Service Catalogue	(Service Design) A database or structured Document with information about all Live IT Services, including those available for Deployment. The Service Catalogue is the only part of the Service Portfolio published to Customers, and is used to support the sale and delivery of IT Services. The Service Catalogue includes information about deliverables, prices, contact points, ordering and request Processes. See also Contract Portfolio.
Service Continuity Management	See IT Service Continuity Management
Service Contract	(Service Strategy) A Contract to deliver one or more IT Services. The term Service Contract is also used to mean any Agreement to deliver IT Services, whether this is a legal Contract or an SLA. See also Contract Portfolio.
Service Culture	A Customer-oriented Culture. The major Objectives of a Service Culture are Customer satisfaction and helping Customers to achieve their business objectives.
Service Design	(Service Design) A stage in the Lifecycle of an IT Service. Service Design includes a number of Processes and Functions and is the title of one of the Core ITIL publications. See also Design.
Service Design Package	(Service Design) Document(s) defining all aspects of an IT Service and its Requirements through each stage of its Lifecycle. A Service Design Package is produced for each new IT Service, major Change, or IT Service Retirement
Service Desk	(Service Operation) The Single Point of Contact between the Service Provider and the Users. A typical Service Desk manages Incidents and Service Requests, and also handles communication with the Users.
Service Failure Analysis (SFA)	(Service Design) An Activity that identifies underlying causes of one or more IT Service interruptions. SFA identifies opportunities to improve the IT Service Provider's Processes and tools, and not just the IT Infrastructure. SFA is a time-constrained, project-like activity, rather than an ongoing process of analysis. See also Root Cause Analysis.

TERM	DEFINITION
Service Hours	(Service Design) (Continual Service Improvement) An agreed time period when a particular IT Service should be Available. For example, 'Monday-Friday 08:00 to 17:00 except public holidays'. Service Hours should be defined in a Service Level Agreement
Service Improvement Plan (SIP)	(Continual Service Improvement) A formal Plan to implement improvements to a Process or IT Service
Service Knowledge Management System (SKMS)	(Service Transition) A set of tools and databases that are used to manage knowledge and information. The SKMS includes the Configuration Management System, as well as other tools and databases. The SKMS stores, manages, updates, and presents all information that an IT Service Provider needs to manage the full Lifecycle of IT Services
Service Level	Measured and reported achievement against one or more Service Level Targets. The term Service Level is sometimes used informally to mean Service Level Target.
Service Level Agreement (SLA)	(Service Design) (Continual Service Improvement) An Agreement between an IT Service Provider and a Customer. The SLA describes the IT Service, documents Service Level Targets, and specifies the responsibilities of the IT Service Provider and the Customer. A single SLA may cover multiple IT Services or multiple customers.
Service Level Management (SLM)	(Service Design) (Continual Service Improvement) The Process responsible for negotiating Service Level Agreements, and ensuring that these are met. SLM is responsible for ensuring that all IT Service Management Processes, Operational Level Agreements, and Underpinning Contracts, are appropriate for the agreed Service Level Targets. SLM monitors and reports on Service Levels, and holds regular Customer reviews.
Service Level Package (SLP)	(Service Strategy) A defined level of Utility and Warranty for a particular Service Package. Each SLP is designed to meet the needs of a particular pattern of business activity. See also Line of Service.
Service Level Requirement (SLR)	(Service Design) (Continual Service Improvement) A Customer Requirement for an aspect of an IT Service. SLRs are based on business objectives and are used to negotiate agreed Service Level Targets.
Service Level Target	(Service Design) (Continual Service Improvement) A commitment that is documented in a Service Level Agreement. Service Level Targets are based on Service Level Requirements, and are needed to ensure that the IT Service design is Fit for Purpose. Service Level Targets should be SMART, and are usually based on KPIs
Service Maintenance Objective	(Service Operation) The expected time that a Configuration Item will be unavailable due to planned maintenance Activity.

TERM	DEFINITION
Service Management	Service Management is a set of specialized organizational capabilities for providing value to customers in the form of services.
Service Management Lifecycle	An approach to IT Service Management that emphasizes the importance of coordination and Control across the various Functions, Processes, and Systems necessary to manage the full Lifecycle of IT Services. The Service Management Lifecycle approach considers the Strategy, Design, Transition, Operation and Continuous Improvement of IT Services.
Service Manager	A manager who is responsible for managing the end-to-end Lifecycle of one or more IT Services. The term Service Manager is also used to mean any manager within the IT Service Provider. Most commonly used to refer to a Business Relationship Manager, a Process Manager, an Account Manager or a senior manager with responsibility for IT Services overall
Service Operation	(Service Operation) A stage in the Lifecycle of an IT Service. Service Operation includes a number of Processes and Functions and is the title of one of the Core ITIL publications. See also Operation.
Service Owner	(Continual Service Improvement) A Role that is accountable for the delivery of a specific IT Service
Service Package	(Service Strategy) A detailed description of an IT Service that is available to be delivered to Customers. A Service Package includes a Service Level Package and one or more core services and Supporting Services.
Service Pipeline	(Service Strategy) A database or structured Document listing all IT Services that are under consideration or Development, but are not yet available to Customers. The Service Pipeline provides a business view of possible future IT Services and is part of the Service Portfolio that is not normally published to Customers.
Service Portfolio	(Service Strategy) The complete set of Services that are managed by a Service Provider. The Service Portfolio is used to manage the entire Lifecycle of all Services, and includes three Categories: Service Pipeline (proposed or in Development); Service Catalogue (Live or available for Deployment); and Retired Services. See also Service Portfolio Management, Contract Portfolio.
Service Portfolio	(Service Strategy) The complete set of Services that are managed by a Service Provider. The Service Portfolio is used to manage the entire Lifecycle of all Services, and includes three Categories: Service Pipeline (proposed or in Development); Service Catalogue (Live or available for Deployment); and Retired Services. See also Service Portfolio Management.
Service Portfolio Management (SPM)	(Service Strategy) The Process responsible for managing the Service Portfolio. Service Portfolio Management considers Services in terms of the business value that they provide.

TERM	DEFINITION
Service Potential	(Service Strategy) The total possible value of the overall Capabilities and Resources of the IT Service Provider.
Service Provider	(Service Strategy) An Organization supplying Services to one or more Internal Customers or External Customers. Service Provider is often used as an abbreviation for IT Service Provider. See also Type I Service Provider, Type II Service Provider, and Type III Service Provider.
Service Provider Interface (SPI)	(Service Strategy) An interface between the IT Service Provider and a User, Customer, Business Process, or a Supplier. Analysis of Service Provider Interfaces helps to coordinate end-to-end management of IT Services.
Service Provisioning Optimization (SPO)	(Service Strategy) Analyzing the finances and constraints of an IT Service to decide if alternative approaches to service delivery might reduce costs or improve Quality.
Service Reporting	(Continual Service Improvement) The Process responsible for producing and delivering reports of achievement and trends against Service Levels. Service Reporting should agree the format, content and frequency of reports with Customers.
Service Request	(Service Operation) A request from a User for information, or advice, or for a Standard Change or for Access to an IT Service. For example to reset a password, or to provide standard IT Services for a new User. Service Requests are usually handled by a Service Desk, and do not require an RFC to be submitted. See also Request Fulfillment.
Service Sourcing	(Service Strategy) The Strategy and approach for deciding whether to provide a Service internally or to outsource it to an External Service Provider. Service Sourcing also means the execution of this Strategy. Service Sourcing includes; Internal sourcing – Internal or Shared Services using Type I or Type II Service Providers; Traditional Sourcing – Full Service Outsourcing using a Type III Service Provider; Multi-vendor Sourcing – Prime, Consortium or Selective Outsourcing using Type III Service Providers.
Service Strategy	(Service Strategy) The title of one of the Core ITIL publications. Service Strategy establishes an overall Strategy for IT Services and for IT Service Management.
Service Transition	(Service Transition) A stage in the Lifecycle of an IT Service. Service Transition includes a number of Processes and Functions and is the title of one of the Core ITIL publications. See also Transition.
Service Utility	(Service Strategy) The Functionality of an IT Service from the Customer's perspective. The business value of an IT Service is created by the combination of Service Utility (what the Service does) and Service Warranty (how well it does it). See also Utility.

TERM	DEFINITION
Service Validation and Testing	(Service Transition) The Process responsible for Validation and Testing of a new or Changed IT Service. Service Validation and Testing ensures that the IT Service matches its Design Specification and will meet the needs of the Business.
Service Valuation	(Service Strategy) A measurement of the total cost of delivering an IT Service, and the total value to the business of that IT Service. Service Valuation is used to help the business and the IT Service Provider agree on the value of the IT Service.
Service Warranty	(Service Strategy) Assurance that an IT Service will meet agreed Requirements. This may be a formal Agreement such as a Service Level Agreement or Contract, or may be a marketing message or brand image. The business value of an IT Service is created by the combination of Service Utility (what the Service does) and Service Warranty (how well it does it). See also Warranty.
Service Warranty	(Service Strategy) Assurance that an IT Service will meet agreed Requirements. This may be a formal Agreement such as a Service Level Agreement or Contract, or may be a marketing message or brand image. The Business value of an IT Service is created by the combination of Service Utility (what the Service does) and Service Warranty (how well it does it). See also Warranty
Serviceability	(Service Design) (Continual Service Improvement) The ability of a Third-Party Supplier to meet the terms of its Contract. This Contract will include agreed levels of Reliability, Maintainability or Availability for a Configuration Item
Shift	(Service Operation) A group or team of people who carry out a specific Role for a fixed period of time. For example there could be four shifts of IT Operations Control personnel to support an IT Service that is used 24 hours a day
Simulation modeling	(Service Design) (Continual Service Improvement) A technique that creates a detailed model to predict the behavior of a Configuration Item or IT Service. Simulation Models can be very accurate but are expensive and time consuming to create. A Simulation Model is often created by using the actual Configuration Items that are being modeled, with artificial Workloads or Transactions. They are used in Capacity Management when accurate results are important. A simulation model is sometimes called a Performance Benchmark
Single Point of Contact	(Service Operation) Providing a single consistent way to communicate with an Organization or Business Unit. For example, a Single Point of Contact for an IT Service Provider is usually called a Service Desk.

TERM	DEFINITION
Single Point of Failure (SPOF)	(Service Design) Any Configuration Item that can cause an Incident when it fails, and for which a Countermeasure has not been implemented. A SPOF may be a person, or a step in a Process or Activity, as well as a Component of the IT Infrastructure. See also Failure
SLAM Chart	(Continual Service Improvement) A Service Level Agreement Monitoring Chart is used to help monitor and report achievements against Service Level Targets. A SLAM Chart is typically color coded to show whether each agreed Service Level Target has been met, missed, or nearly missed during each of the previous 12 months.
SMART	(Service Design) (Continual Service Improvement) An acronym for helping to remember that targets in Service Level Agreements and Project Plans should be Specific, Measurable, Achievable, Relevant and Timely
Snapshot	(Service Transition) The current state of a Configuration as captured by a discovery tool. Also used as a synonym for Benchmark. See also Baseline.
Source	See Service Sourcing.
Specification	A formal definition of Requirements. A Specification may be used to define technical or Operational Requirements, and may be internal or external. Many public Standards consist of a Code of Practice and a Specification. The Specification defines the Standard against which an Organization can be Audited.
Stakeholder	All people who have an interest in an Organization, Project, IT Service, etc. Stakeholders may be interested in the Activities, targets, Resources, or Deliverables. Stakeholders may include Customers, Partners, employees, shareholders, owners, etc. See also RACI.
Standard	A mandatory Requirement. Examples include ISO/IEC 20000 (an international Standard), an internal security standard for Unix configuration, or a government standard for how financial Records should be maintained. The term Standard is also used to refer to a Code of Practice or Specification published by a Standards Organization such as ISO or BSI. See also Guideline.
Standard Change	(Service Transition) A pre-approved Change that is low Risk, relatively common and follows a Procedure or Work Instruction. For example, password reset or provision of standard equipment to a new employee. RFCs are not required to implement a Standard Change, and they are logged and tracked using a different mechanism, such as a Service Request. See also Change Model.
Standard Operating Procedures (SOP)	(Service Operation) Procedures used by IT Operations Management.

TERM	DEFINITION
Standby	(Service Design) Used to refer to Resources that are not required to deliver the Live IT Services, but are available to support IT Service Continuity Plans. For example a Standby data centre may be maintained to support Hot Standby, Warm Standby or Cold Standby arrangements.
Statement of requirements (SOR)	(Service Design) A Document containing all Requirements for a product purchase, or a new or changed IT Service. See also Terms of Reference
Status	The name of a required field in many types of Record. It shows the current stage in the Lifecycle of the associated Configuration Item, Incident, Problem, etc.
Status Accounting	(Service Transition) The Activity responsible for recording and reporting the Lifecycle of each Configuration Item.
Strategic	(Service Strategy) The highest of three levels of Planning and delivery (Strategic, Tactical, Operational). Strategic Activities include Objective setting and long-term Planning to achieve the overall Vision.
Strategy	(Service Strategy) A Strategic Plan designed to achieve defined Objectives.
Super User	(Service Operation) A User who helps other Users, and assists in communication with the Service Desk or other parts of the IT Service Provider. Super Users typically provide support for minor Incidents and training.
Supplier	(Service Strategy) (Service Design) A Third Party responsible for supplying goods or Services that are required to deliver IT Services. Examples of suppliers include commodity hardware and software vendors, network and telecom providers, and outsourcing Organizations. See also Supply Chain.
Supplier and Contract Database (SCD)	(Service Design) A database or structured Document used to manage Supplier Contracts throughout their Lifecycle. The SCD contains key Attributes of all Contracts with Suppliers, and should be part of the Service Knowledge Management System
Supplier Management	(Service Design) The Process responsible for ensuring that all Contracts with Suppliers support the needs of the business, and that all Suppliers meet their contractual commitments.
Supply Chain	(Service Strategy) The Activities in a Value Chain carried out by Suppliers. A Supply Chain typically involves multiple Suppliers, each adding value to the product or Service. See also Value Network.
Support Group	(Service Operation) A group of people with technical skills. Support Groups provide the Technical Support needed by all of the IT Service Management Processes. See also Technical Management

TERM	DEFINITION
Support Hours	(Service Design) (Service Operation) The times or hours when support is available to the Users. Typically these are the hours when the Service Desk is available. Support Hours should be defined in a Service Level Agreement, and may be different from Service Hours. For example, Service Hours may be 24 hours a day, but the Support Hours may be 07:00 to 19:00
Supporting Service	(Service Strategy) A Service that enables or enhances a core service. For example, a directory service or a backup service. See also Service Package.
SWOT Analysis	(Continual Service Improvement) A technique that reviews and analyses the internal strengths and weaknesses of an Organization and the external opportunities and threats that it faces SWOT stands for Strengths, Weaknesses, Opportunities and Threats
System	A number of related things that work together to achieve an overall Objective. For example: A computer System including hardware, software and Applications. A management System, including multiple Processes that are planned and managed together. For example, a Quality Management System. A Database Management System or Operating System that includes many software modules that are designed to perform a set of related Functions. System Management. The part of IT Service Management that focuses on the management of IT Infrastructure rather than Process
System Management	The part of IT Service Management that focuses on the management of IT Infrastructure rather than Process.
Tactical	The middle of three levels of Planning and delivery (Strategic, Tactical, Operational). Tactical Activities include the medium-term Plans required to achieve specific Objectives, typically over a period of weeks to months.
Tag	(Service Strategy) A short code used to identify a Category. For example tags EC1, EC2, EC3, etc. might be used to identify different Customer outcomes when analyzing and comparing Strategies. The term Tag is also used to refer to the activity of assigning Tags to things.
Technical Management	(Service Operation) The Function responsible for providing technical skills in support of IT Services and management of the IT infrastructure. Technical Management defines the Roles of Support Groups, as well as the tools, Processes and Procedures required.
Technical Observation	(Continual Service Improvement) A technique used in Service Improvement, Problem investigation and Availability Management. Technical support personnel meet to monitor the behavior and Performance of an IT Service and make recommendations for improvement.
Technical Service	See Infrastructure Service
Technical Support	See Technical Management.

TERM	DEFINITION
Tension Metrics	(Continual Service Improvement) A set of related Metrics, in which improvements to one Metric have a negative effect on another. Tension Metrics are designed to ensure that an appropriate balance is achieved.
Terms of Reference (TOR)	(Service Design) A Document specifying the Requirements, Scope, Deliverables, Resources and schedule for a Project or Activity
Test	(Service Transition) An Activity that verifies that a Configuration Item, IT Service, Process, etc. meets it's Specification or agreed Requirements. See also Service Validation and Testing, Acceptance.
Test Environment	(Service Transition) A controlled Environment used to Test Configuration Items, Builds, IT Services, Processes, etc.
Third Party	A person, group, or business that is not part of the Service Level Agreement for an IT Service, but is required to ensure successful delivery of that IT Service. For example, a software Supplier, a hardware maintenance company, or a facilities department. Requirements for Third Parties are typically specified in Underpinning Contracts or Operational Level Agreements.
Third-line Support	(Service Operation) The third level in a hierarchy of Support Groups involved in the resolution of Incidents and investigation of Problems. Each level contains more specialist skills, or has more time or other resources.
Threat	Anything that might exploit a Vulnerability. Any potential cause of an Incident can be considered to be a Threat. For example a fire is a Threat that could exploit the Vulnerability of flammable floor coverings. This term is commonly used in Information Security Management and IT Service Continuity Management, but also applies to other areas such as Problem and Availability Management.
Threshold	The value of a Metric that should cause an Alert to be generated, or management action to be taken. For example 'Priority 1 Incident not solved within four hours', 'more than five soft disk errors in an hour', or 'more than 10 failed changes in a month'.
Throughput	(Service Design) A measure of the number of Transactions, or other Operations, performed in a fixed time. For example, 5,000 e-mails sent per hour, or 200 disk I/Os per second.
Total Cost of Ownership (TCO)	(Service Strategy) A methodology used to help make investment decisions. TCO assesses the full Lifecycle cost of owning a Configuration Item, not just the initial cost or purchase price. See also Total Cost of Utilization.
Total Cost of Utilization (TCU)	(Service Strategy) A methodology used to help make investment and Service Sourcing decisions. TCU assesses the full Lifecycle Cost to the Customer of using an IT Service. See also Total Cost of Ownership.

TERM	DEFINITION
Total Quality Management (TQM)	(Continual Service Improvement) A methodology for managing continual Improvement by using a Quality Management System. TQM establishes a Culture involving all people in the Organization in a Process of continual monitoring and improvement.
Transaction	A discrete Function performed by an IT Service. For example transferring money from one bank account to another. A single Transaction may involve numerous additions, deletions and modifications of data. Either all of these complete successfully or none of them is carried out.
Transition	(Service Transition) A change in state, corresponding to a movement of an IT Service or other Configuration Item from one Lifecycle status to the next.
Transition Planning and Support	(Service Transition) The Process responsible for Planning all Service Transition Processes and coordinating the resources that they require. These Service Transition Processes are Change Management, Service Asset and Configuration Management, Release and Deployment Management, Service Validation and Testing, Evaluation, and Knowledge Management.
Trend Analysis	(Continual Service Improvement) Analysis of data to identify time-related patterns. Trend Analysis is used in Problem Management to identify common Failures or fragile Configuration Items, and in Capacity Management as a Modeling tool to predict future behavior. It is also used as a management tool for identifying deficiencies in IT Service Management Processes
Tuning	The Activity responsible for Planning changes to make the most efficient use of Resources. Tuning is part of Performance Management, which also includes Performance monitoring and implementation of the required Changes
Type I Service Provider	(Service Strategy) An internal service provider that is embedded within a business unit. There may be several Type I Service Providers within an Organization.
Type II Service Provider	(Service Strategy) An internal service provider that provides shared IT Services to more than one business unit.
Type III Service Provider	(Service Strategy) A Service Provider that provides IT Services to External Customers.
Underpinning Contract (UC)	(Service Design) A Contract between an IT Service Provider and a Third Party. The Third Party provides goods or Services that support delivery of an IT Service to a Customer. The Underpinning Contract defines targets and responsibilities that are required to meet agreed Service Level Targets in an SLA

TERM	DEFINITION
Unit Cost	(Service Strategy) The cost to the IT Service Provider of providing a single Component of an IT Service. For example the cost of a single desktop PC, or of a single Transaction.
Urgency	(Service Transition) (Service Design) A measure of how long it will be until an Incident, Problem or Change has a significant Impact on the Business. For example a high Impact Incident may have low Urgency, if the Impact will not affect the Business until the end of the financial year. Impact and Urgency are used to assign Priority
Usability	(Service Design) The ease with which an Application, product, or IT Service can be used. Usability Requirements are often included in a Statement of Requirements.
Use Case	(Service Design) A technique used to define required functionality and Objectives, and to design Tests. Use Cases define realistic scenarios that describe interactions between Users and an IT Service or other System. See also Change Case.
User	A person who uses the IT Service on a day-to-day basis. Users are distinct from Customers, as some Customers do not use the IT Service directly.
User Profile (UP)	(Service Strategy) A pattern of User demand for IT Services. Each User Profile includes one or more patterns of business activity.
Utility	(Service Strategy) Functionality offered by a Product or Service to meet a particular need. Utility is often summarized as 'what it does'. See also Service Utility.
Validation	(Service Transition) An Activity that ensures a new or changed IT Service, Process, Plan, or other Deliverable meets the needs of the Business. Validation ensures that Business Requirements are met even though these may have changed since the original design. See also Verification, Acceptance, Qualification, Service Validation and Testing.
Value Chain	(Service Strategy) A sequence of Processes that creates a product or Service that is of value to a Customer. Each step of the sequence builds on the previous steps and contributes to the overall product or Service. See also Value Network.
Value for Money	An informal measure of Cost Effectiveness. Value for Money is often based on a comparison with the Cost of alternatives. See also Cost Benefit Analysis.
Value Network	(Service Strategy) A complex set of relationships between two or more groups or organizations. Value is generated through exchange of knowledge, information, goods or Services. See also Value Chain, Partnership.

TERM	DEFINITION
Value on Investment (VOI)	(Continual Service Improvement) A measurement of the expected benefit of an investment. VOI considers both financial and intangible benefits. See also Return on Investment.
Variable Cost	(Service Strategy) A cost that depends on how much the IT Service is used, how many products are produced, the number and type of Users, or something else that cannot be fixed in advance. See also Variable Cost Dynamics.
Variable Cost Dynamics	(Service Strategy) A technique used to understand how overall costs are affected by the many complex variable elements that contribute to the provision of IT Services.
Variance	The difference between a planned value and the actual measured value. Commonly used in Financial Management, Capacity Management and Service Level Management, but could apply in any area where Plans are in place.
Verification	(Service Transition) An Activity that ensures a new or changed IT Service, Process, Plan, or other Deliverable is complete, accurate, and reliable and matches its design specification. See also Validation, Acceptance, Service Validation and Testing.
Verification and Audit	(Service Transition) The Activities responsible for ensuring that information in the CMDB is accurate and that all Configuration Items have been identified and recorded in the CMDB. Verification includes routine checks that are part of other processes. For example, verifying the serial number of a desktop PC when a User logs an Incident. Audit is a periodic, formal check.
Version	(Service Transition) A Version is used to identify a specific Baseline of a Configuration Item. Versions typically use a naming convention that enables the sequence or date of each Baseline to be identified. For example Payroll Application Version 3 contains updated functionality from Version 2.
Vision	A description of what the Organization intends to become in the future. A Vision is created by senior management and is used to help influence Culture and Strategic Planning.
Vital Business Function (VBF)	(Service Design) A Function of a Business Process that is critical to the success of the Business. Vital Business Functions are an important consideration of Business Continuity Management, IT Service Continuity Management and Availability Management
Vulnerability	A weakness that could be exploited by a Threat. For example an open firewall port, a password that is never changed, or a flammable carpet. A missing Control is also considered to be a Vulnerability.
Warm Standby	See Intermediate Recovery

TERM	DEFINITION
Warranty	(Service Strategy) A promise or guarantee that a product or Service will meet its agreed Requirements. See also Service Validation and Testing, Service Warranty.
Work in Progress (WIP)	A Status that means Activities have started but are not yet complete. It is commonly used as a Status for Incidents, Problems, Changes, etc.
Work Instruction	A Document containing detailed instructions that specify exactly what steps to follow to carry out an Activity. A Work Instruction contains much more detail than a Procedure and is only created if very detailed instructions are needed
Workaround	(Service Operation) Reducing or eliminating the Impact of an Incident or Problem for which a full Resolution is not yet available. For example by restarting a failed Configuration Item. Workarounds for Problems are documented in Known Error Records. Workarounds for Incidents that do not have associated Problem Records are documented in the Incident Record
Workload	The Resources required delivering an identifiable part of an IT Service. Workloads may be Categorized by Users, groups of Users, or Functions within the IT Service. This is used to assist in analyzing and managing the Capacity, Performance and Utilization of Configuration Items and IT Services. The term Workload is sometimes used as a synonym for Throughput.